PSYCHOLOGY AND THE DEPARTMENT OF VETERANS AFFAIRS

Psychology and the Department of Veterans Affairs

A Historical Analysis of Training, Research, Practice, and Advocacy

Rodney R. Baker and Wade E. Pickren

American Psychological Association • Washington, DC

Published by
American Psychological Association
750 First Street, NE
Washington, DC 20002
www.apa.org

To order
APA Order Department
P.O. Box 92984
Washington, DC 20090-2984
Tel: (800) 374-2721
Direct: (202) 336-5510
Fax: (202) 336-5502
TDD/TTY: (202) 336-6123
Online: www.apa.org/books/
E-mail: order@apa.org

In the U.K., Europe, Africa, and the Middle East, copies may be ordered from
American Psychological Association
3 Henrietta Street
Covent Garden, London
WC2E 8LU England

Typeset in Goudy by World Composition Services, Inc., Sterling, VA

Printer: United Book Press, Inc., Baltimore, MD
Cover Designer: Mercury Publishing Services, Rockville, MD
Technical/Production Editor: Devon Bourexis

The opinions and statements published are the responsibility of the authors, and such opinions and statements do not necessarily represent the policies of the American Psychological Association.

Library of Congress Cataloging-in-Publication Data

Baker, Rodney R.
    Psychology and the Department of Veterans Affairs : a historical analysis of training, research, practice, and advocacy / by Rodney R. Baker and Wade E. Pickren.—1st ed.
        p. cm.
    Includes bibliographical references.
    ISBN-13: 978-1-59147-453-1
    ISBN-10: 1-59147-453-1
    1. Mental health policy—United States—History. 2. Psychology—Research—United States—History. 3. Psychologists—Training of—United States—History. 4. Veterans—Medical care—United States—History. I. Pickren, Wade E. II. Title.
    [DNLM: 1. United States. Dept. of Veterans Affairs. 2. Mental Health Services—history—United States. 3. Veterans—history—United States. 4. Government Agencies—history—United States. WA 11 AA1 B168p 2006]

RA790.6.B35 2006
362.20973—dc22
                                                            2006013193

British Library Cataloguing-in-Publication Data
A CIP record is available from the British Library.

Printed in the United States of America
First Edition

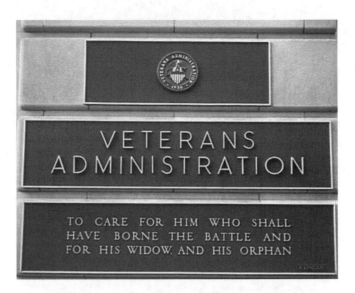

The VA's motto and mission statement is taken from Abraham Lincoln's second inaugural address given March 4, 1865, and appears on a plaque on the front of the VA Central Office building at 810 Vermont Street, NW, in Washington, DC. The photo above was taken circa 1984, prior to the agency's name change on the plaque in 1989 when the VA was elevated to Cabinet status and renamed the Department of Veterans Affairs.

CONTENTS

ACKNOWLEDGMENTS

This history of psychology and the Veterans Administration, now the Department of Veterans Affairs (VA), benefited from the contributions of many. Formal interviews and personal correspondence with psychologists and other mental health leaders who helped shape psychology in the VA were of immeasurable assistance in filling information gaps in published material and providing insights into some of the forces shaping key events in this history.

Current staff of the Mental Health Strategic Health Group (MHSHG) in the VA Central Office supplied material and helped us acquire information not otherwise easily obtained. James Williams, Executive Assistant for the Chief Consultant of MHSHG, was especially helpful in this regard. The staff of the VA Central Office Library were also helpful in accessing archival material in their collection. Special thanks are due to Caryl Kazen, Chief of the VA Central Office Library, and Cindy Rock, VA Central Office Librarian.

J. Jack Lasky, C. James Klett, Lee Gurel, John Overall, William Paré, and Paul McReynolds not only provided richly nuanced oral histories of their careers in the VA but also proved to be reliable and critical reviewers of the research chapters. VA retirees Charles Stenger and Walter Penk reviewed and helped refine and focus the chapter on treatment, and Robert Gresen and Edmund Nightingale helped with the update on the current status of psychology in the VA in the summary chapter. Many thanks to all of them.

The staff of the Arthur Melton Library at the American Psychological Association—Rennie Georgieva, Helen Suprunova, and Jay Staton—also provided generous assistance in obtaining obscure articles and books, checking facts, preparing materials for transcription, and many other thankless tasks. Our deep appreciation is extended to them. David Baker and his staff at the Archives of the History of American Psychology at The University of Akron were similarly helpful in locating archival materials and deserve our thanks.

Finally, several staff members at the American Psychological Association Books Department generously supported research that went into the development of the book. We especially thank Gary VandenBos and Susan Reynolds for their support, guidance, and encouragement.

Psychology and the Department of Veterans Affairs

INTRODUCTION

Several agencies of the federal government played important roles in promoting psychology as a practice and research profession after World War II. These agencies included the Department of Defense, the National Science Foundation, the National Institute of Mental Health (NIMH), and the Veterans Administration (now the Department of Veterans Affairs). This is a historical resource volume on psychology and the Veterans Administration/ Department of Veterans Affairs (VA), which provided significant funding support for the training, research, and employment of psychologists that helped direct and establish the profession of psychology. The volume offers important insights into the expansion of psychology since World War II. It is one of many narrative threads in the story of the major changes in psychology and the reciprocal influence of psychology and government that was begun in the volume on the history of psychology and the NIMH (Pickren & Schneider, 2005). This book highlights the role of government in shaping the lives of its citizens through the assistance provided its veterans. This book is also intended to serve as a resource for scholars wishing to add to the specialized history of post–World War II psychology and government.

The literature on the VA's contributions to the development of psychology has been largely confined to overview accounts of its role in the training of psychologists and the large-scale employment of psychologists after World War II (e.g., Benjamin & Baker, 2004; Moore, 1992; Wolman, 1965). This volume adds needed detail to available information and provides an analysis of historical forces shaping those training and employment contributions. The volume similarly chronicles the forces promoting psychological research and practice. The role of the VA and its psychology leaders in influencing training accreditation and the credentialing of psychologists is provided similar coverage.

PAST AS PROLOGUE

This history of the contributions of VA psychology to the health care of veterans serves as prologue to the care being providing to veterans by psychologists today. Each war introduces new challenges for the care of veterans. The wars in Iraq and Afghanistan are no exception.

Improved health care for those wounded in combat in our latest wars has increased the numbers of severely injured veterans with multiple and complex traumas. This complexity of injury led the VA to create four regional polytrauma centers in 2005 where psychologists join other health care specialists to coordinate needed rehabilitation care for these veterans. Treatment provided by psychologists in these centers for the pain and sequelae of head injury, irreversible physical disability, and the resulting emotional problems is complemented by their efforts in providing needed counseling to the wives, husbands, children, and parents of these veterans. In addition, psychologists are providing similar rehabilitation services to veterans in traumatic brain injury sites closer to the veterans' homes after discharge from the regional polytrauma centers.

The extensive and prolonged use of National Guard and reserve units in the second Iraq war (Operation Iraqi Freedom) presented still another challenge. The disruption of the careers and family lives of these men and women, who were older than other combatants, and their response to extended periods of danger and stress resulted in treatment issues (including posttraumatic stress disorder, depression, and substance abuse) similar to those that emerged from the enlisted military population. In addition, reentry into community life after deployment raises adjustment issues of a magnitude not seen since World War II. The age and maturity of National Guard participants may, however, give them an edge over younger personnel in coping skills, although this factor has not yet been adequately researched. Special joint funding by the VA and the NIMH is being provided for studies looking at coping skills and resiliency factors for all returning veterans, with special attention to personnel from National Guard and reserve units. With eligibility for care in the VA for 2 years after their deployment, these veterans add still another responsibility for care by psychologists.

PSYCHOLOGY AND THE VA: A BRIEF PREHISTORY

From its earliest history, the U.S. government followed a tradition established in ancient Rome of providing benefits to disabled soldiers. That tradition of providing assistance to citizens who fight in their nation's wars has been continued in almost every subsequent society. In America, benefits to disabled soldiers were established in the colonies and were expanded during the Civil War and World War I (Skocpol, 1992; Veterans Administration, 1967). In 1930, President Herbert Hoover established the VA by executive order to consolidate and coordinate government activities affecting war veterans. The consolidated agencies were the Veterans' Bureau (including those Public Health Service hospitals serving veterans), the Bureau of Pensions, and the National Homes for Disabled Volunteer Soldiers. Fifty-four VA hospitals were created under the consolidation.[1]

Although a role had been determined for psychology in the military in personnel selection for the Army in World War I (Seidenfeld, 1966; Sokal, 1987; Yerkes, 1921), it was not until the end of World War II that psychology became established in the VA. Prior to 1946, there were very few psychologists with a doctorate employed by the VA. Psychological services were primarily offered by individuals with master's degrees in psychology who provided assessment services to veterans, usually as part of a vocational rehabilitation program.

GI BILL OF RIGHTS

The development of psychology in the VA, and medical care in general, were promoted by two significant pieces of legislation. The first was the Servicemen's Readjustment Act (Public Law 78-346) commonly referred to as the *GI Bill of Rights*, passed on June 22, 1944. The second legislation was passed on January 3, 1946 (To Establish a Department of Medicine and Surgery; Public Law 79-293) and created an integrated health care mission for the VA, as described in the following section. The GI Bill of Rights legislation is credited with helping the country recover and adjust to the post–World War II era. The entire society benefited from the educational and vocational rehabilitation opportunities given millions of veterans. More

---

[1] Readers interested in a more detailed history of these benefit programs and the social forces and legislative actions leading to the creation of the VA are invited to read the Veterans Administration 1967 report *Medical Care of Veterans*, prepared for the House Committee on Veterans Affairs. This report is one of many on file in the VA psychology archive collection in the Archives of the History of American Psychology at The University of Akron.

than 6 million veterans entered college after the end of the war, representing the most profound democratization of higher education in U.S. history (O'Neill, 1986). The health care benefits for veterans, including significant funding for VA hospital construction, set the stage for the development of the VA as one of the most comprehensive health care systems in modern history. The legislation required the VA to expand its capability to provide health care to veterans, directly led to the growth of psychology in the VA, and spurred the growth of psychology, especially clinical psychology, in the United States.

The GI Bill and the end of World War II created a number of problems for the VA. The end of the war was projected to bring over 16 million veterans back into the mainstream of society, many needing medical care or other assistance in redirecting their social and vocational lives. Initially, the VA attempted to arrange vocational guidance services through a contract system with colleges and universities. These institutions furnished the facilities and the personnel to provide vocational assessment and counseling services to veterans, usually alongside service to their traditional clientele (Darley & Marquis, 1946). This proved problematic as issues of quality and credentials were raised. The VA then sought to have at least one representative at each site and expanded the vocational and rehabilitation program to mental hygiene clinics and veterans' hospitals (Schneidler, 1947).

The personnel problem remained a major issue. The American Psychological Association (APA) leadership objected to the poor quality of the work being done by the colleges, because much of that work was performed by undergraduate students who worked at the counseling centers or by individuals who had little or no training beyond the bachelor's degree (Darley & Marquis, 1946; Darley & Wolfle, 1946). What APA leaders feared was that the public trust in psychology as a science and as a profession would be undermined by the less than professional services provided under the aegis of psychology. This was a critical reason for the VA and the APA agreeing that the entry-level degree for psychological practice had to be the doctorate (Farreras, 2005). That agreement also made salient the woefully inadequate supply of qualified personnel and gave great urgency to the need to develop training standards and establish a pipeline of scientifically trained professional psychologists. As Jane Morgan, in her characteristically direct way, wrote, "The need for clinical psychologists—in large numbers and in a hurry—is obvious" (Morgan, 1947, p. 32).

Medical treatment in the VA was also not well organized to deliver the needed care. The shortage of doctors and nurses was critical. At the end of June 1945, 1,700 of the VA's 2,300 doctors were personnel on active military duty who were on loan from the military and would soon be discharged (Veterans Administration, 1947a). The Civil Service qualification and hiring procedures were cumbersome and delayed recruitment.

Many of the returning veterans needed treatment of medical and psychological problems resulting from their war experience. Veterans with psychiatric disorders occupied 58% of VA hospital beds at the end of the 1946 fiscal year (Grob, 1991; Veterans Administration, 1947a), and the shortage of trained mental health workers in the VA was as critical as it was for other medical care providers. The VA mental health leadership, with Daniel Blain as head of the new Neuropsychiatry Division and James G. Miller heading the Clinical Psychology Section, realized the importance of developing mental health programs for the large numbers of recently discharged veterans. A system of mental hygiene clinics was authorized to serve as a first stop for troubled veterans in the hope that outpatient care would be sufficient and serve to reduce the number of discharged soldiers admitted to hospitals (Blain, 1948). These clinics were located in large urban areas, such as New York, Boston, and Los Angeles, and were immediately overwhelmed with service demands far beyond the capacity of their personnel and space to provide such services (Campbell, 1947; Hildreth, 1954). A team approach was developed where possible, consisting of a psychiatrist, psychologist, and social worker, to provide diagnosis, treatment, and hospital aftercare (Adler, Futterman, & Webb, 1948; Adler, Valenstein, & Michaels, 1949; Campbell, 1947). Still, it was clear that no matter how the various service components were arranged, there were simply not enough personnel to meet the demands.

PUBLIC LAW 79-293

As newly appointed administrator for the VA in August 1945, General Omar N. Bradley made strong pleas to Congress to pass legislation that would help correct some of these problems. On January 3, 1946, less than 5 months after the end of World War II, President Truman signed Public Law 79-293, which created the VA Department of Medicine and Surgery (DM&S) with the responsibility for providing medical care for veterans. The Neuropsychiatry Division was established in the DM&S at this time to coordinate the efforts of psychiatry, neurology, and psychology in treating patients with mental health disorders. In the first organization of these services in the field, counseling psychology became a separate service, with clinical psychology a division or section under psychiatry, which, in some hospitals, was a division under the medical service. Psychologists were expected to provide assessment and therapy as part of the mental health team. In addition, psychologists were expected to conduct research that was relevant to the mental health needs of veterans, although initially, this was defined rather broadly (Bronfenbrenner, 1947; J. G. Miller, 1946; also see chaps. 3 and 4, this volume).

Public Law 79-293 had two major benefits to the VA. The law first established a more responsive recruitment and employment system outside of regular Civil Service procedures to hire doctors, dentists, and nurses. By June 30, 1946, less than 6 months after passage of the law, the number of full-time VA staff physicians had grown to 4,000, almost double the 2,300 physicians on duty a year earlier (Veterans Administration, 1947a). The 1,700 physicians working in the VA who were on loan from the military had dropped to fewer than 400 during the same time period. Second, Public Law 79-293 enabled the VA to establish a system of affiliations with medical schools to both improve the quality of care within the VA and provide training to meet the health care manpower needs of the organization. It was within the provisions of Public Law 79-293 and a subsequent policy decision that the VA began its psychology training program (see chaps. 1 and 2, this volume).

Although the GI Bill had a major impact on society in general, Public Law 79-293 came to be referred to as the "Magna Carta" for organizing medical care in the VA (Veterans Administration, 1967, p. 212). The law's use to establish the psychology training program in the VA led to the training of over 25,000 clinical and counseling psychologists from 1946 to 2005 for leadership and clinical roles in academic, public service, and independent practice settings, as documented later in this volume (see chap. 2).

PSYCHOLOGY AND VA GROWTH IN CULTURAL CONTEXT

Pickren (2005) summarized a number of factors leading to the growth of psychology in the aftermath of World War II and the cultural context of that growth. In that account, Pickren noted that the federal government became involved in the large-scale support of training, research, and practice in the mental health field. The public was becoming more sensitized to the prevalence of mental illness in society. Psychoanalysis was popular, and psychotherapy became part of the middle-class experience as citizens dealt with Cold War anxiety (Capshew, 1999; Hale, 1995; Herman, 1995).

Within the profession, psychologists were also trying to decide how to handle and respond to some of this growth. In 1946, Dael Wolfle, the executive secretary of the newly reorganized APA, editorialized that the "ivory tower had literally been blown out from under psychology" by the demands for application from various government agencies, including the VA, as well as from the private sector (Darley & Wolfle, 1946, p. 180). Although psychology was emerging as a legitimate helping profession in the minds of the public (Cook, 1958), the applied practice of psychology was not always seen as a legitimate career goal by mainstream academic psychologists. This made applied work problematic for the first generation of psychologists trained after World War II. Many of these men (the overwhelming majority of the first post–World War II cohort was male) were veterans themselves and were interested in clinical or counseling psychology primarily for its potential usefulness in ameliorating the suffering that they and their fellow soldiers had experienced. Psychologists interested in being employed by public service organizations and government agencies to perform their clinical practice, like those in the VA and those working for state hospitals, were considered outliers by mainstream psychology, even more than those interested in a clinical independent practice. In his address as outgoing president of the APA Division of Psychologists in Public Service, L. S. Rogers (1956) noted the shift from most psychologists being employed by universities as teachers or researchers before the war to the increase of those in applied practice settings other than colleges and universities after the war. He pointed out that one third of all APA members were employed by a government agency (Clark, 1957) and commented on the puzzlement of academic psychologists as to what a government psychologist does or how they could ever function in a bureaucracy. To some academic psychologists, public service positions were second rate and held only by those unable to qualify for university positions.

Despite academics' puzzlement over the role of psychologists in bureaucracies, psychology and the VA were growing. Most members of Congress were veterans themselves and were eager to support legislation and benefits for their fellow veterans. Veteran service organizations like the American Legion, the Disabled American Veterans, and the Veterans of Foreign Wars were powerful political forces also promoting benefit programs for veterans. Even today, a consortium of these and other veterans' organizations submits a proposed funding bill to Congress in the budget cycle process for issues of importance to veterans, and these organizations conduct site visits of VA medical centers to document and report to the VA and Congress the quality of care received by veterans or concerns about that treatment.

IMPACT OF FEDERAL FUNDING

The influx of federal funding in the VA after World War II resulted in significant growth for the psychology profession in employment numbers, treatment programs, research, and training. By the early 1950s, the federal government was supporting the training of nearly half of all the psychology interns in the country, primarily through training stipends from the NIMH and the VA (Laughlin & Worley, 1991). A large percentage of psychologists receiving training in the VA assumed jobs in the VA after their training, many emerging as leaders who helped shape the profession and its role in treatment and research. The VA became an employer of choice for many psychologists interested in the applied practice of psychology, and the VA shortly became the largest employer of psychologists in the country, a distinction still held today. In what was an annual report by the VA to the APA convention from 1946 through the mid-1950s, R. A. Wolford, deputy chief medical director of the VA, reported in 1956 that the VA employed 628 clinical psychologists as of August 1, 1956 (Wolford, 1956). At the time it was estimated that 3,500 psychologists in the country met VA qualification standards (doctoral degree and internship), and the reported VA employment figures represented almost one fifth of those clinical and counseling psychologists in the country qualified to work in the VA.

Research by VA psychologists saw similar growth trends. Although medical research was not officially added to the VA's medical care program mission until 1958 (Veterans Administration, 1974), psychologists were involved early on in using their skills and interests in research. In a review of research in progress in 1948 (Veterans Administration, 1948), VA psychologists were involved in 57 studies of specific patient diagnostic groups, 52 studies of the effectiveness of therapy, and 103 studies of assessment instruments. In the 1950s, VA psychologists were involved in as many as 500 studies a year, many emerging from the dissertation research of psychology students. In a typical month, about 20 articles were being prepared by VA mental health personnel, with a psychologist being the senior author in three fourths of them (Veterans Administration, 1955b). In his review of the 1st decade of VA psychology, Wolford (1956) cited a report by the National Science Foundation that looked at all research being conducted by psychologists in federal government (Air Force, Navy, Army, Civil Service Commission, Public Health Service, and the VA). Of the 900 research projects studied, VA psychologists were involved in 336, or 37%, of the projects. VA psychologists were also conducting 89% of the clinical research projects, 72% of studies in personality, and 33% of studies in learning and perception topics. Wolford's report noted that psychologists conducted one third of all research in the VA, both in mental health and non–mental health areas. The Annual Report of the Administrator of Veterans Affairs for 1956 (Veterans Administration, 1957) identified 409 of 653 mental health research projects as being conducted by psychologists. Psychological research in the VA in the 1950s and 1960s was critical for the development of psychopharmacology, and VA psychologists' investigations in psychosomatic medicine were important for the later development of behavioral medicine and health psychology (see chaps. 3 and 4, this volume).

The federal funding of VA psychology saw still other benefits in the area of treatment programming. Beginning immediately after the end of the war, VA psychologists were deeply involved in the development of mental hygiene outpatient clinics, where many new treatment programs were pioneered in the 1950s and 1960s (Adler et al., 1948; Hildreth, 1954). The VA credited mental hygiene clinics with reducing the need for hospitalization for more than one in four patients (Veterans Administration, 1950).

VA psychology was also able to promote the profession's role in nontraditional mental health care in the United States because of the comprehensive medical care being given veterans. Despite their significant contributions to mental health treatment, the growing number of community mental health centers did not offer the type of "one-stop" health care resource that the VA provided for veterans. In VA hospitals and mental hygiene clinics the veteran in need of mental health care could receive not only that care but also treatment for a vast array of medical problems, today including transplant surgery, burn care, spinal cord injury care, and other state-of-the-art treatments. The VA pioneered the development of prosthetic devices designed to help the veteran deal with amputations and other physical disabilities resulting from combat. As veterans aged, they were eligible for a full continuum of programs developed by the VA as part of its comprehensive health care programming that were not easily available to nonveterans, ranging from nursing home care to home health care. Support for housing in the VA's community residential care program (with the majority of patients in this program having a psychiatric diagnosis) and other social support systems were also available, as was vocational training and rehabilitation provided by counseling psychologists.

These services were significant for the support of mental health care. Stable housing after hospital discharge helped patients remain in outpatient mental health care programs. Along with other rehabilitation professionals, psychologists played critical roles in assisting the veteran's vocational rehabilitation and return to independent living. Because psychologists practiced their profession embedded in this comprehensive health care organization, their communication and interactions with their colleagues in the other health care professions facilitated an involvement of psychologists and their skills in these programs. A small sample of such programs includes tuberculosis research and treatment, biofeedback treatment for convulsions, treatment of psychological complications in renal dialysis, involvement in geriatric care, spinal cord injury care, and traumatic brain injury care.

THE RELATIONSHIP AND ROLE OF MENTAL HEALTH DISCIPLINES IN THE VA

Psychologists in the VA had similar interprofessional relationship issues with their psychiatry colleagues as existed in other treatment settings, as described by Buchanan (2003). Psychologists developed and practiced their profession, as one early VA chief of psychology noted, as "guests in the house of medicine" (S. Cleveland, personal communication, circa 1978). Once psychiatry and medicine established that they were in charge, however, the need for additional staff to treat large numbers of veterans clearly opened the way for psychology, social work, and nursing to build programs and provide needed services.

Early psychiatry and psychology leaders in the VA Central Office modeled and promoted an interprofessional collaboration model that for the most part existed among the mental health professions in the field (Blain, 1947; Shaffer, 1947). When turf battles emerged between psychiatry and psychology in a facility, a central office psychiatrist and psychologist would both visit that facility. They would both meet with their counterparts and give them a "shape up" message reminding them that they were all here to treat the veterans (J. Davis Jr., personal communication, March 1992).

Early treatment program guides for mental hygiene clinics and day hospitals clearly supported a multidisciplinary team treatment model (Campbell, 1947). These guides typically encouraged the use of psychiatrists, psychologists, and social workers as core treatment team members needed to successfully implement these programs. The multidisciplinary treatment approaches promoted on a large scale in the VA became accepted practices in institutional psychiatric care across the country (Hildreth, 1954).

The first mention of the Neuropsychiatry Division in the VA's annual report to Congress appeared in the report that covered the period ending June 30, 1948 (Veterans Administration, 1949). That report gave several indications of the importance that the VA placed on the Neuropsychiatry Division and the expectations that the VA had for the mental health disciplines. At one point the report stated, "The integrated team approach in treatment, utilizing physicians, nurses, attendants, clinical psychologists, social workers, medical and vocational rehabilitation workers, and special service facilities has enhanced the rapidity and completeness of recovery and rehabilitation" (p. 22). The report went on to note that although clinical psychologists had been in the VA only since the reorganization 2 1/2 years earlier, they had made sizable contributions to the medical care of veterans. For example, psychologists' involvement in individual and group psychotherapy had increased and they were assuming a larger part of the administrative and training duties in the VA. The report finally commented on the importance of training in the VA and indicated that at the end of fiscal year 1948 there were 25 residents in neurology, 385 residents in psychiatry, and 459 trainees in clinical psychology.

It is important to note that counseling psychology became a separate service in the VA Central Office and in VA hospitals in 1952. It was not until after 1957 that clinical psychology was firmly established as an independent service in VA hospitals. In the VA's annual reports to Congress, counseling psychology had its own coverage of vocational rehabilitation activities distinct from that of psychiatry and psychology, in which it reported on programs and on the numbers of veterans being served. The VA established separate internship training positions for counseling psychology starting in 1953. Counseling psychology in the VA (and in other clinical settings) eventually suffered from a lack of status and attention compared with clinical psychology, however. As counseling psychology sought the same treatment privileges and status as clinical psychology in the 1980s, its role in vocational rehabilitation in the VA was "given away" to physical medicine. This abandonment of its work rehabilitation roots was a worst-case scenario of the giving away of psychology recommended by G. A. Miller (1969), who wanted psychology to share knowledge, not forsake it.

OVERVIEW OF THE VOLUME

This volume focuses on psychology training, research, practice, and advocacy activity in the VA. The primary time period covered is 1946 through 1988, although some reference is made to events before and after those dates. The reciprocal relationships between the VA and other organizations, such as the APA, are noted throughout that time period. Chapters 1 and 2 on the training of psychologists describe the VA's contributions to the expansion of the emerging applied field of clinical psychology through its training program for graduate study in clinical psychology and counseling psychology. The VA's role in influencing training accreditation and credentialing is also described in these chapters. Included in chapter 2 are descriptions of the first joint federal advocacy activities of VA psychologists and the APA in the 1970s and 1980s in promoting and maintaining funding for the VA's training program. Chapter 2 also documents the development of postdoctoral psychology training in the VA.

Chapters 3 and 4 focus on the research contributions of VA psychologists. Chapter 3 describes the leadership role of psychologists in some of the cooperative research programs developed by the VA in the 1950s, including programs involving prefrontal lobotomy, psychopharmacology (called *chemotherapy* at the time), issues in treating tuberculosis, and evaluation of treatment settings (the Psychiatric Evaluation Project). Of these, the psychopharmacological research was perhaps the most critical because of its focus on behavioral issues in serious mental illness. This emphasis contributed to the reconfiguration of official diagnostic classification schemes, as evidenced by the third edition of the *Diagnostic and Statistical Manual of Mental Disorders* (3rd ed.; American Psychiatric Association, 1980). Chapter 4 describes in detail two local VA hospital research programs, those of the Perry Point VA Hospital in Maryland and the Palo Alto VA Hospital in California, to illustrate the nature and scope of research by psychologists occurring at the local level. Other contributions of VA psychologists in the development of clinical assessment and rating scales and the study of suicide and other topics are briefly noted. In both chapters, the role of clinical psychologists as scientist–practitioners is key to understanding their research contributions. At the time, it was not common for psychiatrists to have research acumen, and their lack of research skills forced them to rely on psychologists for methodological and statistical guidance.

Chapter 5 highlights some of the treatment programs in the VA and the contributions of psychologists in developing group therapy and vocational rehabilitation programs and treatment programs for specialized patient populations. Chapter 6 addresses professional and mental health advocacy issues in defining and defending the profession in the VA and the advocacy interactions between the VA and other organizations such as the APA.

Chapter 7 provides a historical perspective on the contributions of psychology in the VA, preceded by a description of VA psychology as it exists today. An appendix to the book contains a timeline of events that were significant for the VA and VA psychology, including dates of significant legislation and appointments of key leaders in VA psychology through 1999.

In preparing this volume we encountered a number of limitations in documenting the contributions of VA psychology to the profession and the interactive nature of VA psychology's relationship to the VA itself. The first limitation is that of space. This volume can serve only to highlight the scope of VA psychology's impact on the profession and to provide a valuable resource to those who wish to expand on particular topics. The space limitation was especially significant in describing the scope of research and treatment activities of psychologists in the VA. Difficult decisions were made in deciding what should receive attention and in what depth.

A second limitation is availability of material. Only the personal recollections of key psychology leaders interviewed during this project were available to help complete some topics. Much of the VA psychology story is contained in publications by the VA itself that have not been widely available to the non-VA community. Today these publications are available in only a very few reference sites, principally the VA Central Office Library in Washington, DC. The information bulletins of the VA's Neuropsychiatry Division and the quarterly newsletters reporting on research by VA psychologists, both available in that library, are rich sources of information about what psychologists were doing in the early years. The information bulletin and newsletter formats also offer a unique opportunity not only to read about program development and research projects but also to read discussions and arguments about directions for research, training, treatment programs, and administrative issues. Many, but not all, of these newsletters and VA publications are in the Archives of the History of American Psychology at The University of Akron. However, neither the Archives nor the VA Central Office Library has copies of these newsletter publications before 1959, and these are feared lost. For example, H. Max Houtchens, chief of the Clinical Psychology Division in the VA noted in the forward to the first issue of the quarterly *Newsletter for Cooperative Research in Psychology* (1959, p. 1) that the publication was previously named the *Newsletter for Psychologists in Tuberculosis* and that the name of the publication was changed to more properly reflect the current interests and activities of psychologists (Houtchens, 1959). Complete copies of that newsletter collection addressing VA psychology's work in tuberculosis research have not yet been found.

Oral history interviews were conducted as part of this book project, and Exhibit 1, which follows, includes a list of those who were interviewed or provided other personal communications to the authors regarding the events shaping VA psychology, including personal correspondence with Rodney R. Baker when he prepared an unpublished brief history of the VA in 1992. As noted earlier, a key collection of material for this volume was found in the VA Central Office Library in Washington, DC. Because scholars have limited access to much of this material, copies of all documents published by the VA that are referenced in this volume, including the VA's annual reports to Congress, have been deposited in the VA psychology archive collection in the Archives of the History of American Psychology at The University of Akron.

EXHIBIT 1
Oral Histories and Personal Communication

Interviewers: Wade E. Pickren and Rodney R. Baker

Interviewees and Correspondents

Robert P. Barrell*
Bernhard Blom
Eugene Caffey Jr.*
Dale Cannon
Sidney Cleveland
Jonathan Cummings
John "Jack" Davis Jr.
Peter Dews
Harold Dickman
Norman Farberow
Allen Finkelstein
Robert Gresen
Lee Gurel*
Philip G. Hanson*
Jack Jernigan
Linda Johnson
James Klett and Shirley Klett*
Julian Jack Lasky*

Philip Laughlin
Paul McReynolds*
James G. Miller
Dana Moore
Jule D. Moravec
William Morse
Edmund Nightingale
John Overall*
William Paré*
Cecil P. Peck
Walter Penk
Alex Pokorny*
Joseph Rickard
Edward Sieracki
Charles A. Stenger*
Leonard Ullmann
Antonette Zeiss

Note. Those whose names are followed by an asterisk supplied detailed interview material that is available for review from the American Psychological Association, 750 First Street, NE, Washington, DC 20002.

1

ORIGINS OF VA PSYCHOLOGY AND THE 1ST DECADE OF TRAINING

The end of World War II and the demobilization of millions of soldiers created the need for a large-scale recruitment of health care professionals to assist veterans with their health care. VA psychology and its training program were established in 1946 as part of this recruitment effort and created a stimulus for the employment of psychologists and the training of clinical psychologists across the nation. The impact on the field of psychology was profound. The professional practice of psychology flourished in ways previously unimaginable to psychology's leaders and resulted in a reorientation of the public identity of psychology, which came to be viewed as a science-based treatment profession (Cook, 1958). Prior to that date there were relatively few psychologists employed in professional practice settings, and the training of psychologists was grounded in the experimental and academic tradition of the university, where research and teaching were the primary considerations.

In late 1945 the VA was preparing for a major reorganization of its medical care for veterans. A number of psychologists on active military duty in the Washington, DC area were consulted by General Omar A. Bradley, recently appointed administrator of the VA, to help develop a formal clinical psychology program to meet the mental health care needs of veterans. These individuals included Henry A. Murray, James G. Miller, and George A. Kelly (Hildreth, 1954). In December 1945, Kelly had just been released

Figure 1.1. James Grier Miller, first chief of the VA clinical psychology program, 1946–1947. Digital scan of slide obtained at the Archives of the History of American Psychology at The University of Akron.

from the Navy and was appointed the first VA psychology consultant by Bradley. Kelly was asked to continue planning for the new clinical psychology program and was also asked to help determine employment standards for clinical psychologists in the VA (Hildreth, 1954). Murray and Miller were also subsequently appointed as consultants. Murray was offered the job of heading up the new clinical psychology program in the VA but declined the offer.[1] In the spring of 1946, Miller was released from the Office of Strategic Services (OSS) and accepted an appointment as the first full-time chief of the new clinical psychology program (see Figure 1.1).

Miller had been Harvard trained, receiving his medical degree in 1942 and his doctoral degree in psychology in 1943. From 1944 to 1946 Miller served in the Army Medical Corps and OSS, the forerunner of the Central Intelligence Agency. As a member of the psychological evaluation staff of

---

[1] In a handwritten letter dated January 7, 1946, Murray described the job to a friend as "an opportunity to influence the course of psychological developments for a generation" but stated that it did not interest him at the time because of other commitments. Relevant portions of the letter are in the VA psychology archive collection in the Archives of the History of American Psychology at The University of Akron.

OSS, Miller worked with Henry Murray, Donald MacKinnon, John Gardner, Nevitt Sanford, and others in developing a psychological assessment program for OSS recruits (Pickren, 2003). For the time that Miller served as chief of psychology in the VA (1946–1947), he was on leave from his position as assistant professor of social relations in clinical psychology at Harvard. It was to Miller that the challenge was given to develop the program to provide the needed psychological care for veterans.[2]

THE VA PSYCHOLOGY TRAINING PROGRAM

The challenge Miller faced in hiring the large numbers of psychologists needed to provide psychological care in the VA was complicated by two facts. The first was the small number of doctoral psychologists involved in clinical practice at the time. The directory of the American Association for Applied Psychology (AAAP) had a total of 650 members in applied settings. Only 17% of doctoral-level members of the American Psychological Association (APA) were doing full-time professional work, and a 1941 report indicated that there were only 64 full-time psychologists and psychometricians working in 174 state psychiatric hospitals (APA & AAAP, 1945). Miller was looking at a recruitment effort to hire a projected 500 doctoral-level psychologists to work in the VA (Veterans Administration, 1947b), almost equal to the total supply of psychologists with doctoral training in clinical practice in the country.

The second problem complicating Miller's mission to hire psychologists for the VA was his assessment that it was almost impossible to find psychologists with a well-rounded program of education for the practice of psychology (J. G. Miller, 1946). He was critical of the absence of an organized curriculum to train clinical psychologists, a conclusion also reached by Sears (1946). The problems Miller encountered in finding qualified psychologists quickly led him to turn his attention to finding ways to help train the psychologists needed in the VA.

As noted in the introduction to this volume, legislation passed in 1946 authorized the VA to establish affiliations with medical schools to train needed medical personnel (To Establish a Department of Medicine and Surgery; Public Law 79-293). With this authorization, Policy Memorandum Number 2 was published by the VA on January 30, 1946, and created a system of affiliations of veterans' hospitals with medical schools that is still in effect today (Veterans Administration, 1967). That memorandum

---

[2]Readers interested in a more detailed history of events and social forces leading up to the development of the VA psychology training program are encouraged to read Dana Moore's chapter on the history of VA training in D. K. Freedheim's *History of Psychotherapy* (Moore, 1992).

assigned the VA responsibility for the care of patients and gave the medical school responsibility for graduate education and training. In the 1st year, affiliations with 63 of the nation's 77 medical schools were developed. Both parties benefited—the VA acquired experienced faculty physicians as patient care attending staff, and medical residents helped provide care and benefited from the clinical training and financial support received from the VA. The arrangement also helped ensure community quality of care treatment standards for VA hospitals and added to the prestige of working for the VA.

Although Public Law 79-293 technically established affiliations only with medical schools for the training of medical residents, Miller found language in the provisions of that legislation that would permit psychology students to be employed as part-time staff with a training assignment in delivering psychological services. He was able to convince General Bradley of this interpretation, and the basis for the VA psychology training program was established (Moore, 1992).

Miller also continued discussions begun by Kelly with a group of university consultants to help him develop the VA psychology program and the criteria for training psychologists in the program established in his agreement with General Bradley. In addition to George A. Kelly at Ohio State, these consultants included Chauncey M. Louttit, also from Ohio State, and E. Lowell Kelly from the University of Michigan. Miller and his consultants successfully argued that psychologists with doctorates were able to provide valuable psychotherapy services to patients, and they noted that psychologists were beginning to seek licensure status in some states, which made it possible for them to practice their profession independent of medical oversight (J. G. Miller, 1946). Miller was also convinced that with their research skills, psychologists with doctoral training could conduct important research and program evaluation in the VA that would benefit patients. These arguments were clearly included in the basis for the scientist–practitioner training model that came out of the 1949 Boulder Conference (Raimy, 1950). The VA's decision to adopt the doctoral degree and internship as the credential for VA employment as a clinical psychologist not only set the stage for discussions of what type of training the VA expected from universities but also helped establish doctoral training and the internship as the journeyman credential for psychological practice in the United States.

Miller's final task in establishing the VA psychology training program was to identify those universities training their students in both scientific and clinical areas from which the VA would recruit students for the training program. In December 1945, the VA had sent a request to the APA board of directors to provide a list of universities with adequate facilities for doctoral training in clinical psychology. The board referred this request to the Committee on Graduate and Professional Training. In the spring of

1946, Paul A. Hawley, the VA's chief medical director, had begun meeting with representatives of leading universities to ask them to help train clinical psychologists for the VA. Miller continued these discussions and also began working with Dael Wolfle at APA to help develop the new psychology program and to identify graduate schools that could provide the kind of research and practice academic training he believed necessary to provide the quality and type of care he was looking for in the treatment of veterans. Records from the Association of Psychology Internship Centers (APIC) provided by APIC member Bernhard Blom indicate that Miller was appointed to the APA Committee on Clinical Psychology in 1946 and participated in early discussions for criteria being developed for doctoral training. Twenty-two universities were eventually identified by APA for the VA as providing appropriate doctoral training for clinical psychologists (Sears, 1946).

Following the initial selection of universities, the VA, with support of the U.S. Public Health Service, asked APA to develop a formal accreditation program for doctoral training in clinical psychology to serve as a guide to federal agencies involved in training (Farreras, 2005; Hildreth, 1954). For the 1947–1948 training year, the APA Committee on Graduate and Professional Training reviewed 40 institutions against 13 criteria they developed for doctoral training (Sears, 1947). Only 18 of the reviewed universities met all criteria, but an additional 11 universities were considered to have an "excellent prospect of early action in fully meeting the criteria" (p. 204) and were added to the list presented to the VA. Thirty-one universities were initially recommended to the VA for its training program (see Exhibit 1.1).

EXHIBIT 1.1
Universities Recommended As VA Training Program Sites, 1947

University of California at Berkeley	Ohio State University
University of California at Los Angeles	Pennsylvania State College
Catholic University	University of Pennsylvania
University of Cincinnati	University of Pittsburgh
Clark University	Purdue University
Columbia University	University of Rochester
Duke University	University of Southern California
Harvard University	Stanford University
University of Georgia	Syracuse University
University of Illinois	Teachers College, Columbia
Indiana University	Tulane University
State University of Iowa	Washington University (St. Louis)
University of Kentucky	Western Reserve University
University of Michigan	University of Wisconsin
University of Minnesota	Yale University
Northwestern University	

In an internal document, the VA had identified four additional institutions (not included in Exhibit 1.1) as being approved by APA for VA training for the 1947–1948 training year: University of Chicago, Fordham University, University of Kansas (Menninger Foundation), and New York University. It was further noted that the universities on this expanded list, with the exception of Northwestern University, would be accepting approximately 450 trainees in the fall of 1947 (Veterans Administration, 1947b).

The VA's request of APA to assist federal agencies involved in training of psychologists is generally acknowledged as the stimulus for the development of the APA doctoral accreditation program. The APA accreditation process was of great value to the VA. It gave the responsibility for educational decisions to an impartial and appropriate scientific organization. It further provided an important relationship between the VA and the training universities on which the VA training program was based over the years (Hildreth, 1954).

MILLER'S OUTLINE FOR VA PSYCHOLOGY

Miller outlined his vision for clinical psychology and its training program in the VA in an article for the *American Psychologist* (J. G. Miller, 1946). In that article, he first noted that the number of psychology positions being authorized in the VA's plan for the Vocational Advisement and Guidance Division and the Clinical Psychology Section exceeded the total of all qualified clinical psychologists in the country (referring to those with a doctorate in clinical psychology and applied practice training) and that the demand would not diminish for many years. Noting the far-reaching importance for the psychology profession, Miller presented a challenge to the nation's psychologists

> to enter into new fields of practice and research, to assume new responsibilities to which they have not traditionally been accustomed, and to take an important place in society's task of renewing and maintaining the mental health of the country's veterans. (p. 181)

Miller's plan was to employ clinical psychologists in a number of clinical sites: mental hygiene clinics, regional offices, neuropsychiatric hospitals, neuropsychiatric convalescent centers, and paraplegia and aphasia centers. The latter sites would be in general medical and surgical hospitals. He noted the important role for psychologists in individual and group treatment in these sites (initially under the direction and referral of a neuropsychiatrist). He was especially optimistic about the potential role for psychologists in

TABLE 1.1
Annual Salaries of VA Psychology Staff, 1946

Staff category	Salary
Predoctoral	$3,640
Doctoral	$4,300
Chief of psychology	$5,180
Branch office chief of psychology	$6,230

Note. Predoctoral employment required that all course work be completed for the doctorate or at least 10 courses in specific areas and 2 years of clinical experience. Doctoral positions required the doctoral degree from a recognized college or university and 3 years of clinical experience. In addition to the doctoral degree, the position of chief psychologist required 4 years of clinical experience. Five years of clinical experience were required of branch office chiefs who were also expected to be "mature."

research, particularly in program evaluation, an initiative that was later fully developed by psychologist Lee Gurel (see chap. 3, this volume).

Miller described the VA's plan to employ only psychologists with doctoral training. Because there were not enough psychologists with doctorates to fill authorized positions, Miller indicated that the VA would hire those who had some psychology course work or other college degrees on a temporary basis without promotion possibilities until they had obtained the doctoral degree. It was later determined that these individuals were to be given until 1951 to obtain the doctoral degree, after which only psychologists with doctorates could be employed (Ash, 1968b).

In what was to be the new direction for training, however, Miller articulated the position that the required training of doctoral psychologists for the VA would not be wholly academic. He urged that "real experience be obtained in the clinical techniques which can be learned only in the doing" (J. G. Miller, 1946, p. 185). With that basis for required practical training for employment, he noted that 13 branch chief psychologists would be appointed who, in addition to other duties, would direct the training and professional activities of psychologists in the VA. He then went on to describe the VA's plan for the training of clinical psychology doctoral students in VA hospitals treating neuropsychiatric patients.

Students were expected to work part time in the VA. They were to be hired in their training positions at one of three levels of hourly rate employment on the basis of their level of academic preparation. First- and 2nd-year appointments were generally what are now regarded as practicum training appointments (at hourly rates of about $0.56 for 1st-year appointments and $0.72 for 2nd-year appointments). Third- and 4th-year appointments were devoted to what is now regarded as internship training (both receiving about $0.88 per hour). These latter hourly rates were fixed at half the salary of predoctoral staff salary rates (see Table 1.1). For all training positions preference would be given to veterans, who also would receive additional benefits for education costs authorized by legislation.

Miller's article also stipulated that the students be selected from "any university recognized by the APA as qualified to give complete training in clinical psychology" (J. G. Miller, 1946, p. 186). The university was to be responsible for the training curriculum and for deciding the amount of time that training was to be carried out at the university and the amount at the VA hospital. The only stipulation was that students spend the required number of paid hours at the VA for their training appointments.

Miller finally noted that faculty at the affiliated departments of psychology would be appointed as part-time consultants to supervise the students in their clinical work. In their consulting role, faculty would be expected to advise on clinical practice matters. Still another important role for these consultants was that they would be expected to supervise both students and other staff in carrying out psychological research, as well as conduct research themselves.

APA DISCUSSIONS ON TRAINING

Miller's proposals for the training of clinical psychologists in the VA merged with a number of formal and informal training issue discussions held by APA. In their review of the development of internship criteria, Laughlin and Worley (1991) noted that training issues first received attention in 1931, when APA sponsored a study to look at training needs, including those of the internship. Formal discussions continued through the 1940s in several forums starting with the Lindsley conference in 1941 as chronicled by Farreras (2005). Early issues surrounding internship training ranged from the length of training to when the internship year should be scheduled. Farreras (2005) further reported that the number of medical courses that should be included and the breadth of focus of training were also debated.

The informal discussions on training were no less important, however, in defining the broad range of training issues faced by the profession. An early sample of these informal discussions was a roundtable discussion on internship training arranged by Division 12 (Society of Clinical Psychology) at the annual APA meeting in Philadelphia in 1946 that was summarized in its journal in 1947 and reprinted later (Dosier, 1947/2000). Edgar A. Doll presided over the discussion among the roundtable participants, who, in addition to Miller representing the VA, included Ernest R. Hilgard (chair of APA's Policy and Planning Board), Laurence F. Shaffer (chair of the APA Committee on Clinical Psychology), Bruce Moore (APA Committee on Internship Training), Lloyd N. Yepsen (New Jersey State Department of Institutions and Agencies), and Joseph M. Bobbitt (U.S. Public Health Service).

Doll's opening comments suggested that the training of clinical psychologists was strongest in assessment and challenged the group to focus on the weaknesses of internship training. Moore argued that a primary weakness was the lack of a broad training background needed to make the clinical psychologist something more than a technician. Moore noted the large disparity between the VA's needs (i.e., the need to hire some 500–600 clinical psychologists) and the available pool to draw from and raised the possibility that some other discipline would take over the functions of clinical psychologists if training did not proceed quickly. Hilgard reported that APA had already decided to accelerate the training of clinical psychologists but still called for an improvement of standards for training, citing these standards as a current weakness.

Miller redefined Doll's challenge to look at weaknesses of internship training as a challenge to decide where clinical psychology was going. He argued that the testing role of the clinical psychologist would eventually lead the psychologist to consultation and treatment. In the VA, the three primary tasks for the clinical psychologist would be diagnosis, research, and therapy, in that order. Miller called for a strong alliance between the VA and universities in preparing psychologists for these tasks.

Shaffer believed a greater integration of training among the mental health disciplines was needed. He reported on what he described as an amicable meeting he had attended of a joint committee of the American Psychiatric Association and APA earlier in the summer of 1946 that called for an integration of training that might also include social work. One recommendation of its report was to introduce some training from each discipline into the training of other disciplines. For example, psychiatrists could benefit from some psychology courses on learning and conflict, and psychologists could benefit from some course work on psychosomatic issues. It was expected that teamwork between psychiatrists and psychologists would benefit as they became more appreciative of each other's contributions.

Yepsen and Bobbitt both suggested that the profession needed to look at the fact that clinical psychologists were also working in sites other than in the VA and would have other training content needs. Yepsen noted that psychologists had been working in correction settings for 25 years but that no real progress had been made in training for work in this specific field or in the fields of public welfare and schools. He appealed to the group to look broadly at the training needs for psychologists who worked in different settings.

In addition to outlining the preliminary plans for the training program in the Public Health Service, Bobbitt noted that the Public Health Service training would emphasize outpatient preventive work and would provide training to a broad spectrum of mental health care workers. He expressed the hope that when thoroughly trained psychologists were produced, many difficulties between psychologists and psychiatrists would disappear as psychiatry learned to depend on psychology as it did on other specialties.

A number of topics were introduced into the discussion when the audience was invited to participate (e.g., whether the dissertation and dual foreign language requirements still had a place in the training of clinical psychologists), and the roundtable group had some disagreement regarding a question about why APA was planning for nonpaid internships. Doll indicated that one argument against paying interns concerned the issue of whether the internship was to be viewed as a low-grade job or a high-grade learning experience, and that there was a tendency for paid interns to underrate the training aspect. Bobbitt noted that the Public Health Service was planning to give stipends to interns to get the best students. Miller indicated the VA was also planning to pay its interns to free them from economic concerns so they could attend better to their learning. He again argued that the profession needed to decide what status the clinical psychologist was to have. Miller wanted the psychologist to have the same status as that of physicians (whose students were being paid during their VA training). He indicated that he was sorry the VA had more buying power than some other organizations, with whom he did not want to be in competition, and hoped that this situation would not last long (Dosier, 1947/2000, p. 325).

In the turmoil that attended the growth of the VA training program, George A. Kelly recalled an instance shortly after the end of World War II in which a large and politically powerful private psychiatric institution had announced on its own that it would train psychologists under a subsidy from the VA (G. A. Kelly, 1965). The institution, not identified by Kelly, had also indicated that it would ensure that these psychologists would not be "contaminated by university departments of psychology" (p. 98). Some 40 trainees had been recruited for that training program. The only problem was that this program had never been discussed with or authorized by the VA. In his role as a consultant to the VA at the time, Kelly advised against approval of this program. He also noted that this was a time when those who hesitated to make a decision had the decision made for them.

From 1946 to 1949, the VA and the Public Health Service led the way in determining many of the practical details of defining internship training that met their individual needs. They needed to move forward and could not wait for APA to study all the issues. The fact that this did not always sit well with those in APA is reflected in a 1949 report on the status of doctoral training by the APA Committee on Training in Clinical Psychology (American Psychological Association, 1949). Although the report concluded that overall an excellent job was being done, some concern was expressed that a too-narrow definition of clinical psychology was emerging from the VA's training of clinical psychologists. The VA training model, it was asserted, was primarily focused on work in psychiatric hospitals and clinics with psychotic, neurotic, and seriously disturbed patients. Some members of the committee believed that this focus needed modification. Their report, however, also reinforced the importance of training and supervision in psychotherapy in internship training programs, a direction well established in the VA by that point.

THE 1ST YEARS OF VA TRAINING

By the fall of 1946, Miller had obtained funding for 225 psychology training positions in the first VA training class (Veterans Administration, 1947b). These training positions were allocated among the 22 schools initially identified by APA as meeting certain staffing and curricula criteria. Student applications for admission to the training program were submitted to the chairs of the psychology departments at these schools. The schools selected candidates for the VA training program according to an allotment based on their enrollment capacity, and the candidates were then reviewed by the chief of the Psychology Section in the VA Central Office. Following an almost routine approval, the students were then hired by the VA. Some 200 students were eventually selected for the first training class in the fall of 1946.[3] Area chief psychologists (originally numbering 13 and later reduced to 6) carried primary responsibility for the oversight of training, provided the liaison between the universities and the VA (later using chiefs of Psychology Training Control Units for this purpose), and assigned 1st- and 2nd-year trainees to nearby hospitals and clinics. Students admitted for the internship training year were encouraged to accept assignments at distant hospitals, which would provide them with a wider variety of experiences in different sections of the country (Hildreth, 1954).

Training assignments in the general medical and surgical VA hospitals were often quite unique and involved training activities with many types of patients. Trainees basically functioned as junior staff members and replaced the psychology technicians and psychometrists that had been used in large numbers in the VA prior to World War II. Trainee research activities built into many training assignments ranged from investigations of psychological factors associated with radical surgical procedures such as duodenal gastrectomy to studies related to personality patterns of psychosomatic patient groups to comparison studies of slow versus rapidly growing cancers (Hildreth, 1954).

---

[3] The names of 215 students (205 male and 10 female) selected for the first training class and their universities were published in the "Psychological Notes and News" section of *American Psychologist* (1947b, pp. 184–185).

One of the problems faced by psychology students in the early days of the VA training program, however, was the small number of on-site psychologists with doctoral training serving as role models and mentors to guide their clinical training activities. Students were often free to develop their own training experiences and interests, which resulted in a wide range of training quality. When interviewed, those in the 1st years of VA training expressed disappointment with the lack of direction and supervision but also noted the opportunities and freedom to develop their professional role in a treatment setting when they were taken under the wing of those psychologists and nonpsychologists, including physicians, in the VA's hospitals and clinics (Lasky, 2003).

From 1946 to 1950, the VA psychology training program saw rapid growth in psychology staffing and supervision as well as in numbers of trainees. The number of VA trainees grew from 200 in 1946 to 650 in 1950 (Ash, 1968a). In July of 1952, the VA began developing formal vocational counseling programs in its hospitals and, in addition, began looking at the training of counseling psychologists for the VA. The difficulty in finding appropriately trained counseling psychologists with the needed training and credentials for these programs was similar to that of the VA's earlier problem of finding appropriately trained clinical psychologists. The strategy used for recruitment and training of clinical psychologists was also used in finding counseling psychologists for the VA. The doctoral degree was established as the minimum employment credential for counseling psychologists, and a counseling psychology training program was begun in the VA in the fall of 1953 with 55 training positions (Hildreth, 1954). Robert S. Waldrop served as the director of vocational counseling in the VA Central Office from 1952 until the consolidation of the clinical and counseling psychology programs. For fiscal year 1956, 771 clinical and counseling psychology students were appointed to training positions in the VA (Veterans Administration, 1957). In a reorganization in the VA Central Office in 1957, the staff and training programs for clinical and counseling psychology programs were combined into one service (Cleveland, 1980a).

Although APA had moved quickly to establish accreditation of doctoral programs, it was not until December of 1956 that it published its first list of accredited internship programs (American Psychological Association, 1956). The listing specifically excluded VA training programs with the explanation that "the practicum training facilities of the Veterans Administration are yet to be evaluated" (p. 710). The first VA-accredited internship training program, that of the VA hospital in Topeka, did not appear until the 1974 listing (see chap. 2, this volume).

The early decision in the VA psychology training program to make extensive use of university faculty members as training consultants served an essential role in providing supervision of students in their clinical work at the VA. Just as the VA psychology program profited from its ties with universities, however, the universities derived important benefits from the liaison. In preparing for a 2003 APA annual meeting symposium, Lee Gurel noted his indebtedness to Jack Lasky for reminding him that early on more than a few of the university faculty had limited clinical experience, particularly with the major mental illnesses found in the VA. In visiting their students at VA training sites, they learned about these illnesses along with the trainees, and this learning no doubt benefited them and the students they saw in class (R. R. Baker & Gurel, 2003). Gurel reported that his favorite personal example was that of Victor Raimy, who had told Gurel how pleased he was to have the Fort Lyon VA Hospital as a placement for his University of Colorado students and how much he, too, was learning. The use of university consultants not only enhanced the classroom and practical aspects of training but also provided an important liaison between the universities and the VA. As Miller had expected, these training consultants would also serve as consultants to VA psychology research and conduct research themselves, activities that emerged as a critical aspect of the university affiliation in VA research programs.

EVALUATIONS OF THE VA TRAINING PROGRAM

In the 1st year of the VA psychology training program, a research contract was awarded the University of Michigan to develop criteria for the selection of candidates for training of clinical psychologists. A similar contract was awarded the Menninger Foundation in Topeka for the selection of candidates for training in psychiatry (Veterans Administration, 1947b). The evaluation research for the selection of clinical psychologists for training was headed by E. Lowell Kelly and was based on the experience of the OSS in selecting spies during World War II (E. L. Kelly & Fiske, 1950). In interviews with some of the early VA psychology students involved in this study, a certain amusement (and lack of reverence) was noted in describing the rigorous assessment methodology that was devised for the study (Lasky, 2003).[4]

In its annual reports to Congress the VA had on a number of occasions expressed its assessment of the positive worth of the VA training program. In its 1950 report, for example, it was noted that the VA had profited in two ways. Under supervision, trainees were serving veterans and helping to supplement the shortage of services available from this scarce professional category. It was also noted that the training program had reached the stage

---

[4]Lasky attributes some of this irreverence to a fellow student in the assessment study who had been a spy for OSS and was suggesting that the students in the study not take it too seriously.

where large numbers were completing the doctoral degree requirement and were assuming positions in the VA as fully qualified clinical psychologists (Veterans Administration, 1951). That report went on to note that "the time when all VA staff psychologists would be fully qualified at the doctoral level was being reached at a satisfactory rate" (p. 25). The 1951 report (Veterans Administration, 1952) also noted the contributions made by psychology students during their training period, referring to a demonstration of "an unusual degree of professional competence" (p. 36), and concluded that the students consistently performed at a higher level than would have been true of the technician group they replaced.

In 1956, 10 years after the inception of the training program, the VA's assistant chief medical director for planning appointed a panel of three physicians to formally evaluate the psychology training program. The charge to the panel was to assess whether the training program was meeting its goals of providing qualified psychologists for the VA and whether the program should be continued. That report noted that the graduates of the training program were in fact accepting roles as staff in the VA after their training and that they tended to stay in the VA. Of 507 graduates of the training program who were hired for a VA staff appointment, 409 of those staff were still employed by the VA and the 98 who had left the VA served for an average of 2 1/2 years (Cranston, 1986). The study also found that psychology trainees provided patient care services at a level compatible with their training background and salary levels. Referencing the report in his 10-year review of psychology in the VA, Wolford (1956) came to the conclusions that the VA was as unable to meet its needs for clinical psychologists as ever, that there was nothing to indicate that the training program could meet the expanding use of psychologists in the VA, and that the VA would do well to continue the psychology training program to keep pace with increasing demands so that the differential between needs and resources did not get worse.

An important objective of the training program was to educate the public and the profession of psychology on the psychological treatment needs of those who had served military duty for their country. Perhaps the most important evaluation of the training program from the VA's perspective was the fact that large numbers of psychologists who received training in the VA accepted subsequent staff positions, even though there was no payback service requirement. By 1968, 72% of the clinical and counseling psychologists in the VA had been VA trainees (Ash, 1968a). The program's early role in "growing its own staff" was very successful. In the 1st years of training, many former trainees assumed clinical leadership roles after their training in the newly established psychology programs in VA hospitals. Included in the early years of the VA training program were Cecil Peck and Charles Stenger; both later served critical leadership roles in the VA Central Office, directing VA psychology as it matured.

The VA training program was credited by Harold Hildreth, successor to James G. Miller as chief of the Psychology Section in the VA, for the growth of the entire VA psychology program (Hildreth, 1954). Wolman (1965) also noted that the large-scale training and employment of clinical and counseling psychologists in the VA provided a significant impetus to the emergence of psychologists as health care practitioners. The training program brought qualified clinical and counseling psychologists to the VA who were attracted by professional practice opportunities. The training program also offered financial support to psychology graduate students and gave them a rich opportunity for combining their academic and research work with clinical experience. Students, universities, the VA, and the profession all benefited from the training program.

EARLY LEADERS OF VA PSYCHOLOGY

One of those first hired by Miller for the new VA Psychology Section in 1946 was Maurice Lorr.[5] Lorr had obtained his doctoral degree from the University of Chicago in 1943 and served in the adjutant general's office of the Army. As he was about to be discharged from the Army, he read an advertisement from the VA and contacted Miller, who interviewed him and hired him to serve as assistant chief of psychology for research. Lorr noted that he had had two extra courses in math during his graduate school training, and it was felt that he had some capability to evaluate research. His primary job was to review research being conducted by psychologists in the VA, but he also became involved in numerous research studies himself, including his early work on the Inpatient Multidimensional Psychiatric Scale (IMPS; see chap. 3, this volume). He served in the VA Central Office until 1953, when the chief of outpatient psychiatry in the central office asked him to organize an outpatient psychiatry research laboratory there. Also added to the new VA Psychology Section in 1946 were Jane D. Morgan, who was given the position of assistant chief for training ("Psychological Notes and News," 1946c), and Jacob V. Golder, who served as assistant chief for personnel (Veterans Administration, 1947b).

In addition to the psychology positions in the VA Central Office, psychology leadership positions were established in 13 branch offices that

---

[5] Urie Bronfenbrenner and Iris Stevenson were Miller's first hires, as published in the "Psychological Notes and News" section of *American Psychologist* (1946a, pp. 168–170), but neither stayed in the VA Central Office for more than a few months.

the VA had established to monitor medical care in the VA hospitals. The positions of branch chief clinical psychologist and assistant branch chief clinical psychologist were established in each of these offices. Some of Miller's early appointments to these positions included Harold M. Hildreth, James Quinter Holsopple, and Harold Max Houtchens ("Psychological Notes and News," 1946b, 1947a), all of whom later assumed leadership roles in the Psychology Section in the VA Central Office. Some of these branch office positions had not been filled by the time of a reorganization in 1949 that reduced the 13 branch offices to 6 and renamed them area offices, each with an area chief psychologist position. As of April 1, 1955, the program guide for the Psychiatry and Neurology Service (Veterans Administration, 1955b) listed the area chiefs of clinical psychology and the location of the area offices as Howard R. White (Boston), N. Norton Springer (Trenton), Carl L. Altmeier (Atlanta), Wendell S. Phillips (St. Louis), William M. Hales (St. Paul), and Wendell R. Carlson (San Francisco).[6] In 1965, area offices were abolished (Veterans Administration, 1967).

When Miller left the VA at the end of 1947 to become professor and chairman of the department of psychology at the University of Chicago, Harold M. Hildreth assumed the position of chief of the Clinical Psychology Section ("Psychological Notes and News," 1947c). Hildreth, a 1935 doctoral graduate of Syracuse, had initially stayed on at Syracuse as instructor and later as professor until 1942, when he went on leave to serve in the Navy. On discharge from the Navy in 1946, he was recruited by Miller to serve as branch chief psychologist in San Francisco ("Psychological Notes and News," 1947a). Hildreth served as chief of the Clinical Psychology Section in the VA Central Office for 8 critical years from 1948 to 1956 and completed much of the planning and development of clinical psychology in the VA begun by Miller (see Figure 1.2).

Though Miller had provided creative leadership and a future-oriented vision for psychology in the VA, it was Hildreth's leadership that was responsible for inspiring the growth of the profession in the VA. Lee Gurel described Hildreth as able to make others believe in the importance of psychology, sketching a glorious and eminently believable future for the profession (R. R. Baker, 1996b). Gurel and others also noted that Hildreth infused psychology with a spirit of pride and had a fantastic memory for personal information from those he met, which endeared him to others. He was credited by Stenger (2005) as engendering a sense of closeness and "family" among psychologists throughout the system.

---

[6]The area offices were staffed by supervisors of each of the medical and allied programs. They had no line authority but were responsible for supervision of their specialty area in the field. A seventh area office was later established in Columbus, Ohio (Veterans Administration, 1967).

Figure 1.2. Harold M. Hildreth, chief of the VA clinical psychology program, 1948–1956. Photo provided with permission from Ed Shneidman.

In 1949, Hildreth brought James Quinter Holsopple into the VA Central Office as an assistant chief of the Clinical Psychology Section. Holsopple, a Johns Hopkins doctoral graduate in 1924, had been a cryptologist in the Navy. Following his release from the military, Miller had recruited him in 1946 to serve as branch chief psychologist in Philadelphia. Holsopple took Lorr's position as chief research psychologist when Lorr was asked to head the new Outpatient Psychiatric Research Laboratory in 1953 (see chap. 3, this volume).

Hildreth similarly brought Harold Max Houtchens into the VA Central Office in 1949 from Houtchens's branch office post. Houtchens, who received his doctorate from the State University of Iowa in 1937, had also been recruited by Miller in 1946 for the position of branch chief psychologist in Seattle ("Psychological Notes and News," 1947a). Initially appointed a second assistant chief of the Clinical Psychology Section, Houtchens was later put into the new role of chief consulting psychologist in 1956 and succeeded Hildreth as chief of what was now called the Clinical Psychology Division of the Psychiatry and Neurology Service. Houtchens served in that role until 1963.

Finally, Hildreth recruited James C. Stauffacher in 1955 to serve as chief research psychologist, replacing Holsopple. A 1936 Chicago doctoral graduate, Stauffacher had been chief of psychology at the American Lake VA prior to coming to Washington. He served only a brief time in the Central Office before returning to American Lake as chief psychologist.

SUMMARY

The 1st decade of VA psychology and its training program was characterized by tremendous growth and a concomitant struggle in recruiting and training psychologists to work in the VA. Under James G. Miller's leadership, a course was set with a far-reaching impact for psychology in both the VA and the profession at large, including the establishment of credentials for practice and affiliations with the major universities involved in the training of clinical psychologists. It was left to Harold M. Hildreth for most of this decade to complete the course set by Miller. By the end of the 1st decade of the program, VA psychology was well positioned to enter its maturation years as a health care, training, and research profession.

2

GROWTH AND MATURATION YEARS OF VA PSYCHOLOGY AND THE VA TRAINING PROGRAM

The rapid growth of the VA psychology training program seen in its 1st decade slowed to about 700 to 800 training positions per year by the 1970s. The growth and influence of the training program, however, appeared in the range of training activities, the focus on predoctoral internship training and accreditation, and the emergence of funding and accreditation for postdoctoral training positions. The 2nd decade of training inaugurated, in 1956, what Ash referred to as a "modest" training program in physiological, social, and experimental psychology in the VA (Ash, 1968a). In his 10-year review of VA psychology Wolford (1956) also noted that some VA stations had already begun hiring social and physiological psychologists with plans to revise VA Civil Service qualification to facilitate appointment of these specialists. These training and staff positions, however, did not survive the many changes in the training program that occurred over the next several years.

In the early years of the training program, the administration of the program was shared by the psychologists stationed in the VA Central Office. From 1946 to 1956, that was primarily Miller, Hildreth, Holsopple, and Houtchens. Chiefs of psychology training control units had also been established by 1954. Chiefs of these units were responsible for negotiating training

Figure 2.1. Cecil P. Peck, chief of the VA psychology program, 1962–1975, and deputy director of the VA Mental Health and Behavioral Sciences Service, 1975–1983. Government publicity photo provided by Charles Stenger.

assignments for VA students in different VA hospitals across a number of states. They also helped manage some of the administrative problems in the training program. Many of these early psychology training control unit chiefs also later assumed leadership roles in the VA Central Office, such as Cecil Peck and Frederick Elton Ash.

From 1956 to 1966, a new psychology leadership group emerged in the VA Central Office that oversaw the next period of development of VA psychology and its training program. During this period many of the new VA psychology leaders came from within the VA psychology training ranks. In 1956, Houtchens brought Cecil P. Peck (see Figure 2.1) into the VA Central Office as chief consulting psychologist. For Peck, this began a psychology and mental health leadership career in the VA Central Office spanning 28 years and numerous mental health reorganizations. In 1962, Peck took over as chief of the Psychology Division, and in 1975 he was appointed deputy director of what was then called the Mental Health and

Behavioral Sciences Service after a 1971 reorganization (Davis & Dickman, 1983).

Peck had obtained his doctorate in 1952 from the University of Kentucky after a distinguished World War II career as fighter pilot and advanced flying instructor. A VA psychology trainee from 1947 to 1951 at the Lexington VA Hospital, Peck took a job as chief of psychology at the VA in Sheridan, Wyoming, after earning his degree. He served as chief of the VA's Western Psychology Training Control Unit in Salt Lake City from 1955 to 1956 before coming to Washington (Davis & Dickman, 1983).

Having worked with Peck in the VA Central Office for almost 20 years, Charles Stenger noted that Peck became well known for his emphasis on problem solving, with problems and obstacles redefined as "challenges." Peck's bottom-line focus was always on assisting veterans who served their country, and he insisted on psychologists using their best skills to help veterans. Stenger also noted that Peck worked effectively with other health care disciplines and helped avoid interdisciplinary rivalries (Stenger, 2005). In his role as chief of VA psychology, Peck also developed a reputation for working closely with area chiefs of psychology and chiefs of psychology in the field in building programs. He also helped advance the leadership and research careers of many VA psychologists (see Figure 2.2).

From 1962 to 1966, Peck was able to add a number of new psychology staff and staff positions to the Clinical Psychology Division in the VA Central Office. He first brought Frederick Elton Ash into the VA Central Office in 1962 to take Peck's previous role as chief consulting psychologist. He similarly recruited Richard Filer, a 1951 doctoral graduate of the University of Michigan, for the position of chief of psychology research. An early proponent of geriatric psychology in the VA, Filer moved to the fledgling Office of Extended Care and Geriatrics in 1970 and while there he helped support the expansion of treatment services for elderly veterans.

In 1964, Peck established the new position of chief of psychology for medical and surgical hospitals and hired Charles Stenger for that role. Stenger, a combat medic in World War II and prisoner of war, a VA psychology trainee, and a 1952 Western Reserve University doctoral graduate had previously served as chief of psychology at the Trenton area medical office as well as chief of psychology for 12 years before that at the VA hospital in Coral Gables, Florida. Stenger succeeded Peck as the VA chief psychologist in 1976 when Peck was promoted to deputy director of the Mental Health and Behavioral Sciences Service. During his tenure, Stenger was given many important roles by the administrator of the VA, including coordination of the VA's programs for Vietnam veterans and for former prisoners of war (Stenger, 2003).

In 1966, Peck established two more psychology positions in the central office: chief of psychology for psychiatric hospitals and outpatient psychology

Figure 2.2. Cecil P. Peck addressing a meeting of area chiefs of psychology in Martinsburg, West Virginia, in October 1963 (at far right of table is Charles Stenger, who was brought into the VA Central Office by Peck in 1964 and served as chief of the VA psychology program from 1976 to 1980). Government publicity photo provided by Charles Stenger.

chief. For the first position he hired Harold Dickman (a VA trainee from the University of Kansas and 1956 University of Kansas doctoral graduate). For the outpatient psychology chief position, Peck chose John E. "Jack" Davis Jr. (a VA trainee in Lexington, Kentucky, with a 1955 doctorate from the University of Kentucky).

From 1956 to 1966, the responsibilities for the training program continued to be shared among the psychologists in the Clinical Psychology Division of the VA Central Office. In 1966, the responsibilities for the training program were consolidated into the position of chief for psychology education and training. Ash moved from his position as chief consulting psychologist into the new position and served there until his retirement in 1974. Ash provided important leadership in the development of the psychology training program in its maturation years.

Prior to joining the VA, Ash had previously headed a state department of social welfare psychology program and, like many psychologists of that era, had served in the military, in his case as a Navy psychologist for 3 years.

In 1946, Ash was appointed the first chief psychologist at the Mental Hygiene Clinic in the VA Regional Office, Des Moines, Iowa ("Psychological Notes and News," 1946b). He immediately began training students from the State University of Iowa in the new VA training program. In 1954 he took his first major VA psychology training position as chief of the Psychology Training Control Unit in Knoxville, Iowa, which covered three states. In 1957 he became area chief psychologist at the Area Medical Office in St. Paul, and in 1962 he went to the VA Central Office as consulting psychologist. His interest and background in training led him naturally to the post of chief for psychology education and training when that post was created in 1966.

In his review of the first 20 years of the VA psychology training program, Ash (1968a) noted that 600,000 new veterans were being added to the VA patient care rolls each year and that the need to continue to expand psychology staff and services was as high as ever. Psychology leaders in the VA Central Office were predicting growth in the training program to 1,200 trainees a year, with psychology staff exceeding that level. (The estimated number of trainees was never reached but the number of doctoral psychologists in the VA exceeded 1,400 in the late 1980s.)

At the time of Ash's 20-year review of the VA psychology training program, the VA was annually training 700 students in 71 graduate schools and departments of psychology approved by APA for training in clinical psychology and 23 schools approved for training in counseling psychology. Of the 800 clinical and counseling psychologists in the VA, 72% had been VA trainees. Ash also noted that over the 20-year history of VA psychology and its training program 1,174 psychologists who had completed the training program had accepted VA staff positions. This included over half of those who had been hired for temporary positions in the VA until they had obtained the doctoral degree by the 1951 deadline (Ash, 1968b). In 1966, there were 685 university faculty appointed as consultants in the training program. Over one third of VA staff psychologists were similarly providing consultation to universities or had faculty appointments in the affiliations.

Ash's article described the current and expanded roles of psychologists and trainees in treating nonpsychotic illness. These included working with patients with physical disabilities and the expanding role of psychology in evaluating and treating conditions with organic involvement. The roles of psychologists and trainees included working with patients with renal dialysis, open heart surgery, and organ transplants. Ash further noted the plans the VA had to expand the training program to community psychology, neuropsychology, and gerontology.

Ash concluded his article with a comment on the value of the training program in exposing trainees to a wide variety of patient populations, including women and children, in a wide spectrum of mental health care settings.

The latter ranged from the traditional inpatient mental health care settings to exit wards, sheltered workshops, foster homes, restoration centers, nursing homes, day treatment centers, day hospitals, night hospitals, and outpatient clinics. He speculated that psychologists would not only become more problem oriented and intervene more effectively as therapeutic agents in the future, but that demands for psychologists and the concomitant preparation of psychology trainees would expand into the field of prevention and help reduce the development and occurrence of psychological disturbance.

In her review of the VA psychology training program, Moore (1992) noted that in the 1960s the training program could no longer continue to measure its success primarily by how many trainees came to work for the VA. Important health care forces were emerging in the country, however, that would provide an important stimulus for the VA training program in all health disciplines. Among these forces was a projected shortage of health manpower for all health care organizations, including the VA. In addition, Medicare legislation was being written to provide new health care benefits for the elderly, and the deinstitutionalization of state hospitals created needs for staffing in community mental health centers.

The Veterans Hospitalization and Medical Services Modernization Amendments of 1966 (Public Law 89-785) gave the VA a mandate to train health care manpower for the nation. Popularly known as the Medical Omnibus Bill, it added training of health care providers for the entire country to the VA's service and research mission as well as training to meet its own manpower needs. Ash (1968a) noted the opportunities this gave the VA for sharing and interacting with community agencies for health resources and education.

CHANGES IN TRAINING: 1963 TO 1991

According to Moore (1992), the VA psychology training program was converted into a stipend program in 1963 in which students were no longer part-time employees. Students were supported from special training funds appropriated by Congress and were no longer paid by the hour but received biweekly stipends on the basis of hours for their appointment. First- and 2nd-year students on part-time appointments were required to train a minimum of 500 hours a year. Third- and 4th-year part-time students were required to train at least 1,200 hours a year. Students for practicum and internship training were still selected by the universities. In 1970, block appointments for full-time internships at the 3rd- and 4th-year level required a minimum of 1,900 hours of training. The final change in the administration of the training program, in effect today, occurred in 1973 with other major changes in all VA training programs and gave the training funds to VA hospitals to select and fund students from APA-approved graduate programs in clinical or counseling psychology.

A reorganization of all VA training programs occurred in the VA Central Office in 1973 when the Office of Academic Affairs (OAA) was created, headed by a new assistant chief medical director (ACMD) position. The training programs that had been run by each discipline's department in the VA Central Office were now consolidated into this new office. Organizationally, the training programs were grouped into the medical and dental service, which oversaw the training of medical and dental residents and students, and the Associated Health Professions and Occupations Service, which was responsible for the training of approximately 40 different health disciplines, including psychology (Moore, 1992).

In 1973 Ash moved from the Mental Health and Behavioral Sciences Service in the VA Central Office to the Associated Health Professions and Occupations Service in OAA and continued his role in managing the psychology training program, one of the largest of the training programs in the new service. After Ash's retirement, Jule D. Moravec became the educational specialist for the psychology training program from 1975 to 1977, and Dana L. Moore assumed that role from 1977 until 1985. Just as Ash and Moravec had done, Moore retained close ties with psychology in the VA Central Office and became a regular participant in psychology meetings during the APA conventions, where she reported on the status of and changes in training. Her leadership role and stewardship of the training program during these years was critical in what was to become a major shift in focus of the training program. When Moore left the position, the role of educational specialist for the psychology training program and other associated health training programs passed to nonpsychologists: Dorothy Stringfellow in 1985, Gloria Holland in 1988, and Linda D. Johnson in 1993. Excellent working relationships continued between these educational specialists in the OAA and the psychology program staff in the Mental Health and Behavioral Sciences Service.

VA and APA Advocacy for Training

Because of an austere national budget for the country and the VA, the VA had proposed a significant cut in psychology training funds for fiscal year 1980 that was to begin in October of 1979. With a proposed cut of $900,000 from the previous year's psychology training budget of a little over $4 million, 30% of the VA's psychology training positions would be eliminated, including training at 28 of the 103 VA hospitals funded in the previous year (Moore, 1979a). In her report, Moore noted that these proposed cuts reflected a decision by William Mayer, then ACMD for the OAA, to change the traditional VA policy of supporting psychology at all training levels to a primary focus on internship training. All of the cuts in the proposed training positions were for practicum-level training, which accounted for approximately half of all training positions. The number of training positions for internship training would remain the same (374 vs. 371 the prior year).

The magnitude of the proposed psychology training cut was of concern to VA psychology leaders, APA, and the training universities. The Association of VA Chief Psychologists (AVACP), formed just 2 years earlier, lodged a series of protests. These protests, together with what was one of the first combined federal legislative advocacy efforts between APA and the VA, eventually resulted in the Senate Appropriations Committee "suggesting" that the funds be reinstated. A subsequent meeting was scheduled between the ACMD for academic affairs, a member of the VA General Counsel's Office, a representative of the Senate Appropriations Committee, and a representative of APA to discuss ways that the psychology training funds could be reinstated (Laughlin, 1979). The compromise resulted in establishing 24 more nonrecurring psychology internship positions and some 50 summer practicum positions.

In the VA's 1981 fiscal year training budget for psychology, however, the same cuts appeared that had initially been proposed for the fiscal year 1980 budget. Once again, APA helped out. Harold Dickman, then president of the AVACP, testified on behalf of APA and the Association for the Advancement of Psychology on the issue of the VA's psychology training program before the Subcommittee on HUD-Independent Agencies of the Senate Appropriations Committee. Following that testimony, the U.S. Senate directed the VA to restore the VA psychology training budget to at least the $4 million budget received in the 1979 fiscal year. Patrick DeLeon noted that in Senate Report 96-926 (1980, p. 97) the Senate Appropriations Committee expressly stated that the Committee was "distressed" that the VA had a demonstrated shortage of mental health professionals and yet was proposing a 21% reduction in psychology training support (DeLeon, 1982).

Although most of the proposed cuts were again reinstated, VA psychology had to reassess the focus of its training program. As reported earlier, the OAA had clearly identified internship training as that part of the training program that it would prefer to support. The general hierarchy for the support of training that emerged from that initial decision to reduce practicum-level training gave top priority to APA-approved internships, then internships in the APA approval process, then internships working toward and with potential for approval, then training programs with potential for internships in shortage areas (geography and specialty), and finally practicum-level training only.

Dialogue among VA psychologists and with the affiliated training universities about the future of the VA psychology training program in newsletters, conference calls, and at APA meetings included predictable arguments. Those VA training sites with internship training programs were generally comfortable with and supported the internship-only training direction. Those sites that did not have the staff and resources to mount an internship training program argued that the practicum-level training programs served an important role in serving the mental health needs in their mostly rural areas. They also argued that practicum training was important in introducing graduate students in psychology to the rewards and opportunities in working with the VA patient population and facilitated graduate students' choice of a VA internship site. The VA's psychology training program, however, was to become primarily focused at the internship level within the next decade with occasional exceptions for summer practicum training that was primarily funded out of unused internship dollars.

ACCREDITED INTERNSHIP TRAINING IN THE VA

Budget issues and the new focus on internship-level training brought a number of obvious changes. The first was an eventual decline in the number of training positions in the VA. The 800 or so training positions in the VA in the early 1970s dropped to 600 in the 1980s and declined to 400 in the 1990s. Because there was no influx of new training funds for most of this period and stipends paid to internship students were two or more times that of practicum-level students, especially for summer-only practicum training positions, the same amount of money could support fewer training positions. In response to pressure from the field to keep VA internship stipends equal to those of non-VA training stipends, stipend dollars paid and the numbers being trained were further reduced. The VA also began adding $1,000 to internship stipends to offset its inability to provide health insurance to trainees, a benefit usually included in non-VA internship settings and not added to VA internship appointments until the 2002 training class. As noted later, real dollar increases in the VA's training budget came only with special training promoted by Congress and the VA in such areas as geriatrics and primary care.

The other change produced by the new focus on internship training followed from the funding priority to be given those VAs with APA-approved internships. Although many VA internship programs had been thinking about APA approval, there was no obvious need to do so other than the prestige factor. For many, the hassles (costs and effort) involved in obtaining APA accreditation were not worth the prestige. In addition, prior to 1973, all VA psychology internship training programs that were reviewed and funded by the VA Central Office enjoyed an unofficial kind of blanket accreditation as captive training agencies for APA-approved doctoral programs. That is, the training programs affiliated with an APA-approved graduate training program were to be evaluated at the time of the APA visit to the graduate school, and this was the rationale for APA not including VA training sites in its first listing of approved internship-level programs (American Psychological Association, 1956).

In their review of the development of internship training standards, Laughlin and Worley (1991) also noted that APA did not have the financial resources to evaluate VA or other federally funded training programs in the early 1950s. Because the federal government was financially supporting the training of nearly half of all interns in psychology, a committee was formed in 1955 composed of representatives from APA, the National Institute of Mental Health (NIMH), and the VA to discuss this situation. Laughlin and Worley noted that it was agreed by this committee that VAs should be independently evaluated for internship training, and 154 VA hospitals subsequently submitted applications for training accreditation. Because of funding problems, APA was still unable to site visit any of these programs, and APA informally divided the VA applications into those that appeared to meet the minimum criteria, those whose compliance was uncertain, and those that clearly did not appear to meet the criteria.

Although Laughlin and Worley noted that 83 VA hospitals had been site visited by the end of 1959, no listing of VA programs appeared in the official list of approved programs. Laughlin and Worley cited an APA Education and Training Board decision in 1960 to put a moratorium on evaluating VA internship programs and urged the VA to establish its own evaluation of its training program.

With the creation of the OAA in 1973 and the decentralization of the psychology training program, the tacit accreditation status for VAs affiliated with APA-approved graduate schools was lost (Cleveland & Patterson, 1979). The VA and the APA Accreditation Office would only acknowledge an internship program as accredited if it went through the formal review procedure. The funding priority status given VAs with APA-approved internships clearly offered an important incentive to internship training programs for obtaining accreditation. This stimulus also added to the numbers and status of APA's internship accreditation program.

In 1974, the psychology internship training program at the VA in Topeka, Kansas, became the first in the VA to be accredited by APA. The following year, the training program at the VA at Highland Drive in Pittsburgh was added as an accredited program. In 1976, the programs at Houston and Seattle were accredited. By the fall of 1977, 13 VA hospitals had independent APA approval of their internships and 2 others were recognized members of approved consortia. Two years later, Moore (1979b) reported that the number had almost doubled (see Exhibit 2.1). In 1982, the VA added an APA-approved internship and licensure within 2 years of appointment to the requirements for employment as a psychologist and

EXHIBIT 2.1
VA Internships With APA Approval: July 1979

American Lake (Tacoma), WA (provisional approval)	Palo Alto, CA
	Pittsburgh, PA
Boston, MA	Portland, OR
Brockton, MA	Salt Lake City, UT
Danville, IL	(provisional approval)
Durham, NC	San Francisco, CA
Hines, IL	Seattle, WA
Houston, TX	Syracuse, NY
Knoxville, IA	Topeka, KS
Los Angeles Outpatient Clinic, CA	West Haven, CT
Martinez, CA	Wood, WI
Minneapolis, MN	
New Orleans, LA (provisional approval)	

Note. In addition to the above independently accredited internship training programs, five VA medical centers were recognized members of APA-approved consortia: Albany, New York; Charleston, South Carolina; Jackson, Mississippi; Memphis, Tennessee; and Wichita, Kansas.

clearly established an important benchmark for professional training of psychologists in the country. By 1985, 84 VA internship training programs had received APA approval (Moore, 1992).

It was in 1984 that the VA started training psychologists in the specialized needs of veterans. That year, 25 new internship positions were funded for geriatric-focused predoctoral training, an important emerging area of practice for the VA with the aging of the veteran population.[1] These training positions were initially allocated only among those VAs that had specialized interdisciplinary geriatric training programs or centers of excellence in the VA's Geriatric Research, Education, and Clinical Care programs. The following year, an additional 12 new psychology internship positions focused on geriatric practice were developed for those VAs without the specialized funded geriatric training and education programs. In 1995, 37 new VA psychology internship training positions were established to fund psychology training in primary care. An interesting consequence of these new internship training positions was that the interns applying for and accepting these specialized training positions still needed to obtain a broad practice training experience in order for the training program to retain APA approval. The VA required that when the intern needed to be assigned to other general training activities, another intern, not selected for the specially funded position, had to be inserted into that training or service track while the selected intern completed the more general training program requirements. As a result many more interns were getting exposure to geriatric training

---

[1] We thank Linda Johnson, educational specialist for the VA's Office of Academic Affairs, for compiling the data for the specialized internship positions noted in this paragraph.

and, later, primary care training, than were specifically chosen for those specialized internship positions.

In 1991, the VA was funding 348 APA predoctoral, accredited psychology positions in VA training programs (Moore, 1992). The 1991 Association of Psychology Internship Centers (APIC) Directory reflected that the number of approved VA predoctoral programs in the country represented over one third of all APA-approved internship training programs in the country; 1991 also represented the year the VA started funding postdoctoral training.

POSTDOCTORAL TRAINING IN THE VA

The VA had begun to recognize the importance of postdoctoral specialty training for its patient care programs in the early 1980s. In 1983, the psychology service at the VA hospital at Palo Alto had applied for and received a training grant from NIMH to provide postdoctoral specialty training in the area of geriatric mental health. The 1-year program offered options in one of four special tracks—neuropsychological assessment, psychotherapy, behavioral medicine, and community outreach. The first four postdoctoral students began their training at the Palo Alto VA in September 1983 (Moore, 1983). The VA in Knoxville, Iowa, received similar NIMH funding for postdoctoral training in geriatrics in 1984.

Discussions in both VA and non-VA settings on the future role of postdoctoral training of psychologists raised many issues, not the least of which was the question of funding for these positions. Stipends or salaries for postdoctoral training positions would presumably be higher than for predoctoral training positions. With the VA's eventual decision to fund postdoctoral training positions at the same entry-level salary as a new doctoral psychologist hired right out of the internship, funding for a postdoctoral position would be approximately twice that of a predoctoral intern. With the continued pressures to reduce training funding for psychologists in the VA, the concern in the field expressed in conference calls and APA meetings was that two predoctoral training positions would be lost for every postdoctoral position established. In meetings with the OAA, the AVACP argued that postdoctoral training should be supported with new funds rather than at the expense of predoctoral training funds. As late as 1987, however, OAA opposed postdoctoral training because of budgeting considerations.

In addition to the funding concerns shared by the non-VA training community, early discussions on postdoctoral training in APA also raised the issue of whether postdoctoral training was more than remedial (i.e., training in areas of practice that should have been taught in predoctoral training). The VA's position stressed the need and importance for advanced practice training in the postdoctoral year. Although very ambivalent about postdoctoral training because of its impact on funding for predoctoral training, and with strong proponents on both sides of the issue, VA psychology made the decision that it needed to get involved in discussions of this issue by APA boards and committees.

Advocacy for Postdoctoral Training

Prior to 1984, VA psychology had made many attempts to place VA psychologists on some of the important APA training boards and committees to represent VA training issues. Attempts to get VA psychologists on APA's Education and Training Board were never successful. In 1980, however, the VA had been successful in getting Tom Patterson, chief of psychology at the Topeka VA, on the APA Committee on Accreditation, and his contributions paved the way for a number of other VA psychology leaders to later serve on this committee (Laughlin, 1985).

VA psychology had been more successful in representing its training issues in APIC, founded in 1970 as an informal group of internship agencies interested in discussing training issues for their members (Fox, 1990). Charles Stenger, assistant chief of psychology for medical and surgical hospitals in the VA Central Office, represented VA psychology in APIC in the late 1970s as APIC evolved into a standard-setting association for predoctoral training and, later, for postdoctoral training. With VA psychology internships representing a substantial portion of all internship training programs in the country, VA psychology had a major role to play in the development of policies related to internship training.

To help promote VA psychology's interests in postdoctoral training and accreditation, AVACP began sending an observer to meetings of the APA Committee on Graduate Education and Training. Beginning in 1984 Edward Sieracki, chief of psychology at the VA in Coatesville, Pennsylvania, attended meetings of that committee as an observer for AVACP and to present the VA's eventual agenda to support both postdoctoral training and accreditation. Dana Moore, representing the OAA, also attended many of those meetings and spoke to the VA's issues in establishing postdoctoral training. In its October 1985 meeting, the committee recommended that postdoctoral accreditation and training be established in clinical, counseling, and school psychology and forwarded that recommendation to the APA Task Force on the Scope and Criteria of Accreditation (Sieracki, 1986).

Two key national conferences on graduate education held in 1987 were attended by VA psychology leaders. The National Conference on Internship Training in Psychology was held in Gainesville, Florida. Sponsored by APIC and the Department of Clinical and Health Psychology at the University of Florida, this conference recommended that internship training be a 2-year process—1 year at the predoctoral level and 1 year at the postdoctoral level—and that all internship training be conducted within programs accredited by the APA. That same year, APA sponsored the National Conference on Graduate Education in Psychology in Salt Lake City, Utah. That conference also promoted the important role of postdoctoral study in the training of psychologists. Although APA did not establish its postdoctoral accreditation program until 10 years after the APA Committee on Graduate Education and Training made that recommendation, the VA continued to look for funding support for postdoctoral training.

First VA-Funded Postdoctoral Training Programs

The first VA-funded postdoctoral psychology training programs were established in substance abuse as part of a specially funded substance abuse interprofessional clinical team fellowship program. These first postdoctoral programs were funded for the training year beginning in October 1991 at the VA medical centers in Dallas and Seattle (one postdoctoral training position per facility). Arguments by VA psychology for the importance of postdoctoral training in the OAA led to that office reversing its position and subsequently submitting a budget initiative to establish postdoctoral fellowships in psychology in posttraumatic stress disorder (PTSD), substance abuse, and geriatrics. Only postdoctoral training in geriatrics was approved, however, and requests for postdoctoral training proposals were announced. Six VA medical centers were each awarded one postdoctoral geriatric funding position for the training year beginning in the fall of 1992 (Gainesville, Florida; Knoxville, Iowa; Little Rock, Arkansas; Milwaukee, Wisconsin; Palo Alto, California; and San Antonio, Texas). Funding for both the substance abuse and geriatric postdoctoral positions was renewed annually. In 1995, additional postdoctoral training positions became available to these training programs to meet APA's emerging requirement for at least two postdoctoral positions per program for postdoctoral accreditation. Unfortunately, funding for the new geriatric postdoctoral positions in 1995 came out of the funding for predoctoral training positions in geriatrics (L. Johnson, personal communication, June 15, 2004).

In 1995, two postdoctoral psychology training positions were funded in the interprofessional fellowship program in PTSD at the VA in Honolulu. Special postdoctoral funding for psychology also came in 2002 following the establishment of the VA's Mental Illness, Research, Education and Clinical Centers (MIRECC; see chap. 7, this volume). In 2003, three more postdoctoral psychology positions were funded in the VA's interprofessional fellowship program in palliative care, and 2004 saw four more postdoctoral psychology positions funded in the interprofessional fellowship program in psychosocial rehabilitation for veterans with chronic serious mental illness.

One of the reasons that VA psychology pushed APA to establish postdoctoral accreditation was a policy by OAA that funded training positions in the VA would only be awarded where the training program had national accreditation status. OAA allowed the first VA postdoctoral psychology training positions to be funded with an understanding that APA was in the process of establishing such accreditation. The VA in San Antonio became the first legally funded postdoctoral training program in 1999 when it received APA accreditation for its postdoctoral psychology training program, the first VA training program to receive this accreditation and only the third such accredited postdoctoral training program in the country.

The VA's postdoctoral training program continued to grow. By 2001, funding for postdoctoral training required APA accreditation or evidence of substantial progress in preparing for accreditation as shown by self-study documents, and a total of 38 postdoctoral positions were funded that year under these requirements. Through 2004, the VA had funded over 300 psychology fellows. For the training year beginning October 2004, the VA was funding 359 predoctoral internship training positions and 73 postdoctoral training positions (L. Johnson, personal communication, July 12, 2004). By the following training year, APA's accreditation Web site noted that almost half of the accredited psychology postdoctoral training programs were housed in VA medical centers.

CONCLUSIONS AND SUMMARY: IMPACT OF THE VA PSYCHOLOGY TRAINING PROGRAM

Although the impact of the VA psychology training program on the profession of psychology has already been noted in a number of areas such as the establishment of training standards, the full impact of the training program can be best appreciated in the sheer numbers of psychologists who received at least part of their professional training in the VA. From Table 2.1, it can be noted that the VA funded almost 36,000 psychology training positions in the 60-year period from 1946 through 2005.[2]

It can also be noted that large numbers of psychologists received internship training in the VA without funding support in what were called *without compensation* (WOC) appointments. Records of these appointments were not generally kept by the VA Central Office, however, and the practice

---

[2] For comparison, the only other major single source of funding of psychology training that approached this level was the funding provided by the National Institute of Mental Health, which supported 32,727 clinical psychology training appointments from 1948 through discontinuation of its training funding in 1986 (Schneider, 2005).

TABLE 2.1
Funded VA Psychology Training Appointments: 1946 Through 2005

Year	Number	Year	Number	Year	Number
1946	200	1966	725	1986	607
1947	460	1967	620	1987	599
1948	459	1968	726	1988	385
1949	550	1969	750	1989	405
1950	650	1970	800	1990	486
1951	700	1971	800	1991	350
1952	700	1972	800	1992	344
1953	700	1973	800	1993	350
1954	700	1974	826	1994	365
1955	765	1975	935	1995	391
1956	771	1976	787	1996	401
1957	775	1977	747	1997	408
1958	775	1978	674	1998	407
1959	775	1979	650	1999	418
1960	775	1980	582	2000	418
1961	675	1981	587	2001	404
1962	700	1982	613	2002	410
1963	700	1983	617	2003	438
1964	700	1984	583	2004	440
1965	802	1985	643	2005	432
Total					35,952

Note. Training counts were obtained from the VA's annual reports to Congress for 1948, 1951, 1955 through 1968, and 1974 through 1987. Because of an error in double-counting training positions from 1974 to 1986, only half of the reported training positions from those reports are recorded. Data for other years were obtained from reports in the VA's Office of Academic Affairs or from other internal VA documents. Data for 8 training years could not be found and are estimated for 1949, 1952 through 1954, 1969, and 1971 through 1973.

of appointing psychology interns to these nonfunded positions was discouraged as the VA moved to accredit all of its training programs. Although they were not included in the training appointment counts in Table 2.1, informal surveys by AVACP indicated that 50 to 70 interns a year were receiving nonfunded internship training in the VA in the early 1980s, adding an estimate of at least 500 or more internship appointments to the training count.

Because the early years of VA training permitted individuals to have multiple-year appointments, an estimate of the number of individuals receiving professional training in the VA was calculated by taking half of the 22,548 appointments from 1946 through 1977 and adding that number to the 13,404 appointments from 1978 through 2005. The resulting calculation indicates that, without counting WOC appointments, almost 25,000 clinical and counseling psychologists received funded training in the VA for their future clinical, academic, research, and administrative roles in the profession. In its 1968 report to Congress, 2 years after passage of the legislation giving the VA a mandate to train health professionals for the entire nation, the VA noted that "VA psychology is making a major contribution to the national health picture . . . [and] is the largest supplier of trained psychologists to the Veterans Administration and to the country through the psychology training program" (Veterans Administration, 1969, p. 37).

The VA's important role in the training of psychologists in this country since 1946 is clearly noted in numbers and scope of activities. As reflected earlier in this chapter, however, this role also reflects a continued and sometimes contentious course of funding support for psychology and other nonphysician training in the VA by the federal government. The introduction to this book notes the fact that in the early years of the VA, most Congressional representatives were veterans themselves and were quite supportive of the VA and its programs. With the loss of veterans in Congress, the funding support for the VA began waning during the federal government budget problems starting in the 1980s. The successful advocacy role of VA psychology and APA certainly contributed to this course of continued financial support, but the cessation of NIMH training funds for psychology and the other mental health disciplines after the 1986 training year, and after a 40-year program of funding support, showed that the federal government support of psychology training was not universal. Nevertheless, the commitment of the federal government to its nation's veterans and Congressional support of that commitment are, and always have been, an important factor in the history of psychology training in the VA.

That VA psychology training has survived and flourished despite the many changes in the training and professional landscape over the past several decades is testimony to its leaders in the VA Central Office and in the field. These leaders changed training directions when those changes were needed. The successful advocacy for training was also always deeply rooted in the contributions of VA psychology and its training program to the nation's veterans. The research and treatment contributions of VA psychology that supplemented and supported the training of psychologists are detailed in the following two chapters.

3

PSYCHOLOGY AND THE VA COOPERATIVE RESEARCH PROGRAMS

After the end of World War II, the context for the extensive research programs developed in the VA was the rapid demobilization of the military. VA leaders, especially the new administrator, General Omar Bradley, recognized that the responsibilities for veterans' health care called for a more proactive and large-scale program than had been the norm for the VA (Bradley & Blair, 1983; Magnuson, 1960). A new ethos of hospital care based on scientific findings was emerging and helped shape the VA's approach to revitalizing and expanding its hospital system (Stevens, 1999). The VA arranged a memorandum of understanding with many medical colleges that made VA hospitals sites for training medical personnel and for the conduct of medical research (see chap. 1, this volume). Clinical psychology was included as an allied health profession (J. G. Miller, 1946). An ambitious program of constructing new hospitals and renovating older ones was also undertaken.

This chapter is devoted to one of the major research innovations of the VA: the *cooperative study*. In cooperative studies, a common research protocol was shared by as many hospitals as wished to collaborate. The advantages were a very large patient pool from many areas of the country, huge data sets, and a fair amount of statistical power in the analysis. As with all large studies, there were problems, including some inconsistency in following the protocol (Pokorny, 2004).

The rationale for ambitious research programs was that medical research would lead to better patient care. Two other benefits were also anticipated: Opportunities for research would aid in recruiting better personnel, and the research would help develop the knowledge base for many diseases relevant to the veteran population. Clinical ends, then, were offered as the justification for VA research, although it did not always prove to be the case that the ends justified the means. Cardiovascular disease, cancer, psychiatric disorders, and tuberculosis (TB) were the leading foci of VA research programs. In 1946, together with the Army and Navy, the VA initiated the first cooperative study, an investigation of the effectiveness of drug treatments for TB, then a major problem in VA hospitals and among nonhospitalized military veterans. Later in this chapter, a major cooperative research program on TB and its treatment that was led by psychologists is described. It was also in 1946 that the VA began an ambitious program of contractual research with a number of medical colleges. Personnel at VA hospitals and medical researchers at multiple sites collaborated on studies of treatment sequelae of several medical conditions frequently found among veterans.

In regard to psychiatric disorders, the VA leadership was particularly worried that the costs of providing care for a flood of veterans with severe mental illness would overwhelm the system. To that end, the VA made prevention of hospitalization, when possible, and early discharge, when not possible, its main emphases. It was hoped that research could play a role in this plan and would help reduce costs (Blain, 1948). By the end of fiscal year 1948, four psychological research laboratories had been established (Veterans Administration, 1949).

By the late 1940s, a research emphasis had emerged in neuropsychiatry, as the field was then called. As has been well documented, large numbers of American military personnel had suffered psychiatric problems during World War II (Shepard, 2000). There were nearly a half million psychiatric discharges, and many more men were unable to return to combat. One immediate consequence was that nearly 60% of all the VA hospital beds were occupied by neuropsychiatric cases. And the number of veterans seeking treatment for psychiatric problems after the war rapidly increased. The neuropsychiatric research emphasis emerged in this context and was then extended into psychosomatic disease, TB, and other relevant areas, such as suicide (Farberow & Shneidman, 1955, 1961).

THE VA COOPERATIVE STUDY OF PREFRONTAL LOBOTOMY

The first cooperative study in which psychologists were key research personnel was the VA study of prefrontal lobotomy conducted at six VA hospitals from 1949 to 1958. Lobotomy as a therapeutic technique was based on chimpanzee research reported by psychologist Carlyle Jacobsen in 1935 (Jacobsen, Wolfe, & Jackson, 1935). In late 1935, Portuguese neurologist Egas Moniz first applied the technique to human psychiatric patients and reported such positive results that it became a widely used treatment for psychotic and profoundly depressed patients for the next 1 1/2 decades (Pressman, 1988; Valenstein, 1986). Moniz was awarded the Nobel Prize for this work in 1949.

So many positive reports of successful psychosurgery had been published since 1936 (e.g., Freeman & Watts, 1942), that the procedure appeared attractive to the VA for its burgeoning population of veterans with psychotic disorders. For example, of the 103,600 patients in VA hospitals in June 1948, 47% (48,692) were listed as psychotic (Veterans Administration, 1949). Few treatments had proved reliable or effective, though many had been tried (Shakow, 1972).

Within the VA system, approximately 1,500 veterans had been lobotomized by the early 1950s, with inconclusive results (Jenkins & Holsopple, 1953). What became clear was that no systematic research on the effects of lobotomy beyond the first postoperative year had been conducted. The cooperative study was the first attempt to evaluate psychosurgery outcomes using standard experimental protocols: control groups and standardized psychometric instruments. The study was planned by psychiatrist Richard L. Jenkins and psychologist James Quinter Holsopple. Jenkins was VA chief of psychiatric research and Holsopple was the assistant chief of clinical psychology service. Although both were principal investigators (PIs), the bulk of the design and analysis of the study fell to Holsopple and psychologist Joseph Zubin. This was certainly typical of the division of responsibilities between the two professions at the time. Psychiatrists were simply not trained in research methodology or design, whereas psychologists were trained. When George A. Kelly and James G. Miller sold the VA on developing a training program for clinical psychology, one of the selling points was that psychologists would bring well-developed research skills to the table of clinical service (Bronfenbrenner, 1947; Farreras, 2005; J. G. Miller, 1946). It was the research skills of the psychologists that were required to make the cooperative studies feasible.

Six VA neuropsychiatric hospitals cooperated on the lobotomy studies: Roanoke (Virginia), Bedford (Massachusetts), Northampton (Massachusetts), Fort Custer (Michigan), North Little Rock (Arkansas), and American Lake (Washington). In all, 373 patients were enrolled in the study: Half of the veterans underwent 1 of 4 lobotomy procedures, and half served as controls. However, random assignment of patients was not used. Choice of lobotomy procedure was apparently made by the preference of the operating physician. Patients were evaluated pretreatment, 3 months and 1 year post-operation, and annually for 5 years after the operation. The major assessment device was the Northport Record, developed for use within the VA, then revised by psychologist Maurice Lorr and published as the Multidimensional Scale for Rating Psychiatric Patients (MSRPP; Lorr, 1953). The MSRPP used medical and allied professionals as raters to indicate patient status. Other assessment methods used included personality and intelligence tests (Scherer, Winne, Clancy, & Baker, 1953).

In 1955, responsibility for the follow-up phase of the study was transferred to the Central Neuropsychiatric Research Unit at the Perry Point, Maryland, VA hospital. Psychologist James Quinter Holsopple left the VA Central Office to head the unit. After Holsopple's untimely death in 1956, the responsibility for the follow-up was given to psychologist Josephine Ball. Catholic University psychologist James Gresock consulted on the follow-up and when C. James Klett transferred to Perry Point, he helped pull together the summary report of the cooperative lobotomy study (Ball, Klett, & Gresock, 1959). Interim reports from one of the cooperating hospitals, Northampton, Massachusetts, were issued (e.g., Scherer, Klett, & Winne, 1957). The results were somewhat surprising. Although many of the lobotomized patients improved in several areas of functioning, so did many of the controls. A major confound caused by the introduction of antipsychotic medications, primarily chlorpromazine, in the 3rd and 4th years of the study made any firm conclusions about the effectiveness of lobotomy versus standard care impossible. Only the controls showed improvement from the new medications. It was also recognized that the extra attention paid to both controls and lobotomized patients may have served as a stimulus for improvement. The inability of the study investigators, principally psychologists, to prevent the introduction of psychotropic drugs to the study patients indicates that research needs were subservient to clinical procedures. The cooperative study was disbanded in 1958, though further assessment work on lobotomy outcomes was conducted in the VA (e.g., McReynolds & Weide, 1960).

THE COOPERATIVE CHEMOTHERAPY STUDIES IN PSYCHIATRY

The remarkable success of the first antipsychotic drugs in the early 1950s formed the background for the VA research program (Healy, 2002). One of the principal problems faced by the VA was the number of veterans with psychosis in the system's hospitals. Many of these were World War II veterans who imposed an increasing financial and care burden on the system. At the close of fiscal year 1953, of 109,035 usable hospital beds, 45,723 were occupied by these veterans. Of that number, 41,937 were in neuropsychiatric hospitals, 3,778 in general medical and surgical hospitals, and 8 were in TB hospitals. More than 3,000 more had to be housed in non-VA hospitals under special contracts (Veterans Administration, 1954). And the waiting list for neuropsychiatric beds had grown steadily since 1946. The negative sequelae of these trends were exacerbated by a severe shortage of psychiatrists within the VA system (Veterans Administration, 1955a). In this atmosphere, the 1955 administrator's report mentions the use of chlorpromazine and reserpine for the first time (Veterans Administration, 1956).

It was at the Perry Point, Maryland, VA hospital that the most ambitious of the cooperative studies was coordinated: the VA Cooperative Studies of Chemotherapy in Psychiatry. The rapid acceptance of the new psychotropic drugs within the VA had already impacted the prefrontal lobotomy study in such a way as to obscure the results, as previously noted. Once the responsibility for the lobotomy study was relocated to the Perry Point Central Neuropsychiatric Research Unit in 1955, the PIs, including psychologist James Quinter Holsopple, immediately called for an evaluation of the drugs across multiple hospital settings. Begun in 1956, the VA Cooperative Studies of Chemotherapy in Psychiatry were large-scale studies of what was then called *chemotherapy*, now termed *pharmacotherapy* or *psychopharmacology*. The program was conceived and planned at about the same time that the National Institute of Mental Health (NIMH) established the Psychopharmacology Service Center under the direction of Jonathan Cole and began a similar multisite investigation of the effects of the new psychotropic drugs. Both the NIMH and the VA programs were part of an enormous interest in these drugs on both basic and clinical research levels (Cole & Gerard, 1959). Psychologists, in fact, had already begun research on the effects of drugs on behavior using nonhuman animals (e.g., Brady, 1953, 1956; Healy, 1998, 1999, 2000; Laties, 2003). From this work, the field of behavioral pharmacology was established and developed in parallel with the research programs of both the VA and NIMH (Laties, 2003). The clinical research, by contrast, has historically been referred to as *psychopharmacology research* (W. Morse, personal communication, May 12, 2005; Uhr & Miller, 1960).

In 1955, at a meeting of VA hospital representatives and clinical researchers called by the VA central office, the idea of a cooperative study of the drugs' effects was discussed, but no action was taken to initiate a study. In 1956, the VA Psychiatry, Neurology, and Psychology Service (PNP) began working toward developing a cooperative research program. The first planning meeting was held in March 1956 with a few of the chemotherapy researchers and Washington-area hospital representatives. This group moved toward instituting a formal cooperative program and called an official meeting to be held the next month to develop and implement a research protocol. It was this group that became the Executive Committee for Cooperative Studies in Psychiatry and that was responsible for planning the research protocols and evaluating the results (Veterans Administration,

1970). In this, the committee relied on the research acumen of psychologists. Indeed, psychologists were members of the committee from the 2nd year (1957) on. (See Table 3.1 for a list of psychologists who were members of the Executive Committee.) The research design and methodology became the responsibility of the psychologists. Using their scientific training in the Boulder model, psychologists were expert at these tasks and the statistics necessary to analyze the massive data sets.

A critical rationale for the development of the VA chemotherapy cooperative research was the lack of controlled studies on the drugs. After the first published report in English on chlorpromazine in 1952 (Delay, Deniker, & Harl, 1952), almost 1,000 studies were published over the next 4 years. However, only 10 used rigorous and standard research approaches (control groups, objective measures, etc.). The case study methodology was, of course, well established in psychiatry and often yielded useful information, but it left doubts about the generalizability and reliability of the results. It was at this nexus that the research tradition of psychology proved critical.

The Executive Committee, made up of psychiatrists and psychologists, devised the main research questions for the cooperative studies. The Central Neuropsychiatric Research Unit was renamed the Central Neuropsychiatric Research Laboratory (CNPRL) and was under the nominal authority of the director of the psychiatry and neurology service in the VA Central Office. The second line of authority was the Executive Committee, which helped define a study area, provided expert advice on pharmaceutical agents, and approved or disapproved protocols prepared by the CNPRL. In fact, the psychologists wrote the research protocols with feedback from the Executive Committee and the investigators at the cooperating hospitals. The most important administrative figure, who worked behind the scenes, was Clyde Lindley. Lindley had earned his master's in psychology from Iowa in 1938 and was tireless in his efforts to keep the cooperative studies and conferences running smoothly from an administrative viewpoint (C. J. Klett, personal communication, August 14, 2005).

The first chief of the CNPRL was psychologist James Quinter Holsopple. After Holsopple's unexpected death in 1956, N. N. Springer briefly served as chief (1957–1958) before returning to his position as area chief of the VA in Trenton, New Jersey. He was succeeded by the more research-oriented J. Jack Lasky (1958–1962). Around the same time, psychologist Mordecai "Maury" Gordon was brought from the Knoxville, Iowa, VA hospital to serve as assistant chief of the CNPRL. When Gordon left after 2 years, C. James "Jim" Klett became assistant chief of CNPRL and in 1962 assumed the position of chief for the duration of the program. (Lasky, Gordon, and Klett had been trainees in the VA clinical psychology training program.) Each of these men was assisted by an able staff of psychologists and worked closely with psychologists at many cooperating VA hospitals

TABLE 3.1
Psychologist Members of Executive Committee, Cooperative Research in Psychiatry, 1956 through 1975

Name	Location	Service period	Position	Degree
Maurice Lorr	Washington, DC	1957–1967	Chief, OPRL	PhD, University of Chicago, 1943
N. Norton Springer	Perry Point, MD	1957–1958	Chief, CNPRL	PhD, New York University, 1936
Julian J. Lasky	Perry Point, MD	1958–1962	Chief, CNPRL	PhD, University of Michigan, 1950 (t)
Clyde Lindley	Washington, DC	1959–1974	Exec. Secretary	MA, University of Iowa, 1938
H. Max Houtchens	Washington, DC	1960–1962	Director, VA Psychology	PhD, University of Iowa, 1937
H. Elston Hooper	Washington, DC	1962–1964	Chief, Psychology Research	PhD, University of South Carolina, 1950 (t)
C. James Klett	Perry Point, MD	1962–1974	Chief, CNPRL	PhD, Washington, 1956 (t)
Richard N. Filer	Washington, DC	1964–1974	Chief, Program Development	PhD, University of Michigan, 1951
Lewis J. Sherman	Brockton, MA; St. Louis, MO	1967–1974	Consultant	PhD, University of Illinois, 1954 (t)
Donald R. Stieper	St. Paul, MN	1968–1971	Assistant Chief, Mental Hygiene Clinic	PhD, Northwestern University, 1952

Note. CNPRL = Central Neuropsychiatric Research Laboratory; OPRL = Outpatient Psychiatric Research Laboratory; t = VA trainee.

and clinics (Lasky, 1960). Over the life span of the cooperative program, 80 different VA hospitals collaborated, and thousands of veterans, primarily male, participated.

The first few studies were program studies derived from the Executive Committee proposals. Later, the Executive Committee came to rely on the CNPRL for suggested studies and served a primarily advisory role. Numerous projects on the psychological effects of various drug treatments were conducted, all using a common protocol devised by the study's Executive Committee. The first annual research conference of the Cooperative Studies of Chemotherapy in Psychiatry was in April 1956. At that meeting, a tentative protocol for the first cooperative project was developed. Recruitment of investigators at VA hospitals began that year. At the second annual meeting in 1957, the protocols for Project 1 and what became Project 2 were refined with input from the local PIs, and work began. The involvement of local PIs in feedback and refinement of research protocols proved to be a critical component of the cooperative program over the years.

The first focus of the Cooperative Studies of Chemotherapy in Psychiatry was the clinical effectiveness of psychotropic drugs: Did they work? Were they effective? Of the extant psychotropic agents, which were more effective? It was these questions that became grouped together under Projects 1 and 2, with the title "Drug Therapy in Schizophrenia: A Controlled Study of the Relative Effectiveness of Chlorpromazine, Promazine, Phenobarbital, and Placebo" (Casey, Bennett, et al., 1960). The term *controlled study* reflected the investigators' aim to bring rigorous research methods to clinical research.

The advantages as well as the problems of multisite research with a large clinical population were apparent right from the beginning. Project 1 was designed to last 12 weeks. Thirty-seven VA hospitals cooperated with 692 male, mostly chronic patients with schizophrenia serving as participants. Patients were randomly assigned to one of the four treatment conditions, the drugs were administered in a double-blind procedure, and attempts were made to keep other treatment conditions equal (i.e., ward transfers and psychotherapy were restricted). Patients were rated on four separate measures at the beginning, at 6 weeks, and after 12 weeks. Over 600 raters were used, as well as the self-rating on anxiety completed by each patient. The four measures generated 25 criteria whose results were available for data analysis. The measure that proved to be the most useful was the total morbidity score from the MSRPP, devised by psychologist Maurice Lorr (1953).

Toward the end of the 12-week period of Project 1, it occurred to the Executive Committee that the study could be extended to test the effect of alternating the treatments in a crossover design. The resultant research became known as Project 2. This process illustrates how one research program generated another; though this was not the always the case over the next

20 years, it often occurred. Over the second 12 weeks, 489 of the patients continued in the study. Random assignment was made to one of 12 groups. Four groups continued with the treatments as in the first project, and in the remaining groups the medications and the control substances were switched. Chlorpromazine was found to be significantly better in reducing total morbidity of patient groups treated with this drug over a 12-week period than were any of the other three agents. Promazine was significantly more effective than either control substance over the 12-week period, but superior only to phenobarbital after 24 weeks of treatment. When chlorpromazine or promazine followed control substances, clinical improvement was increased, especially with chlorpromazine. The substitution of control substances following tranquilizing drugs maintained the gains from the tranquilizing drugs surprisingly well for an additional 12-week period.

After 24 weeks, reduction of specific symptoms was greatest with chlorpromazine, less with promazine, and little with the control agents. The value of chlorpromazine in treating patients with schizophrenia was confirmed by this study. Promazine was effective compared with control substances, but it was not as effective as chlorpromazine. Phenobarbital and placebo caused insignificant changes and fulfilled their role as control substances. Finally, the feasibility of conducting large-scale drug studies of seriously ill psychiatric patients was demonstrated. Thirty-seven hospitals contributed 805 patients over 24 weeks of treatment (Casey, Bennett, et al., 1960). This conclusion led to Project 3.

Projects 1 and 2 also brought to light some unexpected problems. Definition of an appropriate participant was an issue from the beginning (Lasky, 1958). The research protocol required that only *newly admitted* patients be recruited for the study. Immediately, local PIs asked for clarification of the term. What generated the confusion was the frequent transfer of veterans from one VA hospital to another. The patient could be newly admitted to one of the hospitals participating in the study, but he may have been a patient in another hospital for several years. The Executive Committee encouraged a liberal interpretation of the requirement, so that any newly admitted patient could be a study participant (Lasky, 1958). This protocol problem was representative of issues in interpretation and administration of the protocols that were quite frequent over the life of the program, according to participants (e.g., Caffey, 2003; Lasky, 2003).

Technological issues also proved to be a serious problem in Projects 1 and 2 and caused serious delays in data analysis. Their resolution also changed the collection and recording of data in future projects. These problems were due to computing technology. At the time, computers were not widely available, especially computers that could handle the massive data sets generated by the VA projects, and computing time was very expensive. Part of the problem stemmed from the lack of foresight about what would be needed to run the basic data analysis. Originally, the psychologists at CNPRL in Perry Point, Maryland, in conjunction with the Executive Committee, planned to have their clerks use desk calculators to tabulate the results. However, once Projects 1 and then 2 were under way, it became clear that doing so was impractical, as more than 6,000 comparisons between drugs and variables had to be computed. It took time to find an organization with available and affordable computing time. The computing contract was given to the National Bureau of Standards. The next problem was the preparation of the data for computer analysis; the CNPRL discovered that the data were not in the form required for the Bureau's computer. Data preparation resulted in a delay of 5 months, and then the Bureau's staff had to write the program to run the IBM cards. Because of project design flaws in the coding of the data, computer problems resulted in further delay. Other errors also created delays, so that a number of months passed before the data analysis was completed. All of these problems were unexpected, and eventually all of them were resolved, and the CNPRL staff was able to learn from them for future projects. What Jack Lasky, then CNPRL chief, fervently wished for was that the VA had its own computer (Lasky, 1958). That did not happen for several years.

PROJECT 3

By the time Projects 1 and 2 were completed, pharmaceutical companies were rapidly creating new compounds on the basis of the success of chlorpromazine. The findings from Projects 1 and 2 led logically to Project 3, a comparative study of four promising phenothiazine derivative drugs— triflupromazine (Vesprin), mepazine (Pacatal), prochlorperazine (Compazine), and perphenazine (Trilafon)—against chlorpromazine (Thorazine), which was the new standard treatment. Each drug was compared with phenobarbital as the active control medication (Casey, Lasky, Klett, & Hollister, 1960).

Results from an analysis of covariance of the data indicated that all five phenothiazines were superior in therapeutic effectiveness to phenobarbital, with mepazine less effective than the others. A separate sequential analysis of the data using the total morbidity score of the MSRPP (Lorr, 1953) as the single indicator of therapeutic effectiveness was conducted by Klett and Lasky (1960). The two statistical methods yielded complementary results. The Klett and Lasky study was an example of how psychologists well trained in the scientist–practitioner model could bring added value to clinical research. Sequential analysis of the data provided a running summary of the study's progress, which made real-time clinical decisions possible even while the study was ongoing.

Other projects over the next few years also addressed the effectiveness of various drugs in treatment of schizophrenia. Psychologists had a major influence in the development of studies comparing drug treatment with psychotherapy and social therapies. This comparative work was extended to depression in Project 5 and later to bipolar disorder. By the early 1960s, the cooperative group believed that their work and that of others had established the effectiveness of drug therapy in treating schizophrenia.

By the mid-1960s, Jim Klett, CNPRL chief since 1962, began a series of cooperative studies to address the question of whether it was possible to determine the right drug for the right patient. In other words, were there patient variables that would predict which drug would be most effective for each patient? Earlier work provided encouraging support of this possibility (Klett & Moseley, 1965), but these positive results did not hold up in a subsequent replication (Galbrecht & Klett, 1968; Platz, Klett, & Caffey, 1967).

During the 1960s, pharmaceutical companies produced new psychotropic medications, many of which were potentially useful to VA in its mandate to care for a large population of veterans with severe mental illness. The VA conducted a series of drug screening studies as part of the cooperative studies. The cooperative approach was deemed ideal to evaluate the new drugs, often in comparison with drugs of established efficacy or in combination with other drugs (e.g., Hollister, Overall, Meyer, & Shelton, 1963; Overall, Hollister, Bennett, Shelton, & Caffey, 1963; Overall, Hollister, Prusmack, Shelton, & Pokorny, 1969).

Two things should be noted here. First, according to early participants in the Cooperative Studies in Psychiatry program, including two chiefs, Lasky and Klett, and one member of the Executive Committee, Caffey, pharmaceutical companies were not allowed any voice in the research program. The companies were eager, of course, to have their drugs tested in the kind of large clinical trials the VA conducted, but the researchers and staff were strongly discouraged from any significant interactions with pharmaceutical representatives (Caffey, 2003; Klett, 2003; Lasky, 2003). Second, the lead investigators in these drug-screening trials were the internist Leo Hollister and the psychologist John Overall. Both are generally recognized as among the chief creators of modern psychopharmacology—Hollister because of his keen insights on the kinds of questions that needed to be asked, and Overall for his methodological expertise. Overall had completed a National Science Foundation postdoctoral fellowship in the L. L. Thurstone Psychometric Laboratory at the University of North Carolina just prior to coming to the VA. The two worked together for many years, long after their association with the VA had ended (see the interview with Hollister in Healy, 1999).

The burgeoning recreational drug scene of the 1960s and 1970s and the attendant fears of the public and policy makers provided the social context for new directions for the Cooperative Studies in Psychiatry. Beginning in the late 1960s and continuing into the mid-1970s, the VA was drawn into an initiative sponsored by the Nixon administration to address the treatment of drug addiction (Stockdill, 2005). This is the same era in which the Nixon administration created two new institutes to address alcohol and drug problems: the National Institute of Drug Abuse and the National Institute of Alcohol Abuse. A new bureaucratic entity was established to harbor these two new institutes and the older NIMH: the Alcohol, Drugs, and Mental Health Administration (ADAMHA; Schneider, 2000). The ADAMHA institutes and the VA were directed by the Nixon administration to make clinical research into problems of alcohol and drug addiction a priority. In this context the VA Cooperative Studies in Psychiatry began multisite research in addiction treatment (Klett, 2003).

A new drug, L-alpha-acetyl-methadol, to treat heroin addicts was chosen for comparative study. In Project 22 twelve VA hospitals participated in the study of the drug, popularly known as long-acting methadone. As in other cooperative studies, random assignment and double-blind procedures were used. A second study, run in parallel with Project 22, only involved one VA hospital (Sepulveda, California), but included a number of other sites. The Perry Point CNPRL coordinated both projects and served as the data-processing center. Nixon's Special Action Office for Drug Abuse Prevention was the sponsoring agency (Klett, 2003).

NEW DIRECTIONS AND UNPLANNED BENEFITS

An unanticipated result of the cooperative research on drug treatment of schizophrenia was a new emphasis on behavior. The results of the research were expressed in terms of how a drug did or did not affect the patient's behavior and this represented a dramatic move away from psychodynamic explanations and treatment for schizophrenia and other mental disorders. A primary tool for measuring behavior became the rating scale. For example, the Brief Psychiatric Rating Scale, which quickly became the primary instrument for assessment of manifest psychopathology in clinical psychopharmacology drug trials and remains so today, originated in the collaboration of Overall and Don Gorham when they were both at the Perry Point VA (Overall & Gorham, 1962). These scales were most often developed by psychologists who had the research and methodological training to develop them. In some sense, it also increased the authority of psychologists in the explanation of mental illness and was part of the change process that led to the reconceptualization of the classification of mental disorders found in the *Diagnostic and Statistical Manual of Mental Disorders* (3rd ed.; American Psychiatric Association, 1980).

Enduring research partnerships, like that of Overall and Hollister, frequently grew out of initial contacts within the VA and lasted beyond the researchers' stint there. For example, Overall and Klett began working together while Overall was at the CNPRL in Perry Point (1959–1961). Their working relationship resulted in one of the first textbooks on applied multivariate analysis a decade later (Overall & Klett, 1972). Klett also developed long-lasting research and publication relationships with psychiatrists Eugene Caffey and Walter Ling (e.g., Cohen, Klett, & Ling, 1983; Prien, Caffey, & Klett, 1971).

A benefit, unanticipated but welcomed, of the Cooperative Studies of Chemotherapy in Psychiatry was the rise in the number of smaller cooperative studies and the expansion of research activities generally in the VA system. These related studies were funded independently of the major projects. A side benefit of this was the encouragement of research by psychologists who were primarily clinicians. In the first 20 years of the cooperative program, hundreds of related studies were conducted. These related studies were not as elaborate or complex as the large cooperative studies. Many of them involved one or two investigators at a few sites and many of them did not address psychopharmacological issues. The involvement in research often served primarily as a morale booster (Caffey, 2003) by encouraging a research ethos among the VA medical staff, particularly among psychologists. By the third Chemotherapy Studies in Psychiatry research conference in 1958, related studies were part of the regular program. By 1959, the program included even more related studies, most of them by psychologists. The CNPRL started a newsletter for the cooperative program in 1957 both as a tool for communication among cooperative PIs and to let personnel throughout the VA system know about the work. By 1959, the newsletter became a venue for communicating information about related studies and recruiting partners. Jack Lasky, the newsletter editor, called this approach the "Small Scale Mutual Aid Research Group" (Lasky, 1959b). Though many of the projects were small in scale, some of them were quite important. For example, psychologists participated in the validation studies of Maurice Lorr's new scale, the Inpatient Multidimensional Psychiatric Scale (Lasky, 1959a). The encouragement of research in the newsletter and the opportunity to present at the research conferences led to a rapid growth in the number of psychologists and other health professionals participating in research and in the conference. In 1958, 20 psychologists participated in the research conference. In the 20th year of the conference (1974), 161 psychologists participated. Of course, other cooperative programs were also initiated in this time period, two of which are briefly described in the following sections.

PSYCHOLOGISTS' COOPERATIVE RESEARCH ON TUBERCULOSIS

The VA Cooperative Studies of Chemotherapy in Psychiatry were clearly a major research effort, in which the work of psychiatrists, psychologists, and other health care professionals impacted patient care. As noted at the beginning of the chapter, the first cooperative study in the VA was an investigation of the effectiveness of drug treatments for TB. From that original cooperative study, psychologists began a number of cooperative studies of their own independent of psychiatry, starting with TB, that paralleled the mostly medical-based, pharmacology cooperative studies developed in psychiatry.

Pulmonary TB was a serious problem among veterans after World War II and required a major allocation of VA resources—personnel and monetary—to deal with it. Beginning in 1946, a cooperative TB research and treatment program using the new antibiotic drugs made it among the very first diseases to be the target of a VA cooperative research program (Veterans Administration, 1967). By 1954, the VA was operating 21 TB hospitals with 14,000 patients, and many of the 109 general medical and surgical hospitals had TB wards (Hildreth, 1954). Psychoanalysis provided the major theoretical framework for guiding psychological treatment. The 20-year period from the end of the war to the mid-1960s has been characterized as the golden age of American psychoanalysis (Hale, 1995); during this period many diseases were viewed through a psychoanalytic–psychosomatic lens, including TB (e.g., Wittkower, 1949).

Psychologists had also contributed to the theoretical and treatment literature of TB (e.g., Barker, Wright, & Gonick, 1943; Harrower, 1955). Psychological factors were found to be important in almost every aspect of TB treatment, especially the problem of *irregular discharge*. The last term refers to patients leaving the hospital or sanatorium before treatment was complete. Irregular discharge was a problem in both VA and non-VA hospitals, of course. The TB patient, when hospitalized, lived in a highly regulated environment, often very different from his or her home life. The confinement and isolation of the patient, often for an indeterminate period of time, typically led to dissatisfaction when the symptoms began to lessen, and the patient would often leave against medical advice. In the VA, psychologists were drawn into treatment and research on TB early on.

In 1949, the Castle Point, New York, VA TB hospital became the first to employ a full-time clinical psychologist, Daniel Casner. The success there led to the addition of clinical psychologists to the staffs of at least five other TB hospitals by 1953, as well as service in general medical hospitals (Barrell, 2003; Casner, 1953). As in other VA medical settings, psychologists provided training supervision to graduate students, worked to improve physician–staff and staff–patient relations, and sought to understand and prevent irregular discharge. The use of psychological tests to determine which patients were likely to leave treatment early (irregular discharge) became an important aspect of treatment and research for psychologists in TB settings (Calden, Thurston, Stewart, & Vineberg, 1955; Hildreth, 1954).

The work of psychologists with TB patients caught the interest of the National Tuberculosis Association (NTA). In 1955, the NTA invited VA psychologists to hold a special session on psychology and TB at the annual NTA meeting in Milwaukee, with six psychologists reporting on their work with TB patients. The NTA was quite enthusiastic about the work and reported on it regularly in their newsletter ("VA Psychologists Conduct Nationwide Study," 1959). It was clear that the NTA hoped that the VA research would improve treatment outcomes for TB patients.

In 1956, a group of psychologists planned a cooperative study of psychological factors in TB (Vernier, Barrell, Cummings, Dickerson, & Hooper, 1961). Robert Barrell, a psychologist from Virginia and a member of the very first cohort of VA trainees at the University of Michigan, had transferred to Downey VA Hospital in 1954 from a VA general medical hospital in New Orleans. Barrell had extensive experience working with TB patients in New Orleans, and he continued to work with TB patients at Downey. In an oral history, Barrell remembered his duties as encompassing diagnostic work and group and individual therapy (Barrell, 2003). It was in this time frame that Barrell and other psychologists who were working with TB patients decided to initiate a cooperative study of psychological aspects of TB patients, thus extending the earlier TB cooperative study that had focused on drug treatment. It also was modeled somewhat after the cooperative study of psychotropic medications that had just begun.

A central committee was formed, with George Calden, of the Madison, Wisconsin, VA hospital, Claire Vernier, chief of the psychology service at the Baltimore VA hospital, and Sanford Brotman, then at the San Fernando, California, VA hospital. Shortly after the committee began its work, Calden stepped down and was replaced by Robert Barrell of the Downey VA. Two other psychologists, Jonathan Cummings and Joseph Dickerson, were also drawn into the planning and direction of the research project. The central committee met separately several times before calling a general meeting of investigators for late August 1956 in Chicago. They developed the protocol for the research, chose the tests that would be used, and, in some cases, developed new tests specifically for TB patients. As with Maurice Lorr in the lobotomy project, the TB team also developed rating scales for both

TABLE 3.2
VA Principal Investigators, Tuberculosis Cooperative Research Program

Principal investigator	Location	Degree
Marian Ruth Ballin	Livermore, CA	PhD, Stanford University, 1954
Robert Barrell	Downey, IL	PhD, University of Michigan, 1954 (t)
Charles Bowdlear	Kansas City, MO	PhD, Western Reserve, 1955 (t)
Sanford Brotman	San Fernando, CA	PhD, University of California, Los Angeles, 1955 (t)
Daniel Casner	Castle Point, NY	PhD, New York University, 1950
Jonathan Cummings	Hines, IL	PhD, University of Illinois, 1954
Joseph Dickerson	Minneapolis, MN	PhD, University of Minnesota, 1958
H. Elston Hooper	Long Beach, CA	PhD, University of South Carolina, 1950 (t)
Charles McCarthy	Sepulveda, CA	MA, Michigan State, 1956 (t)
Mildred Mitchell	Dayton, OH	PhD, Yale University, 1931
Joseph Rickard	Temple, TX	PhD, University of Chicago, 1955 (t)
Saul Rotman	Sunmount, NY	PhD, Boston University, 1954 (t)
Herman Schubert	Buffalo, NY	PhD, Columbia, 1932
Harold Segel	Butler, PA	PhD, Penn State (t), 1955
Claire Vernier	Baltimore, MD	PhD, University of California, Berkeley, 1941
John Watkins	Portland, OR	PhD, Columbia University, 1941
Ranald Wolfe	Chillicothe, OH	PhD, The Ohio State University, 1948
Lewis Yager	Omaha, NE	PhD, University of Chicago, 1944

Note. t = VA trainee.

patients and staff (Barrell, 2003). There were also scales designed to measure ward behavior and responses to treatment. The research protocol was designed with clinical ends in mind; the hope was to improve the VA treatment programs for TB patients and to reduce irregular discharge.

There were 15 individuals who attended the Chicago meeting and only one, P. J. Sparer, was stationed at a TB hospital. The others were either at neuropsychiatric or general medical and surgical hospitals. This is an indirect indication of how widespread the problem of TB was in the VA system and how many resources were directed toward improving treatment.

The basic report of the cooperative research program was published as a monograph in 1961 (Vernier et al., 1961). Eighteen hospitals participated in the study, with a psychologist functioning as PI at each hospital (see Table 3.2 for hospitals and psychologists who served as PIs). All of the PIs had extensive experience in the VA system.

A total of 814 TB patients at the 18 hospitals were recruited for the study. Data were collected from September 1957 until March 1958. Of the total sample recruited, 47 were women patients and were subsequently excluded, leaving 767 male patients. The overwhelming percentage were White, with 22% African American and 2% other ethnicities. Not all patients were available for assessment in all three studies of the program.

Psychological adjustment in the evolutionary sense of adaptation had become a°critical aim of clinical psychology early in the 20th century (see Wells, 1917) and was the focus here, in the study of adjustment to treatment, hospitalization, and posttreatment community life. For each of these foci, measures were developed to assess adjustment. Additional measures of intelligence and personality were also taken. Factor analyses were used to parse the relationships among the data.

Those patients who were "good" hospital patients were also those who had a very difficult time adjusting to community life upon discharge. Being a good hospital patient was indicated by passivity and low activity levels. Conversely, those whose behavior was problematic during hospitalization were much more likely to make a positive community adjustment. Problem patients were characterized as demonstrating higher activity levels, more independence, and greater intelligence than good patients. The authors suggested some possible clinical implications for patient management in the TB hospital: The hospital should be reorganized to allow for higher activity levels and find ways for more independent patients to care for themselves and develop roles similar to the ones they were accustomed to in the community; for those passive patients, the hospital should be used to foster social skills and greater independence for later community living. The authors concluded that this type of research held great promise as a model for investigating the relationships among psychological variables and various disease states.

The TB cooperative psychology studies led to other follow-up cooperative studies as VA psychologists developed a broader research focus. With the start of the cooperative studies in TB by psychologists, the *Newsletter for Psychologists in Tuberculosis* was begun in 1956, initially edited by Shalom Vineberg. By 1959 the Cooperative Psychology Research Laboratory had been formed, located at the Baltimore, Maryland, VA hospital with Claire Vernier as coordinator. In 1959, the newsletter was renamed the *Newsletter for Cooperative Research in Psychology*, edited by Vernier, to more properly reflect current research interests and activities (Houtchens, 1959). The newsletter continued to report on TB studies but also began to report on psychologists' work on other medical disorders (e.g., dependency in epilepsy and paraplegia) and new areas of research (e.g., the domiciliary as a setting for care and treatment of psychiatric patients; an investigation of time perception in chronically hospitalized patients with brain damage; and applications of a general feedback model to the group therapy process). Although annual cooperative psychology research conferences were similarly dominated by TB research presentations for some time to come, the 1960 conference in Chicago featured a symposium on the current status of psychosomatic research presented by Cecil Peck, then chief consulting psychologist in the VA Central Office.

In 1960 the Cooperative Psychology Research Laboratory was briefly moved to Augusta, Georgia, before being discontinued in 1961. H. Elston Hooper took over as editor of the newsletter in 1960, and in 1961 the publication continued as the *Newsletter for Research in Psychology*, dropping the reference to cooperative studies, and Neil Coppinger took over as editor, publishing the newsletter from Hampton, Virginia. Coppinger continued as editor when he moved to Bay Pines in 1970. By the time of his death in 1974 he had diligently chronicled the scope of research of psychologists in the VA over a 13-year period as editor of the psychology research newsletter.

With the first issue of 1973, the psychology research newsletter was renamed the *Newsletter for Research in Mental Health and Behavioral Sciences*. The name change reflected the reorganization of the PNP into the Mental Health and Behavioral Sciences Service in early 1972. The newsletter now was meant to more accurately reflect the multidisciplinary nature of mental health care and research in the VA. Psychologists James Klett and Robert Prien became coeditors of the newsletter in 1975 and the newsletter was published by CNPRL at the Perry Point, Maryland, VA hospital until it was discontinued in 1976.

THE PSYCHIATRIC EVALUATION PROJECT

At the suggestion of the Bureau of the Budget, the VA established the Psychiatric Evaluation Project (PEP) in 1955 to evaluate the effects of different types of treatment settings on patient outcomes. Like other VA multisite studies begun about this time, the PEP was conceived as a cooperative research project. Part of the inspiration for the PEP project came from the massive hospital-building program that the VA engaged in after the end of World War II. New types of neuropsychiatric hospitals were built, usually smaller, and staff–patient ratios were experimented with, especially the attempt to provide higher staff–patient ratios. For example, the new Haun-style psychiatric hospitals, smaller than the older-style hospitals, were designed to allow greater freedom of movement for patients; they also featured more staff than patients. The study of size and patient–staff ratios was initiated, at least in part, as a way to evaluate the effectiveness of this new approach compared with the older approach and to determine if the newer approach was more cost-effective (Ullmann, 1967).

Initial planning of the PEP study was supervised by Richard L. Jenkins, then chief of psychiatry research, and James Stauffacher, then assistant chief of psychology research; these two became director and assistant director, respectively, of the project. Lee Gurel (see Figure 3.1), then chief psychologist at the VA hospital in Fort Lyon, Colorado, replaced Stauffacher in December 1956, and replaced Jenkins as director in January 1961. Gurel

Figure 3.1. Lee Gurel. Photo courtesy of Lee Gurel.

earned his doctorate at Purdue University (1952), where he had also been a VA clinical trainee from 1949 to 1952. He served the VA first at the Martinsburg, West Virginia, VA hospital and then went to Fort Lyon, where the VA was a primary training site for clinical students from the University of Colorado at Boulder. The PEP headquarters office was housed in the Washington, DC, VA hospital to facilitate the extensive communication with participating hospitals around issues of data collection.

Phase 1 of the PEP project measured hospital effectiveness by type of hospital and patient–staff ratio. The 12 hospitals were divided into three types. Four were large old-style VA hospitals distinguished by large patient populations and low staff–patient ratios. Three were small old-style hospitals (652–1,337 beds), also with low staff–patient ratios. There were four new Haun-style hospitals characterized by small nursing units constructed so as to enforce higher staff–patient ratios, that is, more staff than patients. One of the hospitals was of the old style but had been rebuilt in the new style and also had a high staffing ratio (Jenkins, cited in Ullmann, 1967).

The research team at each hospital consisted of a psychologist, a social worker, and a research assistant (see Table 3.3 for a listing of hospitals and the psychologists who were local directors). The intent of the research was to provide guidance on how to make VA hospitals more effective. Newly admitted patients were to be followed for 5 years. A major criterion was

TABLE 3.3
Locations of VA PEP Study Hospitals and Research Psychologists (1961)

Location	Research coordinator	Degree
Brockton, MA	Robert G. Walker	PhD, University of South Carolina, 1950 (t)
Ft. Lyon, CO	Hiram Gordon	PhD, Duke University, 1952 (t)
Houston, TX	Philip Hanson	PhD, University of Texas, 1960
Lyons, NJ	Herman Efron	PhD, New York University, 1953
Marion, IN	David Rosenberg	PhD, Vanderbilt University, 1953
Montrose, NY	Elmer Struening	PhD, Purdue University, 1957
Palo Alto, CA	Leonard Ullmann	PhD, Stanford University, 1955 (t)
Roanoke, VA	Roy Eck	PhD, University of North Carolina, 1954
Salisbury, NC	William Morris	PhD, University of Tennessee, 1952
Salt Lake City, UT	William Dobson	PhD, Purdue University, 1951 (t)
St. Cloud, MN	Esther Toms	PhD, University of Minnesota, 1955 (t)
Sepulveda, CA	Robert Gunn	PhD, Western Reserve, 1956

Note. t = VA trainee.

the number of days that patients spent in community, that is, not in a psychiatric hospital or penal facility. The results suggested that type of hospital and patient–staff ratio made a significant difference in the first 2 years after initial admission to a VA facility, with smaller hospital and higher staff–patient ratios predicting the greater number of days in the community. These results were interpreted to mean that smaller facilities with high staff–patient ratios provided more effective treatment. However, as Gurel and Ullmann showed, these correlations diminished with the passage of time, leading to some questions about the relative importance of hospital style and staff–patient ratios (Gurel, 1964; Ullmann, 1967).

Not content to limit the PEP study to the administratively mandated variables, Gurel and his group gathered data on all 41 VA psychiatric hospitals in an attempt to define the much discussed concept of *hospital atmosphere*. They were able to quantify a dimension of nontraditionalism, which was then shown to be related to patient outcomes, especially for a separate sample of long-stay patients.

The chief of the PEP project at the Palo Alto, California, VA hospital was Leonard "Len" Ullmann. Ullmann earned his doctorate at nearby Stanford University, where he had also been a VA trainee. (He is better known for the seminal series of books and articles on the use of behavior modification strategies he coauthored with Leonard Krasner [e.g., Ullmann & Krasner, 1965].) Ullmann summarized the PEP results in *Institution and Outcome* (1967).

A number of other studies evolved out of this first phase and included the research of psychologists like Philip Hanson in Houston. Significantly, the research expertise of psychologists in these evaluation studies led the

VA to establish the Program Evaluation Office within the Office of the Chief Medical Director, with Lee Gurel as the first director. This in-house evaluation program conducted studies on extended community care, nursing homes as out-placement resources, and gerontological programs. Gurel was able to recruit an elite group of researchers for these projects, both within the VA Central Office and at local VA hospitals. At least as important as the management contributions of the centrally directed PEP studies were the professional contributions of the wide-ranging individual research conducted by staff in participating hospitals. Their roughly 300 publications prior to PEP's termination amply validated the rational that recruitment of superior staff required that they have adequate opportunity to pursue related studies of their own design and execution. In-house evaluation programs also brought with them many problems and at times created barriers between local VA hospital personnel and the Central Office–based program evaluation staff (Gurel, 1975). As Gurel later recounted, the cost of such an evaluation program, in salaries and benefits, came to be seen as too costly by VA administrators and the program was dramatically reduced in 1969 (Gurel, 2003). For a period, however, evaluation research represented a new area of professional development for psychologists and the idea of program evaluation was picked up by the NIMH in the 1970s (Stockdill, 2005).

SUMMARY

The cooperative research projects described in this chapter formed an important part of the history of research within the VA and also added greatly to the clinical science literature of the 1950s and 1960s. The idea of multisite investigations following a common research protocol was validated by the results of the various VA cooperative projects. The NIMH was stimulated by the VA projects to initiate such programs, and they are now common practice.

Of course, the VA cooperative projects did experience problems, some of which were significant. One problem cited by several participants was the failure of investigators at some sites to consistently follow the research protocol (Caffey, 2003; Gurel, 1999; Pokorny, 2004). Another problem, especially in the early days, was the lack of research sophistication among some participants. Lee Gurel relates the anecdote of one presentation at an early Chemotherapy in Psychiatry conference, where the presenter noted that he assigned participants into experimental and placebo control groups. It emerged that the patients assigned to the placebo control group were those patients the investigator assumed would not improve on the medication! There were also technical problems associated with data analysis, typically because the data sets were so large and the computer technology still so crude.

It should be noted, however, that the cooperative studies provided an incentive and an official sanction for psychologists trained as scientists to actually practice science. This was perhaps the major benefit from the VA cooperative studies, whether in drug evaluation, TB research, hospital effectiveness, or any of the myriad smaller cooperative studies from the mid-1950s until the mid-1970s. Although clinical rationales were typically offered to justify the research, the reality was that funds and time were available for those psychologists who wanted to continue in research to do so. Of course, not all VA psychologists did research; in fact, probably fewer than half of them did. However, the opportunity was there, and that opportunity facilitated the recruitment of highly skilled psychologists into the VA system for at least the first 25 years after the establishment of the VA Clinical Psychology Training Program in 1946.

Following the 1973 research conference of the VA Cooperative Studies in Psychiatry, a reorganization in the VA Central Office resulted in all research being consolidated under the aegis of the assistant chief medical director for research and development. The 1974 conference in New Orleans was renamed the Annual Conference of VA Studies in Mental Health and Behavioral Sciences to reflect the breadth of activity in both research and clinical applications in mental health and behavioral sciences. In addition to updates on cooperative studies, symposia included mental health involvement in medical and surgical problems, innovative therapeutic approaches, brain function and age, and human rights in mental health care.

In 1978, the organization of research within the VA was changed. Research in VA settings east of the Mississippi River was coordinated from Perry Point, Maryland, under the direction of William Paré, and west of the Mississippi River research was coordinated from the Livermore, California, VA. Monies for research were also dramatically reduced at this time as well. After 1978, research, including psychological research, became much more focused on specific clinical questions. All multicenter clinical research was channeled through the office of the chief of cooperative studies Veterans Administration Central Office and assigned to one of several cooperative studies project coordinating centers for statistical and computing support.

4

VA PSYCHOLOGY AND INTERNAL
RESEARCH LABORATORIES

When the VA made a commitment to develop clinical psychology as one of the four mental health professions—psychiatry, psychiatric nursing, and clinical social work were the others—there was a realization that research was one of the foundation stones of psychology. To enhance the appeal of the VA program to extant and future generations of psychologists, a research ethos was incorporated into the recruitment effort (Bronfenbrenner, 1947; Hildreth, 1954; J. G. Miller, 1946; Morgan, 1947). This was meant to reassure psychologists who were in mainstream departments of psychology that the VA did not intend to create a different kind of psychologist, that is, a purely professional psychologist oriented to practice. Another aspect of the VA commitment to research was the very real worry over the status of the VA medical system. It had fallen on hard times and low-quality care by the end of World War II, and those among the leadership who were forward thinking believed that one way to keep the VA from becoming a second-rate system of care was to make the VA an attractive place for high-level intellectual pursuits, such as research. It certainly was part of the attraction for many newly minted VA psychologists.

For at least the first 30 years after World War II, the VA was able to maintain a research effort within its institutional boundaries, though those efforts began to diminish by the late 1960s. This chapter is about research at two VA hospitals that were somewhat exemplary of internal VA research efforts. The Palo Alto, California, VA hospital was among the most active of all the VA hospitals in the western United States in regard to research, and the Central Neuropsychiatric Research Laboratory at the Perry Point, Maryland, VA hospital was the foremost center for psychiatric research in the VA system for many years.

PSYCHOLOGICAL RESEARCH AT THE PALO ALTO VA HOSPITAL: 1947 THROUGH 1969

In this section, some of the psychological research conducted at the Palo Alto VA from 1947 to 1969 is described. The focus is on psychologist Paul McReynolds, who, in many ways, was a model of the new kind of clinical psychologist that was articulated at the Boulder Conference in 1949 (Farreras, 2005; Raimy, 1950). McReynolds began working at the Palo Alto VA hospital in 1947, while enrolled in the clinical psychology doctoral program at Stanford University. He earned his doctorate in 1949. However, he already had extensive clinical experience through his work in the U.S. Army Air Force. McReynolds had earned his bachelor's degree at Central Missouri State University (1940) and then began graduate work at the University of Missouri. However, after World War II began he enlisted in the Army Air Force. For the first half of the war, he did psychological testing for the Army Air Force in San Antonio and Miami Beach. In the second half of the war, McReynolds became involved in psychopathology research, with a focus on test development and rehabilitation of disturbed returning airmen. He completed his master's degree in psychology at the University of Missouri (1946) right after the end of the war.

At the time McReynolds first came to the Palo Alto VA, Robert E. Kantor was the chief clinical psychologist. Kantor only held a bachelor's degree until 1953, then earned his doctorate in 1956. This was somewhat unusual, but it was not unusual for a bachelor's or master's level psychologist in the VA to be a chief psychologist until well into the 1950s.

In the late 1940s research in the VA was encouraged by the new Department of Medicine and Surgery. At the Palo Alto VA, a research committee was formed in December 1948 and McReynolds was appointed chief of psychological research in 1951. The presence of psychological interns, primarily from the Stanford clinical psychology program, also enhanced the research program and provided a source of personnel for both clinical work and research. This relationship was enhanced by McReynolds's appointment as consulting associate professor at Stanford. His Stanford appointment, made in 1956, allowed Paul to serve on thesis and dissertation committees and to apply for outside funding from the National Science Foundation and the National Institute of Mental Health (NIMH).

Much of the research was multidisciplinary: psychologists working with psychiatrists, neurologists, social workers, vocational counseling, and so forth. The ethnologist Gregory Bateson was on staff and had begun his work on communication patterns among persons with schizophrenia and their families, including the famous double-bind work. McReynolds (1954a) described the various research projects under way. There were studies of group therapy, selection of psychiatric aides, mothers of schizophrenic patients, chlorpromazine, and the development of a lobotomy prognosis scale (McReynolds & Weide, 1959). This range of research topics became broader and is described in this chapter, with an emphasis on the work of McReynolds.

In 1956, McReynolds published a monograph on anxiety and motivation that provided the backdrop for much of his later research. In fact, a broad overview of McReynolds's research at the Palo Alto VA indicates that his work fell into two broad categories: experimental psychopathology (nature of schizophrenia and anxiety) and clinical assessment. The assessment or psychometric emphasis actually undergirds almost all of his work and stands out because of his expertise in assessment. However, the concept of motivation and the role of cognitive processes were, in McReynolds's view, relevant to all of his work, so, on a metalevel, his work was an attempt to understand motivational and cognitive processes in individuals with serious mental illness.

Early in his career, McReynolds developed the Hospital Adjustment Scale (HAS). This scale was completed between 1951 and 1953; it was the first scale for rating hospitalized individuals with psychosis on behavior alone (Ferguson, McReynolds, & Ballachey, 1953) and was widely used as an objective criterion in various treatment programs (McReynolds, 1968b). The HAS was designed to be completed by a nurse or psychiatric aide who could observe a patient's daily behavior. Each of the 90 items could be marked *true*, *not true*, or *doesn't apply*. The scale included such items as "The patient likes to do the opposite of what he's asked to do"; "The patient helps out when needed"; "The patient spends a lot of time talking to himself"; and "The patient knows the names of all the doctors, nurses, and aides." The total score was meant to be an indicator of how well the patient adjusted to the demands of hospitalization in spite of the psychopathological symptomatology. Or, as McReynolds later put it, the HAS was meant to measure a kind of functional social intelligence (McReynolds, 1968b).

The HAS is of a piece with rating scales such as those developed by Maurice Lorr (e.g., the Multidimensional Scale for Rating Psychiatric Patients [MSRPP] and the Inpatient Multidimensional Psychiatric Scale [IMPS]) and other patient rating scales of the era (Lorr, 1953, 1954; Lyerly & Abbott, 1966). This was an era rich in the development of many kinds of assessment instruments. There was also a tradition of the development and use of paper and pencil tests to assess a range of abilities, traits, and conditions. McReynolds, Lorr, and other young psychologists were simply following the trail already blazed for them. The post–World War II clinical psychologist was trained to be a scientist–practitioner and was drilled in psychometric theory and the development of assessment instruments. In the VA hospital setting, where the bulk of the work was done with patients with serious mental illnesses, and with the behavioral ethos of the time, a natural result was the proliferation of rating scales and many other assessment devices.

Of course, most of these assessment instruments dropped out of use over time, but one far-reaching consequence of this work was the shift toward behavioral and then cognitive explanations of serious mental disorders and away from psychoanalytic or psychodynamic explanations. The concurrent development of effective antipsychotic medications amplified this trend. Not to be underestimated in this regard is the development of rating scales to measure the behavioral changes induced by the medications. What psychologists like McReynolds contributed to this shift was the attitude that what could be observed could be measured and those measurements then could be interpreted to indicate change and improvement, or their absence.

In 1948, not long after McReynolds began working at the Palo Alto VA hospital, he initiated work on a cognitive assessment instrument that he came to call the Rorschach Concept Evaluation Technique (CET; McReynolds, 1951, 1954b, 1965). His aim had been to develop an objective approach to the Rorschach Projective Technique. CET administration called for the presentation of 50 selected areas of the Rorschach cards to a participant, who was asked to answer yes or no to whether the area presented could be a certain item, that is, a bat, a shoe, a boat, and so forth. Several studies (e.g., McReynolds, 1966) showed that individuals who had been diagnosed with schizophrenia differed significantly and meaningfully on the CET from "normals." McReynolds asserted that the test measured conformity and idiosyncrasy in cognition and also measured ability to form and evaluate concepts, which McReynolds saw as a critical component of the cognitive dysfunction found in patients with schizophrenia. The CET, then, combined his psychometric interests with his interests in cognition and schizophrenia. In this time period, McReynolds was unusual for his interest in cognition.

In 1960, McReynolds became chief of the new Behavioral Research Laboratory (BRL) at the Palo Alto VA hospital and remained in that position until he left the VA in 1969 (see Figure 4.1). The staff of the BRL varied over the years; usually, there were two other psychologists, postdoctoral fellows, graduate students, technical assistants, and clerical personnel. The primary mission of the BRL was research in psychopathology, with the end in mind of generating knowledge that would lead to increased efficacy in treatment. A range of topics loosely fitting within the mission

Figure 4.1. Paul McReynolds and staff of Behavioral Research Laboratory, Palo Alto VA Hospital. Photo courtesy of Paul McReynolds.

of the BRL was investigated by psychologists on staff. Examples include hallucinations, delusional behaviors, and verbal conditioning in patients with schizophrenia. In addition to publications in psychological journals, the BRL issued frequent research reports, for example, Sidle (1962) and Uribe and Tryk (1967).

McReynolds's most important theoretical work of this era was an attempt to apply his interests in cognition and motivation to the problem of schizophrenia. The centerpiece of this work was his chapter in Don Jackson's seminal edited volume, *The Etiology of Schizophrenia* (1960). Jackson was a psychiatrist colleague of McReynolds and, along with ethnologist Gregory Bateson, Jay Haley, and others, formulated the noted *double-bind* theory of communication in schizophrenic families.

Several studies relevant to McReynolds's formulation of his theoretical work on schizophrenia had been published in the mid- to late 1950s (McReynolds, 1953, 1956, 1958). The chapter in Jackson's book was meant to draw this material together into a theoretical formulation of psychological causation in schizophrenia. McReynolds proposed that anxiety was the principal causal factor in schizophrenia. Anxiety stemmed from the person's inability to integrate new information (*percepts* was the term McReynolds used) into existing cognitive structures or conceptual schemes. McReynolds did not deny that there were innate biological factors or physiological dispositions; rather, he suggested that the cognitive or psychological factors were fundamental in schizophrenia.

McReynolds's research in the 1960s followed up on the approach to schizophrenia that he had outlined in his chapter in Jackson's book (McReynolds, 1960). Highlights included a study on conceptual ability in patients diagnosed with schizophrenia; delusional thinking in schizophrenia (McReynolds, Collins, & Acker, 1964); and reduction in the appeal of novel stimuli in withdrawn persons with schizophrenia (McReynolds, 1963). The latter theme led to the Obscure Figures Test to assess the need for novelty, which McReynolds termed *cognitive innovation* (Acker & McReynolds, 1965) and to a series of studies using mice as subjects to determine whether novel experiences in infancy led to enhanced exploratory behaviors in adulthood (McReynolds, 1971). They do, at least in mice. McReynolds also made a film of his mice research (McReynolds, 1969).

In 1968, taking a broader perspective, McReynolds began what became a series of edited books on psychological assessment (McReynolds, 1968a). In 1969, faced with concerns about changes in VA research policies at the national level as the VA Central Office sought to make its research grants program similar to that of NIMH, he resigned from the VA and accepted a position as professor and director of clinical training at the University of Nevada at Reno. His position at the Palo Alto VA was not filled and the BRL was discontinued.

OTHER PSYCHOLOGICAL RESEARCH AT THE PALO ALTO VA HOSPITAL

Although this section has focused on the work of Paul McReynolds and his staff at the BRL, there were a number of other psychologists doing interesting and, as it turned out, historically important research during this period. Leonard Ullmann, as noted in chapter 3 of this volume, headed the Psychiatric Evaluation Project (PEP) at the Palo Alto VA. But he and fellow psychologist Leonard Krasner began a fruitful collaboration in behavior modification studies even before Ullmann completed his doctorate. Krasner became the director of the VA training program at Palo Alto in 1956. From 1957 to 1965, he served as chief of the Psychology Training Control Unit for all the VA-funded psychology training programs on the West Coast.

Ullmann and Krasner became well known for their work on verbal conditioning and behavior modification of patients with schizophrenia. Their volume, *Case Studies in Behavior Modification* (1965), has become a classic of the early behavior therapy literature. Essentially, Krasner and

Ullmann found that they could condition schizophrenic speech and then modify it with behavioral interventions. The net result of this was a model of behavioral treatment that was widely copied around the world. It became another important piece of the trend toward conceptualizing psychological disorders primarily in behavioral terms rather than in terms of intra-psychic factors.

One of the research and treatment programs begun at the Palo Alto VA had an important impact on the emergence of the community mental health emphasis of the 1960s. George W. "Bill" Fairweather became a staff member of the Palo Alto VA in 1957. He began his VA career at the Houston VA in 1953 after completing his doctorate at the University of Illinois. From Houston he moved to the Perry Point, Maryland, VA in 1956 and on to Palo Alto in 1957. According to his memoir, Fairweather became convinced of the importance of supportive environments for successful treatment of individuals with mental illness while still in graduate school (Fairweather, 1994). After initial attempts to develop a research and treatment program on the basis of his ideas at the Perry Point VA, he was able to fully develop and document such a program while at the Palo Alto VA.

The Palo Alto VA hospital, like other major VA hospitals, had a large population of patients with chronic mental illness who seemed destined for very long hospital stays. Fairweather and his colleagues developed the idea of forming some of the patients into small self-help, self-directed *lodge societies* to determine whether such a society would prove more supportive and ameliorative than long-term hospital care. He gained permission to do the experiment on two wards of the hospital. Patients were given a chance to volunteer for the opportunity to live in a lodge society. Those patients who volunteered were then randomly assigned to either the lodge society or to serve as a control group. Fairweather reported that there was a great deal of resistance to his plan from most of the other mental health professionals, as his proposal meant that the patients would be trusted to care for themselves and one another and direct their own lives, rather than relying on direction and guidance from mental health professionals (Fairweather, 1994).

The patients assigned to the lodge society group were given a month to develop plans for their move off campus into an independent living arrangement. They had to figure out how to feed themselves and what they would do to earn money. A dwelling was found and, after a couple of aborted attempts, the group settled on a janitorial service as their mode of earning an income. Mental health professionals, chiefly Fairweather, served as consultants to the group, but the group was expected to learn how to govern themselves. Of course, many mistakes were made, including sloppy janitorial work that had to be redone for them to be paid, and the group did experience discrimination from some of its neighbors. What Fairweather and his colleagues found, however, was that patients with chronic mental illness could learn to govern themselves and avoid the usual pattern of being recommitted to long-term psychiatric care. In fact, Fairweather found that only 5% of the lodge patients returned to the hospital in comparison to an average of 75% return of other VA patients with chronic mental illness.

The reports of this work (e.g., Fairweather, 1964, 1967; Fairweather, Sanders, Cressler, & Maynard, 1969) provided an important positive stimulus for the new federally funded community mental health centers movement begun in the 1960s (J. G. Kelly, 2005). They also coincided with the emergence of community psychology as a subfield within mainstream psychology. As a result, Fairweather became an important influence on the development of new treatment approaches for individuals with chronic mental illness. Several states adopted his lodge society approach in their state mental hospitals, with a fair amount of success. Fairweather eventually left the VA and held a professorship for many years at Michigan State University.

The Palo Alto VA was a critically important site for psychological and psychiatric research and the full importance and story of it is beyond the scope of this chapter. A list of psychologists who were on staff at the Palo Alto VA in the years covered here can be found in Table 4.1. A check of their names in PsycINFO will indicate the richness of psychological research at the site. In addition, Palo Alto was an important site for the new research in psychopharmacology, as the internist Leo Hollister was located at the Palo Alto VA for many years. The richness of psychological research at Palo Alto was rivaled by that occurring across the country at the Perry Point, Maryland, VA hospital.

WILLIAM PARÉ AND THE RESEARCH LABORATORY AT THE PERRY POINT VA

At the height of funding of its research efforts (1961–1966), the VA averaged $31 million a year in medical research, with nearly $40 million allocated in 1966 (Veterans Administration, 1967). It was in this period that William "Bill" Paré was recruited by the noted physician and medical researcher W. Horsley Gantt to come to the Pavlovian Research Laboratory at the Perry Point VA in 1965. Paré remained at Perry Point for nearly his entire career and played important roles in keeping the VA psychological research ethic alive and organized. At the time of his retirement in 2000, he had been continuously funded for his research for over 30 years, the longest such funding stream in the VA.

The Pavlovian Research Laboratory at Perry Point had been established in 1955 as the Psychophysiology Research Unit, with psychologist Clinton Brown (PhD, 1953, Cincinnati) as its first director. Horsley Gantt was then

TABLE 4.1
Psychologists Associated With the Palo Alto VA Hospital, 1951–1969

Name	Degree	Position	Years
Glen A. Brackbill	PhD, University of California, Los Angeles, 1950	Staff Psychologist	1953–??
John M. Daily	PhD, Iowa, 1953	Staff Psychologist	1954–1961
George W. Fairweather	PhD, Illinois, 1953	Staff Psychologist	1957–1962
		Chief, Social Clinical Research	1962–??
Ben C. Finney	PhD, University of California, Berkeley, 1951	Chief, Psychotherapy (Clinical Psychology Service)	1949–1961
Stanley Goldstein	PhD, Michigan, 1952	Chief, Counseling Psychology Service	1960–1969
William R. Grove	PhD, Pittsburgh, 1937	Chief, Clinical Psychology Service	1951–1957
Richard C. Hamister	PhD, Stanford, 1950	Chief, Psychodiagnostics	1949–1955
		Assistant Chief, Clinical Psychology	1955–1958
		Chief, Clinical Psychology	1958–1968
Robert E. Kantor	PhD, University of California, Berkeley, 1956	Chief, Clinical Psychology	1946–1951
Thomas W. Kennelly	PhD, Columbia, 1941	Director, Psychological Services	1958–1970
Leonard Krasner	PhD, Columbia, 1950	Chief, Psychology Training	1956–1957
		Assistant Director and Coordinator of Training	1957–1965
Melvin Lerner	PhD, New York University, 1957	Social–Clinical Research Psychologist	1960–1961
Bernard Light	PhD, Illinois, 1951	Chief, Counseling Psychology	1956–1959
Donald Lim	PhD, University of California, Berkeley, 1961	Coordinator, Training	1963–1970
Robert McFarland	PhD, Chicago, 1951	Research Associate	1952–1955
Paul McReynolds	PhD, Stanford, 1949	Research Psychologist	1947–1951
		Chief of Psychological Research	1951–1960
		Chief, Behavioral Research Lab	1960–1969
H. Edward Tryk	PhD, Oregon, 1965	Research Associate, Behavioral Research Lab	1965–1967
Leonard Ullmann	PhD, Stanford, 1955	Coordinator, PEP	1956–1963
Robert L. Weiss	PhD, Buffalo, 1958	Assistant Chief, Research Psychology Service	1959–1960
		Assistant Chief, Behavioral Research Lab	1960–1969
Wirt Wolff	PhD, Stanford, 1953	Chief, Counseling Psychology	1954–1956

Note. PEP = Psychiatric Evaluation Project.

recruited by psychiatrist William Reese, a consultant to the Perry Point VA from the Johns Hopkins Medical School, to bring his respondent conditioning approach to Perry Point, and the laboratory there became a kind of branch of the Pavlovian Research Laboratory at Johns Hopkins University. This was important in that it established behavioral research as central to the VA research effort. Gantt, of course, was internationally known and recognized as one of the leading behavioral researchers of the 20th century. He had studied with Ivan Pavlov in St. Petersburg in the 1920s and, along with Howard Liddell, had founded the field of experimental psychopathology in the United States (Pickren, 1995). It was considered a coup to have him associated with the VA.

When Gantt recruited him, Paré was a recently tenured professor at Boston College. Paré earned his doctorate at Carnegie-Mellon University (1960) and the position at Boston College was his first appointment. There, he established a small operant laboratory where he and his students investigated the effects of environmental stressors on rats. One of his Boston College students, Jim Lynch, went on to earn his doctorate at Catholic University and while there had the opportunity to do some research at the Pavlovian laboratory in Perry Point. He met Gantt and told him about Paré. Gantt then invited Paré to give a talk and used the occasion to recruit him to come to Perry Point. After only 1 year there, Paré was named chief of the Pavlovian Research Laboratory, a position he held until his retirement.

A source of occasional conflict between Paré and Gantt was their different research approaches. Gantt was very committed to a Pavlovian or respondent conditioning approach, but Paré was committed to a Skinnerian or operant conditioning approach. Paré recounted how much of Gantt's research was extremely time consuming, for example, his failed efforts to condition kidney function in dogs. Paré also objected to the reliance on a medical case study approach, with results never subjected to statistical analyses. Paré knew this was unacceptable to psychology journals and believed, probably correctly, that if he went in that direction he was committing a kind of professional suicide in terms of his work being accepted by the psychological community (Paré, 2003).

Once established at Perry Point, Paré returned to his investigations of stress–disease relationships. He described the first few years at Perry Point as part of a golden age of psychological research in the VA. He had almost an unlimited budget for research and this was typical, he recounted, across most of the VA hospital system. Four experimental rooms were built for his work. Internal VA grants provided support for technicians, animal caretakers, and secretarial support. Paré and his staff built much of the apparatus that was used in the laboratory. Because he lived on site for the first few years, he could come over at almost any time of day or night and work in the laboratory.

Paré had begun his work on stress–disease relationships while still at Boston College (e.g., Paré, 1962). He expanded and extended this work for the remainder of his long career. Early American research on possible stress–disease relationships dated back to the 1930s, much of it psychoanalytically oriented. Especially well known was the work of the Hungarian-born psychoanalyst Franz Alexander (Alexander, 1934; Pickren, 1995). By the 1950s, researchers from many disciplines were investigating psychological factors in disease and health and new perspectives were emerging. Hans Selye's work on stress and disease was becoming widely known and very influential, as it was for Paré (2003; Selye, 1952). Typically, in Selye's work, stress was induced through the use of restraint and was intended to produce a large physiological response. Other models that emerged were the conflict model (Sawrey & Weisz, 1956) and the control and predictability model of Jay Weiss (1970).

Paré found that he didn't like the intense physical insult to the animals that these methods inflicted. As an alternative, he developed an activity stress model in which one animal (rat) was placed in a running-wheel cage and allowed to eat 1 hour a day, while yoked to another rat that was not in an activity cage. Both animals received the same amount of food. The nonactivity rat survived nicely on the amount of food provided, but the activity wheel rat ran excessively and developed significant ulcers within about 12 days. The problem was that it took, by experimental psychology standards, a long time to run one study and additional time to replicate it with additional subjects. The rat strain that Paré started out with was the Wistar Long-Evans. However, in 1989 he discovered that the Wistar Kyoto strain was very susceptible to the stress induced by the activity wheel so that ulcers developed much quicker. He concluded that this resembled the typical stress situation in the general population where some people develop stress reactions and others are capable of handling much more stress without any ill effects. He pursued this for many years and found that the critical issue is to determine the relative impact of behavior, environment, physiology, and, eventually, genetic heritage. Paré argued that the finding that stomach ulcers are caused by the *helicobacter* bacterium does not negate his work, because about 80% of the population carries *helicobacter* in their digestive systems and only a small percentage have ulcers. The role of behavior, physiology, and environment remain crucial factors in the onset of ulcers.

Toward the end of Paré's research career, he began working with a research team at the University of Pennsylvania on the question of stress, depression, and neurotransmitter changes (e.g., Redei, Solberg, Kluczynski, & Paré, 2001; Tejani-Butt, Paré, & Yang, 1994). He had found that the Wistar Kyoto strain exhibited some of the behaviors described in the animal depression literature. Paré did the behavioral work with the rats at the Perry

Point VA, then sent the brains to his Penn colleagues, who evaluated the neurotransmitter changes. The group also was able to administer different antidepressant drugs and evaluate both behavior and transmitter changes. What is remarkable is how Paré maintained scientific agility even as his scientific field changed rapidly over the course of his career.

FUNDING PSYCHOLOGICAL RESEARCH IN THE VA

According to Paré (2003), the way the funding worked in his first few years was through the local medical director. The director, Paré stated, was the key. A director who was committed to research and felt it necessary and important could make sure the conduit for funds was always working. Some of the directors articulated that what they wanted was research that was good science, whether or not it had direct clinical relevance. Others, according to Paré, were more oriented to clinical research. Of course, the attitude of "good science and the rest be damned" only lasted as long as the money was flowing freely. By the early 1970s, the VA had become much more cost conscious, and research funds became more restricted. This cost-consciousness was part of the greater scrutiny of medical and psychological research that was characteristic of the Nixon administration (Pickren & Schneider, 2005).

Funding from the VA Central Office was apportioned to each VA hospital or medical center. Investigators submitted a proposal requesting support for a certain number of years. The proposals were reviewed by the Central Office and funds allocated to the VA site. For at least one period, VA hospitals were able to get money above and beyond their operating budget, depending on how many research programs were being conducted at the site. This led to some padding of research proposals by a few medical directors (Paré, 2003). For the investigators, however, it was generally a boon as it put them and the medical directors on the same side, rather than creating an atmosphere of opposition between clinic and research laboratory. In some years, Paré reported, the central office's Director of Behavioral Science Research, psychologist Richard Filer, would call him and ask whether he could use another $10,000. It was a golden age indeed!

Later, in the 1970s, this changed as a result of funding decreases to the VA. Under Marguerite "Rita" Hayes, then in charge of medical research in the VA, the process of funding research became much more like that of the National Institutes of Health (NIH). Peer review panels were set up, in a program called Merit Review in the VA, and both the allocation of funds and the conduct of research were placed under tighter controls. Finally, in 1978, under Operation Scissors, with the VA facing a $10 million shortfall, research funding was cut back drastically. Although VA hospitals with large research programs continued to operate independently, the administrative components of small VA programs were consolidated into two centralized offices to reduce administrative overhead costs. The Eastern Research and Development Office (ERDO) was located at Perry Point, and the Western Research and Development Office was located at the Livermore, California, VA. Many local programs were scaled back or cut out altogether. The ERDO was headed by Paré and was responsible for VA research east of the Mississippi. This division lasted for 22 years.

OTHER VA LABORATORIES

There were many other major research efforts by psychologists within various VA settings in the years between 1950 and 1975, but space considerations preclude extensive discussion of each of them. A few are described here to give a flavor of the range of research that was carried out.

In chapter 3, we mentioned Maurice Lorr's work on the VA Cooperative Studies of Chemotherapy in Psychiatry. His major strengths were assessment methodology and research design. Lorr earned his doctorate in 1943 at the University of Chicago, one of the major centers of psychometrics at the time under the leadership of Louis L. Thurstone. After World War II ended, Lorr was recruited to the new VA Clinical Psychology Program under the direction of James G. Miller. His first position was as assistant chief of psychology service for research (1946–1953). Lorr then became chief of the Outpatient Psychiatric Research Laboratory in the VA Central Office, a position he held until he left the VA in 1967 to become a professor of psychology at Catholic University. Throughout his career, Lorr focused on measurement and classification issues in personality and psychopathology.

One of the first assessment instruments Lorr developed was the MSRPP (Lorr, 1953). The MSRPP was predicated upon the old Northport Record, which was in use in the VA hospital system. Lorr refurbished it by using factor analysis to identify the relevant domains being measured by the scale (Lorr, Jenkins, & O'Connor, 1955). The MSRPP was developed in response to the need to reliably evaluate patient change following lobotomy, a technique in regrettably wide use within the VA hospital system at the time. Just as the MSRPP came into use, the VA, like other mental hospitals, began moving away from lobotomies toward greater reliance on the new antipsychotic medication, as discussed in the previous chapter. However, the MSRPP proved to be a reliable and valid way to measure patients' behavior change with the new medications as well.

As previously stated, this focus on behavior rather than on the intrapsychic factors of the older psychodynamic systems contributed to the move away from psychodynamic formulations of the etiology and treatment of mental disorder and helped the acceptance of the rather radical third revision of the *Diagnostic and Statistical Manual of Mental Disorders* (3rd ed., DSM–III; American Psychiatric Association, 1980). Before he left the VA, Lorr contributed to this trend as well with two other major assessment instruments, the Psychotic Reaction Profile (PRP; Lorr, O'Connor, & Stafford, 1960) and the IMPS (Lorr, Klett, McNair, & Lasky, 1962, 1963). The PRP used nurse or psychiatric aide observations of ward behavior of hospitalized psychiatric patients. The scale used the ratings to derive scores of disorganized thinking, withdrawal, paranoid belligerence, and anxious depression. Severity of psychosis (i.e., open vs. closed ward patients) could be detected with the profile. The IMPS was a much more ambitious scale. With it, Lorr and his colleagues sought to provide a reliable and valid measure of classification of the major psychotic syndromes, thus reducing the ambiguity of the original DSM (American Psychiatric Association, 1952). Again, the focus was on behavior, physical and verbal, of patients with psychosis, as rated by trained clinicians, and not on psychodynamic theory or unseen intrapsychic factors. The method of obtaining the data was through a clinical interview, and no other data were allowed. Clinicians were trained to an acceptable level of interrater reliability. The result was a scale that was highly usable in clinical settings both to identify psychotic types (classification) and to formulate treatment, especially drug treatment, on the basis of type.

Lorr left the VA system in 1967. He had grown disenchanted with the struggle to get funding for his projects, and personality clashes with his superior left him drained. He accepted a professorship at Catholic University, where he continued to develop assessment instruments and work on psychometric methodology.

Born in Pittsburgh in 1918, Norman Farberow has spent his entire career in the Los Angeles area. He was one of the first trainees in the VA clinical psychology training program and earned his doctorate at UCLA in 1950 with a dissertation on the personality patterns of suicidal veteran mental hospital patients. He spent 10 years (1949–1959) as a clinical psychologist in the Los Angeles VA Mental Hygiene Clinic. An early interest in the phenomenon of suicide became the shaping force of his career. In 1958, he and Edwin Shneidman became principal investigators of the newly established VA Central Research Unit for the Study of Unpredicted Deaths. After Shneidman left in 1966, Farberow continued in his position as principal investigator until his retirement in 1981 (N. Farberow, personal communication, April 14, 2004).

Suicide of veterans became of great concern to the VA during the 1950s, when the rate of suicide among veterans both within the VA hospital system and outside it, already higher than in the nonveteran population, suddenly increased alarmingly over the pre–World War II rates (N. Farberow, personal communication, April 14, 2004). Farberow and Shneidman were charged with the task of determining why there was a higher suicide rate among veterans and with developing strategies to identify warning signs of suicide and prevent it. Data from across the VA hospital system were sent to the research unit for analysis by the investigators. One of the surprising findings was a link between the use of the new psychotropic medications thorazine and rauwolfia and suicide (see chap. 3 for more information on the use of antipsychotic medications). Many psychiatrists were enthralled with the success of the new medications in quieting and controlling patients. They quickly became the primary method of treatment over other treatment methods, such as psychotherapy, craft therapy, and occupational therapy. Absent these interventions, many patients took their own lives when they stopped taking their medications or took them irregularly. Farberow and Shneidman found that there were often signs of an impending suicide or suicide attempt. This work led to their well-known and now internationally used phrase "cry for help" and their equally familiar list of "ten suicide myths" (Farberow & Shneidman, 1955, 1961; Shneidman & Farberow, 1961). These proved useful in helping mental health professionals and the general public in understanding the diverse range of risk behaviors that often signaled potential suicide behavior.

It was also in 1958 that Farberow and Shneidman cofounded the Los Angeles Suicide Prevention Center. The center allowed the two psychologists to gather data from a broader swath of the population than the VA and thus helped them discover and articulate more effective strategies for preventing suicide. The center and the VA research unit formed a symbiotic system in which techniques and strategies from each site were used to increase effectiveness at the other site. The work of Farberow and Shneidman in the VA and at the center was crucial for the development of the new field of suicidology. The idea of crisis intervention centers, often staffed by trained laypeople, grew out of their work in Los Angeles. Farberow continued at the center until 1988, Shneidman left Los Angeles and the VA in 1966 to become chief of Studies of Suicide Prevention at the NIMH in Maryland. Their work is a landmark in the history of mental health interventions.

Contributions by VA psychologists to life span research and research in neuropsychological assessment and brain functioning deserve mention. In his review of research contributions of VA psychologists since World War II, Penk (2005) noted that the work of James Fozard and other VA psychologists on the influence of developmental variables on adjustment to treatment helped justify the establishment of the National Institute on Aging and the foundation of gerontological research centers and units in many medical schools and VA medical centers. VA psychological research also contributed to major discoveries in brain functioning on the basis of the concepts of behavioral neurology (Penk, 2005). In support of this latter contribution, Penk cites the Aphasia Research Center established by Harold

Goodglass at the Boston VA, which became the longest-running extramural NIH research center in the history of NIH. The work of Gerald Goldstein and his colleagues in Kansas and later at the Pittsburgh VA provided fundamental contributions to computer-assisted neuropsychological assessment and the use of these assessments in studying the cognitive processes of schizophrenia (Penk, 2005).

CONCLUSION

The 1950s and 1960s were the golden age of psychological research in the VA system. Most VA psychologists were primarily focused on clinical work, yet many of them also conducted research on many different issues relevant to clinical concerns. And a few even did research that was not immediately applicable to treatment. Even as the VA began reducing funding for research in the 1970s, there were still many investigations going on. For example, in 1973 psychologist Richard Filer, chief of the Research Division of the Mental Health and Behavioral Sciences Service, reported that there were more than 1,000 approved research projects dealing with mental health issues in the VA system (Filer, 1973). The Boulder model of the psychologist as a scientist–practitioner was on display.

5

VA PSYCHOLOGY AND
TREATMENT SERVICES

The development of clinical services by psychologists beyond the traditional roles of assessment and diagnosis was initially fueled by wartime needs. Military psychiatry was overwhelmed with psychiatric casualties and was forced to involve psychologists as psychotherapists, a role zealously reserved for medically trained personnel up to that point (Capshew, 1999; Shepard, 2000). Similarly, the number of psychiatrists in the VA after World War II was simply too small to deal with the increased needs for treatment and psychiatrists were faced with having to request the aid of psychologists in treatment, including adult individual and group psychotherapy (Farreras, 2005). It was this shortage of mental health professionals that prompted both the VA and the National Institute of Mental Health (NIMH) to generously fund training for a massive expansion of the mental health field after World War II.

In the immediate post–World War II mental health treatment environment, VA psychologists were trendsetters of mental health services. Later, VA psychology paralleled developments in the broader world of professional psychology. From its inception, however, psychology's role in the VA in mental health treatment was influenced by the internal needs of the VA health care system—to treat large numbers of patients and to deal with the problems of the patient population with serious mental illness (see chap. 1, this volume). The role of VA psychology in addressing the treatment needs of veterans from 1946 to 1988 can be characterized by three major contributions. First, psychologists helped increase mental health care programs and services for veterans, especially group therapy programs; second, psychologists played a pivotal role in the shift of mental health care from a focus on inpatient care to outpatient care; and third, psychologists helped develop specialized mental health care programs for veterans.

Psychologists in the early post–World War II years, like other mental health professionals, were enamored of psychoanalytic theory and practice (Hale, 1995). However, the mental health needs of large numbers of veterans generated pressure to find relatively quick and effective treatments. Psychologists helped shift the therapeutic focus from the intrapsychic conflict of psychoanalysis to interpersonal conflict and from a psychosexual emphasis to an emphasis on psychosocial processes. The emergent psychotherapy systems of Carl R. Rogers and George A. Kelly, for example, provided viable alternatives for the provision of mental health services and also had the added advantage of direct correspondence to American White middle-class norms and values (G. A. Kelly, 1955; Pickren, 2005; C. R. Rogers, 1951). Group therapy, which quickly became a prominent treatment modality across much of the VA health care system, also found great acceptance among the first generation of "modern" clinical and counseling psychologists, thus providing an important linkage between VA psychologists and the rest of the profession (Moreno, 1953).

In considering the links between VA and non-VA psychology in the first post–World War II generation, it is not surprising to see similarities in the development of psychology as a mental health field. Many of the key leaders in developing American psychology in academic and other treatment settings were also involved in helping guide VA psychology. Of those invited by Donald B. Lindsley to the first conference on graduate training in clinical psychology in 1941, Donald Marquis, David Shakow, Henry Murray, Chauncey M. Louttit, and James Quinter Holsopple were all involved with the VA after the war (Farreras, 2005). Marquis and Shakow were on the first VA psychology subcommittee formed to advise the VA Neuropsychiatric Division. Murray and Louttit were early consultants working with James G. Miller to design the new VA psychology program, and Holsopple joined the VA Central Office in 1949 as the assistant chief of clinical psychology. Other noted consultants to either the VA Central Office or the branch offices in 1947 included Carl R. Rogers, Gordon Allport, J. McV. Hunt, George A. Kelly, Rensis Likert, Laurence Shaffer, Leona Tyler, Ernest R. Hilgard, and Edward Tolman ("Psychological Notes and News," 1947c). Allport and Rogers had already served as presidents of the American Psychological Association (APA), and the others were all future presidents of APA. On the D. B. Baker and Benjamin (2005) list of participants at the NIMH-sponsored 1949 conference on graduate education in clinical psychology at Boulder, Colorado, were James G. Miller, the first director of the VA psychology training program, and his replacement, Harold M. Hildreth, who later had a distinguished career at the NIMH. David Shakow, Victor C. Raimy, E. Lowell Kelly, and others attending that conference were also serving as consultants to either national VA psychology or local psychology planning or training advisory committees. In 1946, Shakow and Kelly had also been appointed to part-time roles as VA branch office chiefs of psychology in Chicago and Columbus, respectively ("Psychological Notes and News," 1946b). As described in chapter 1, many academic psychologists held paid consultancies to various VA training sites. It is clear that, at least in the immediate post–World War II period, there were unusually strong ties among psychologists in the VA system, the NIMH, and psychologists in academic settings.

THE EARLY NEED FOR MENTAL HEALTH SERVICES IN THE VA

In his article on priorities for psychiatric treatment of veterans, Daniel Blain, chief of the newly formed Neuropsychiatric Division in the VA, outlined the problems that psychiatry, neurology, and clinical psychology faced in treating veterans seeking mental health care in the VA after World War II (Blain, 1948). He categorized the problems into three areas: prevention of hospitalization, earlier discharge, and the problems of chronic mental illness.

Using projections from World War I and the then current experience of the VA, Blain estimated that 134,000 beds would be needed for neuropsychiatry patients, reaching this peak in 1965. If reached, this estimate would more than double the 55,000 psychiatric beds in the VA in 1947. Blain noted that the VA would not be able to staff the projected bed increases as this would exhaust the supply of mental health personnel in the country. In 1947, for example, 3,000 psychiatric beds in the VA were closed because of shortages of personnel. By March of 1947, only 149 of the 546 authorized positions for clinical psychologists in the VA had been filled, including only 70 of the 305 positions assigned for hospital care (Veterans Administration, 1947b). Similar shortages existed for psychiatry. Even the VA's new training programs for psychiatry and psychology could not produce the numbers of staff needed.

Veterans with psychiatric disorders occupied 58% of VA hospital beds at the end of the 1946 fiscal year (Grob, 1991; Veterans Administration, 1947a). According to Blain (1948), however, the number of admissions for these patients represented only 12% of all hospital admissions. Similarly, there was not much change in the average length of stay for chronic psychiatric patients from the 519 days reported in 1940 for all patients with psychiatric disorders (Veterans Administration, 1941). Patients with chronic mental illness were historically given only custodial care and, Blain noted, the prevailing medical opinion was that there was not much a doctor could do for such patients so that little money and staff were assigned for their care.

In his report to the field in 1947, Blain outlined a number of steps that were being taken to address these problems (Veterans Administration, 1947b). In its planning for new VA hospitals, the VA would be making significant shifts in the location and size of hospitals. Formerly built in rural or suburban areas, hospitals were now to be built in or very near to major cities with proximity to medical schools and with better transportation and accessibility of patients to care. New hospitals would be built with 1,000 beds with medical, surgical, and neuropsychiatric services available in all new hospitals. General medical and surgical hospitals would have about one third of their beds assigned to patients with psychiatric disorders, and two thirds of the beds in neuropsychiatric hospitals would be devoted to such patients. A minimum of 50 beds would be reserved for female patients.

Blain reported that several new committees had been formed to advise the new Neuropsychiatry Division on treatment programming and other matters. These committees were composed of representatives of the mental health professions from universities as well as from other treatment and health care programs in the country, such as the U.S. Public Health Service. Donald G. Marquis (University of Michigan) represented psychology on the main advisory committee and also served as chair of the Psychology Subcommittee, which included Henry W. Brosin (University of Chicago), Frank Fremont-Smith (Josiah Macy Junior Foundation, New York), Allen Gregg (Rockefeller Foundation), and David Shakow (Illinois Neuropsychiatric Institute, Chicago).

The advisory committees helped evaluate potential mental health treatment programming for the VA and, equally important, helped to justify to Congress the need for funding of the VA's mental health treatment programs. However, the health professions had not previously encountered the magnitude of the problems in the VA, and the VA often had to rely on its own staff to develop the new treatment program strategies needed to care for the problems of its veterans and address the unique treatment issues created in wartime experience. An important alliance with the Medical Rehabilitation Service in the VA Central Office, for example, introduced substantial increases in occupational therapy, corrective therapy, and recreational care services for the patient with an acute or chronic psychiatric disorder. Foster home care programs and the work and training programs of the Vocational Rehabilitation and Education Office were stepped up, and by the end of 1947 Blain was able to report that one third of the neuropsychiatric discharges from the VA were for patients averaging more than 5 years of hospitalization.

MENTAL HYGIENE CLINICS AND GROUP THERAPY

The most important impact on reducing hospitalization of patients with psychiatric disorders came with the development of mental hygiene clinics (MHCs) in the VA. Although MHCs were established in the country in the early 1900s for outpatient care for children and adults (Cushman, 1992), the countrywide development of MHCs for the treatment of veterans with psychiatric disorders provided a proving ground for therapeutic and administrative procedures unparalleled anywhere in the world (Adler, Futterman, & Webb, 1948). MHCs had been earlier authorized in the VA, but none had been started until the fall of 1945, when the first MHC was established at the regional office in Los Angeles.

In July 1946, VA Circular 169 was published and defined the function of the MHC as alleviating minor neuropsychiatric illness, preventing the development of a more serious illness, and reducing the number of veterans requiring hospitalization. The first MHCs were placed in the VA's regional offices. These offices served as business offices for helping veterans apply for disability compensation, educational programs, and other benefits authorized by law. It was believed that this first point of contact for many veterans would also be an ideal site to provide veterans with outpatient care for minor readjustment problems that might otherwise interfere with their ability to take advantage of the training offered veterans under the GI Bill of Rights (Servicemen's Readjustment Act of 1944; Public Law 78-236).

The success and growth of MHCs was substantial. In January 1946, the VA was operating only five VA-staffed MHCs and 12 contract clinics that collectively served 5,000 patients. By April 1947, the number of VA-staffed clinics had increased to 30. Together with 49 contract clinics, they served 12,800 veterans. Although the VA had some success in recruiting psychiatrists and psychologists who had experience with child guidance clinics and adult clinics before the war, recruitment problems still existed for MHCs. All of these clinics were operating at capacity with long waiting lists. Though VA hospitals were often forced to use less than adequately trained staff, an early decision was made by the VA not to start an MHC until properly trained staff were available (Blain, 1948.)[1]

---

[1] VA Circular 169 defining the operation of Mental Hygiene Clinics (MHCs) required that a fully qualified psychiatrist must be recruited to provide administrative and professional oversight before an MHC could be established.

The strategy of placing MHCs only in regional offices was changed after a 1947 pilot study showed the benefits of placing MHCs in the hospital setting, although for the next 2 decades outpatient care in hospitals was officially limited to follow-up care after hospitalization.[2] The Program Guide for the Psychiatry and Neurology Service reported in late 1954 that the VA was operating 62 MHCs—39 in regional offices, 14 in hospitals, and 9 in other VA offices (Veterans Administration, 1955b). Staffing for these MHCs included a total of 165 psychiatrists, 151 clinical psychologists, and 162 social workers. Also included were 45 psychiatry residents, 160 psychology trainees, and 42 social work students. The number of staff ranged from 2 to 54 with a median staff of three psychiatrists, three psychologists, and three social workers. The aforementioned program guide also described typical activities in an MHC as including screening and intake, therapy, teaching and research. Of particular note was the fact that 25% of the patient load included work with veterans who had a major psychotic diagnosis.

In his review of clinical psychology in the VA, Hildreth (1954) used actual reports from the field to describe the wide range of activities of clinical psychologists in MHCs. In addition to individual and group therapy and assessment activities, psychologists supervised both psychiatry and psychology students in their clinical activities. They assisted the personnel divisions of the regional offices in testing personnel for promotion and were consulted on problems of personnel relationships. They also worked closely with the regional offices supporting their counseling psychology colleagues in the vocational rehabilitation and education offices who were providing vocational counseling services to veterans and helping them obtain education and training for their vocational goals. Two special contributions of psychologists in MHCs, however, were their roles in developing group therapy programs and research and program evaluation designed to help develop specific therapeutic or rehabilitation programs.

The VA had decided early to include research duties in all staff psychologist positions, a decision subsequently incorporated into the U.S. Civil Service Commission Classification Specifications of 1949, which included service and research in the position descriptions for all psychologists employed in the VA and other federal agencies. This early decision led to a significant role of psychology in research and program evaluation in the VA and a research leadership role among psychologists employed in other federal government institutions (see the introduction to this volume). The early decision by the VA to include research activities in all psychologist

<hr />

[2] Resourceful VA personnel, however, shortly developed a method to serve new outpatients without hospitalization by using paper-only admissions and discharges.

positions also reflected and supported the aforementioned claim by Adler, Futterman, and Webb (1948) that the MHC served as a proving ground for new treatment program approaches.

Psychologists at the VA MHCs were involved in cooperative studies of psychotherapy as noted in the annotated bibliography of cooperative studies in mental health from 1956 to 1975 (Veterans Administration, 1975; see also chap. 3, this volume). The MHC role in research was also expanded in the mid-1950s when the study of group psychotherapy with outpatients with psychosis was given a high research and program evaluation priority. MHCs were also often used as a site for dissertation research by psychology students and interns.

Although group therapy advocates had been promoting the usefulness and importance of group therapy as a direct rather than incidental therapeutic approach before World War II, it was again the need to treat large numbers of veterans in the post–World War II era that gave group therapy its eventual status as an important mental health treatment in the VA. Among the mental health professionals assigned to MHCs, psychologists tended to emerge as leaders in developing therapy groups. This leadership was due in part to the fact that psychiatrists in the VA initially insisted that individual therapy be supervised by a psychiatrist, but there was not the same insistence that psychiatrists supervise the group therapy work of psychologists (Lasky, 2003).

Early therapy groups, however, were not given much value. In describing the MHC clinic operation established at the Boston Regional Office in 1946, Adler, Valenstein, and Michaels (1949) reported that psychologists were doing group therapy in the clinic but that the usefulness of group therapy was primarily limited to reducing isolation and the stigma of mental illness so that the patient became more accessible for treatment. An early VA technical bulletin (Veterans Administration, 1947c) noted that the benefits of group therapy were in reducing the feelings of uniqueness of patients through discovery that others had the same problems, the encouragement of one's progress by the group, and the stimulating effect of friendly competition as to who could show the most improvement. That publication continued by observing that the indications and advantages of the many group techniques had not yet been worked out, but it seemed that any form of group therapy was better than none at all. For the fiscal year ending June 30, 1956, over 14,000 patients had received group psychotherapy services compared with some 6,000 patients receiving individual psychotherapy (Veterans Administration, 1958).

Part of the problem with the perceived limited value of group therapy was that group therapy did not fit well with psychoanalysis and the psychodynamically oriented individual therapy modalities that were the treatments of choice for VA psychiatry at the time and that were also dominant in mental health treatment outside the VA. There was also an emerging literature on group therapy that was characterized by a confusing array of claims and counterclaims and different schools of thought about the use and role of group therapy in treatment (Luchins, 1959). A historical review of the development of group psychotherapy (Rosenbaum, Lakin, & Roback, 1992) noted that many mental health professionals regarded group therapy as ancillary or supplementary rather than a primary treatment vehicle in the years following World War II. They also observed that the pioneers of the group therapy movement did not always speak with one voice and that the post–World War II years served as a fertile period of study and experimentation in academic settings.

To assist the VA psychologist interested in developing group therapy skills, the VA published the *Manual of Group Therapy* (Luchins, Aumack, & Dickman, 1960). Written by three VA psychologists and consultants, this manual not only reviewed the theoretical bases for group therapy but was one of the first publications giving the beginning group therapist practical guidance in conducting effective group therapy. Its chapters discussed such topics as different kinds of groups and desired outcomes, where to conduct groups, the time and frequency of group meetings, the optimal number of members in a group, preparing the patient for group therapy, and how to handle hostile, dependent, silent, and talkative patients. The popularity of the manual led to a second printing a year later and helped establish a sound theoretical and therapeutic basis for group therapy in the VA.

In addition to the significant impact of MHCs and group therapy in keeping patients functioning in the community in work and family activities, the reduction in days of care and costs for hospitalization were significant. A 1952 VA study indicated that over 10% of the patients receiving care in MHCs were being kept out of hospitals. Over a 3-year period, it was estimated that some 2,200 patients would have required hospital care if not treated in MHCs, with an 80% or $4 million cost savings over care in a hospital. The average length of stay for all patients with psychiatric disorders had also been substantially reduced from the 519 days of care reported in 1940 to 226 days of care in fiscal year 1953 (Veterans Administration, 1954). Fifty percent of patients admitted for psychiatric care were being discharged within 30 days, and an additional 25% of admitted patients were being discharged within 3 months. However, the days of care for patients with chronic psychiatric disorders, especially for the World War I patient, was still high. Although the median length of stay of such patients was 81 days at the end of 1952, the average length of stay was still 514 days, and the VA had to develop other programs to address the treatment needs of these patients.

COUNSELING PSYCHOLOGY IN THE VA

Counseling psychologists were active in the immediate post–World War II period in the provision of vocational assessment, counseling, job placement, and consultation (Schneidler, 1947). Counseling psychology was officially established as a service in the VA in 1952, with Robert Waldrop as the first chief of the service in the VA Central Office. Admiral Joel T. Boone, then VA chief medical director, supported the establishment of a vocational counseling program in 1952 on the basis of his belief that the medical job was not complete until the individual has been restored to a life that was as socially productive and personally satisfying as possible (Wolford, 1956). In Boone's view vocational problems and conflicts were often inextricably interwoven with illness in regard to etiology and recovery, and he was convinced that postdischarge vocational placement was an essential and integral part of general treatment for all veterans.

As the VA's deputy chief medical director, Wolford commented in his 1956 APA address that in the 4 years following the establishment of the VA counseling psychology program, the program had turned in an impressive record in evaluation, counseling, job placement, follow-up, and research. Wolford especially described the job placement activities of counseling psychologists as their "pay-off" function in that this support helped avoid rehospitalization of veterans (Wolford, 1956, p. 245). These placement and follow-up activities of counseling psychologists became important in the work therapy programs developed by the VA in the 1950s to help reduce hospitalization of veterans, including the veteran with chronic mental illness.

Work therapy programs did much to help reduce the cycle of dependency on the hospital that was frequently found in patients with chronic psychiatric disorders. The concept of employing patients to work in the hospital as part of their rehabilitation goals had existed in the VA domiciliary program in the Veterans Bureau as early as 1868. In describing these early programs and the adoption of what were called *member–employee programs* to a psychiatric patient population in the early 1950s, Peffer (1955) noted the successes of member–employee programs in helping discharge some of the patients with chronic mental health in the VA. The first member–employee program for patients with psychiatric disorders was established at the VA in Roseburg, Oregon, in March of 1949. By September 1954, there were 19 VA hospitals with established member–employee programs. In his survey of 342 patients in member–employee programs, later called Compensated Work Therapy, Peffer reported that 61% of the patients had a diagnosis of schizophrenic reaction of various types. Although 48% of the studied patients were still participating in these programs, 24% had been successfully discharged to community employment with only 3% readmitted to the hospital.

The roles of counseling psychologists in the member–employee programs were varied and ranged from appointments as managers of these programs to helping screen applicants and providing counseling services (Veterans Administration, 1957). Counseling psychologists and social workers were almost universally assigned to the member–employee programs regardless of which service was administratively responsible for the program. Counseling psychologists provided critical functions in vocational assessment, counseling, placement, and follow-up services. Social workers were equally important in these programs for those patients who needed housing after hospital discharge, as many of these patients had alienated themselves from family or otherwise had no ties in the community.

In his survey of work therapy and employment programs in the VA, Dickman (1981) noted that VA psychologists had pioneered important and productive work therapy programs, but that the VA had begun to pull away from programs aimed at providing employment for socially and vocationally marginal veteran patients. It was not until the resurgence of the psychosocial rehabilitation model in mental health in the VA in the 1990s that the VA again reinvested significant resources in this treatment model (see chap. 7, this volume).

SPECIALIZED HOSPITAL TREATMENT PROGRAMS

By the mid-1960s, psychologists had helped pioneer numerous specialized treatment programs for veterans in the VA. It was in this same historical moment that NIMH sponsored its third national conference on psychotherapy research. In many ways, the 1960s were a turning point for psychology as a mental health profession. For example, the NIMH conferences on psychotherapy research in 1958, 1961, and 1966 revealed the proliferation of therapy forms, techniques, and applications over that time period (Rosner, 2005). During this period, there was a trend away from psychoanalytic theory and practice and toward behavior therapy (Hale, 1995; Ullmann & Krasner, 1965). The post–World War II cohort of modern clinical and counseling psychologists was maturing and there was an increasing controversy about the direction of psychology as a mental health profession, especially over issues of appropriate training and independent practice (e.g., Pottharst & Kovacs, 1964).

The same trends noted in the NIMH psychotherapy research conferences were occurring in the VA. In May 1965, the VA sponsored a psychology conference in Chicago to focus on the professional programs and techniques being developed to meet the challenging treatment objectives of the VA. The conference was titled "VA Psychology in the Mid-Sixties: Trends and Developments" (Veterans Administration, 1965).[3] The emphasis was on nontraditional treatment approaches being used by psychologists. The papers represented some of the early work of Earl Taulbee at the VA in Tuscaloosa on attitude therapy, Joseph McDonough's work at the VA in Palo Alto on systematic reinforcement (token economy), Julian Meltzoff and Richard Blumenthal at the VA outpatient clinic in Brooklyn on day treatment centers, and Fred Spaner at the Downey VA in Chicago on the unit system. Other papers like that of Philip M. Carman at the VA in Wadsworth (Los Angeles) described activities of VA psychologists in renal dialysis, open heart surgery, automated retraining of persons with aphasia, and other medical programs of the general VA hospital. Harold Dickman at the VA in Roseburg, Oregon, described unit therapeutic milieu programs, and Roy Brener at the VA in Hines (Chicago) reviewed the work of psychologists in domiciliary restoration centers. Discussants also offered critiques and voiced their views of what was happening and what should be happening. A review of the papers and discussions during that conference offers an important insight into the activities of VA psychologists in the 1960s as they experimented with different treatment programming ideas, and the trends that emerged from that conference are summarized in this section.

The conference clearly reflected two major changes occurring in VA psychology. The first was the shift from psychodynamic treatment approaches to behavioral approaches. The second was the creative development of treatment programs to meet the special needs of the VA to reduce the need for hospitalization and to treat large numbers of patients, especially those who had histories of long-term hospitalization.

A clear consensus emerged from the conference that the traditional one-on-one psychodynamic therapies favored by psychiatry in the VA were not adequate to meet the treatment needs of veterans. In his presentation of the attitude therapy program at the Tuscaloosa VA hospital, Taulbee expressed the concern of other presenters that there would never be enough therapists for the one-on-one therapies. He also made the observation that understaffed hospitals, clinics, and domiciliaries were crowded with what psychodynamic therapists considered poor diagnostic risks for their treatment techniques.

The new treatment programs being developed by VA psychologists placed an emphasis on behavior, including both the behavior of health care staff and the behavior of patients. Taulbee's attitude therapy approach, for

---

[3] The collected papers and discussions of that conference were reproduced and widely disseminated throughout the VA but were never officially published. A copy of the conference papers is on file in the VA psychology collection at the Archives of the History of American Psychology at The University of Akron.

example, argued that the total hospital environment must become the "therapist" and that all hospital personnel who came in contact with the patient, including custodians and food service personnel, must present a united and consistent approach in interacting with the patient—approaches that Taulbee outlined in his five "attitudes," one of which was to be selected for each patient.

The presentation by Spaner similarly focused on changing behavior of staff. He noted that staff would frequently avoid dealing with patients who presented management problems by transferring them to other treatment units. He found that these interward transfers and lack of continuity of care contributed to problems with discharge and readmissions. The unit system he helped develop at the Downey VA Hospital required psychiatric units to take care of their own patients, severely restricting transfers. New admissions were rotated among the units, and all readmissions had to be accepted by the unit from which the patient had last left.

VA psychologists were also taking advantage of the behavior therapies gaining popularity in the 1960s. McDonough described a token economy program for patients with acute psychiatric disorders that rewarded desired interpersonal and other social behaviors and made it possible for many of these patients to be more quickly discharged. In addition to helping patients leave the hospital earlier and for longer periods of time, the token economy program was also reported as helping patients who could not be realistically discharged by providing a better hospital adjustment with a reduction in patient management problems.

To help reduce length of hospitalization and readmissions, VA psychologists were also instrumental in developing day treatment centers for treatment of patients with chronic psychiatric disorders. Focused on patients needing more outpatient care than could be provided in MHCs, the day treatment center used what was called a partial hospitalization treatment model. Patients would attend a 4- to 6-hour day of treatment activities up to 5 days a week but would return to their homes in the evening.[4]

The new treatment approaches were in fact showing successes in reducing the need for hospitalization and readmissions. In an 18-month study of the day treatment center at the Brooklyn Outpatient Clinic, for example, Meltzoff and Blumenthal reported during the conference that patients in their program study had half the readmission rate of control subjects. In a 3-year study, Taulbee noted that the attitude therapy program at the Tusca-

---

[4] Psychologists were also in leadership or team member roles in the later development of day hospitals, another partial hospitalization program in the VA that was designed to use the same daily treatment structure of Day Treatment Centers, with patients living at home, to provide short-term, intensive outpatient treatment for a nonchronic patient population to help reduce the need for hospitalization.

loosa VA resulted in the highest turnover rate of patients in all VA hospitals; the 16% turnover rate was, in fact, among the highest for all psychiatric hospitals in the nation at the time. His study also showed that attitude therapy with the confused, elderly patient was helping discharge some of these patients after 20 years of hospitalization.

The focus on behavioral treatments not only ushered in a new focus for treatment in the VA but, combined with the development of behavioral rating scales in research (see chaps. 3 and 4, this volume), supported the emerging field of treatment outcome research. For example, Spaner used a philosophy of treatment questionnaire in his evaluation of the unit system at the Downey VA Hospital and found that staff members from all disciplines were scoring higher in that program on scales measuring awareness of the needs of patients.

Discussants at the conference helped illustrate some of the issues with which psychologists were struggling regarding the new treatment interventions. Some criticized the single-minded focus on program goals for keeping the patient out of the hospital. Others called for psychologists to do more work looking at what types of programs led to what kinds of results and to do more theorizing about the changes being produced in their work that could be used in planning for further action and research. Still others noted that the opportunities for innovation were often missed or delayed because of the demands of heavy patient loads.

The conference clearly illustrated that the 1960s were a period of program experimentation as well as self-examination for psychologists in the VA. Concomitant with this experimentation and examination was a divergence from what was happening in psychology outside of the VA; this divergence bears brief mention.

From 1946 to 1965, the primary interface and synergy of effort between VA psychologists and their non-VA colleagues in academia occurred in the affiliation agreements, to which each side brought different interests. As noted in the VA psychology conference in 1965, VA psychologists were trying to handle the problem of treating many veterans and tended to focus much of their effort on what worked in keeping the patient stable and out of the hospital. Their first interest was typically not in the theoretical base of their activities, which was often the interest of their academic colleagues. These different interests, however, complemented each other in the affiliation arrangement.

It is important to point out that psychologists initially drawn to work in the VA were largely motivated by their interest in helping patients. Their professional needs were often met in these treatment activities (see the introduction to this volume). Psychologists drawn to academia were often meeting their professional needs in teaching and research. Those VA psychologists interested in teaching could and did have those professional needs met in the VA's training program. Those interested in research could and did take advantage of the ready access to research funding through the 1960s and most of the 1970s.

Two other observations can be made about the differences between VA and academic psychologists. It can first be noted that other than at APA meetings, VA and academic psychologists attended different professional meetings, with either a more practical treatment focus (VA psychologists) or a theoretical emphasis (academic psychologists). VA psychologists also tended to identify and communicate about organizational and treatment issues with their VA psychology colleagues across the nation. Academic psychologists tended to relate with other psychologists in their own institutions, an observation made by Rosner in describing some of the limitations of the NIMH psychotherapy research conferences in trying to encourage an interaction among the academic community and VA researchers (Rosner, 2005).

HUMAN RELATIONS TRAINING, COMMUNITY CONSULTATION, AND EMPLOYEE INTERPERSONAL TRAINING

The Human Interaction Training Laboratory (HITL) developed by psychologists at the VA hospital in Houston serves to illustrate an innovative treatment program that gained importance beyond patient care application. First, the HITL was based on industrial-organizational psychology and the laboratory method of learning and change, neither of which were usually thought of as contributing to mental health treatment. The program further provided an example of how VA psychologists contributed their social relations expertise within the community and, finally, how that expertise served as an internal resource for the VA in dealing with system problems.[5]

In the 1950s, organizational consultants were beginning to use experiential learning groups as planned interventions for organizational change (Hirsch, 1987). At the University of Houston, Robert Blake had begun experimenting with changes in organizational learning groups. He found success in removing the traditional trainer in these groups and substituted the use of rating scales to help learning group participants process their own experiences and direct their own learning. Blake also argued for the use of experiential learning and human relations training with other populations.

In early 1961, Blake and his colleague Jane Mouton made a management training visit to the Houston VA hospital. Afterward, Robert Morton,

---

[5]The material in this section was primarily provided by Philip G. Hanson (2004).

the chief of psychology at the Houston VA, convinced Lee Cady, then director of the Houston VA, of the potential usefulness of human relations training and learning groups as a treatment focus for patients with psychiatric disorders. Cady turned over a 30-bed treatment unit to psychology to be used to develop this treatment approach.[6] Initially directed by Morton and Dale Johnson, a staff psychologist at the VA at the time, the program was started with VA Central Office funding in May 1961.

In 1964, Sidney Cleveland, who had become chief of psychology at the Houston VA in 1962, turned the program over to Philip G. Hanson. Hanson continued developing the program and helped transport the program to other VA and non-VA treatment settings. The HITL, as it came to be called, adopted Blake's laboratory model with self-directed patient treatment groups using psychosocial and interpersonal rating forms to focus their group discussion activities. Staff served primarily as consultants to the treatment groups. Giving patients a major responsibility for their treatment and its success was an important philosophical base of the HITL.

The data produced by patients in the program were used to monitor patient progress and direct program changes; equally important, the results provided outcome data for research studies. The HITL was acknowledged by the National Training Laboratories for Applied Behavioral Sciences for its innovations in the use of human relations training as a patient treatment approach (Hirsch, 1987; *Problems of the Veterans Wounded in Vietnam*, 1970), and the first publication describing the program appeared in the *Journal of Applied Behavioral Science* (Hanson, Rothaus, Johnson, & Lyle, 1966). By the end of 1981, the VA's survey of mental health treatment programs showed that 52 VA hospitals were using some form of human relations training in their treatment programs.

The human relations training model used for patient care by the psychology staff at the Houston VA also came to the attention of the city of Houston when it needed help with a racial crisis. Following a confrontation between police and the African American community in May 1967, 4 hours of gunfire erupted between police and students at Texas Southern University, a historically Black university in Houston. A police officer was killed and student rooms were ransacked by police in search of hidden weapons. The resulting tensions convinced the city administration that some type of intervention was needed. Mel Sikes, a Black psychologist associated with the Houston VA HITL and a member of the Houston Community Council,

---

[6]This may have been the first instance, or among the first instances, in which psychology was given responsibility for managing an inpatient acute psychiatric treatment program, either within or outside of the VA.

was approached to develop a human relations training program to improve relations between police and the community.

The police–community relations program eventually developed by the Houston VA psychology service drew on the experiences in the HITL as well as its staff and other Houston VA psychologists, who served as small group leaders in a series of training sessions. Groups of police officers and community members met for 3 hours once a week for 6 weeks. The original design was provided by Hanson using a Blake and Mouton program design on intergroup conflict. This 18-hour program was repeated until the entire police force of 1,400 had attended one of the training sessions. The program activities and evaluation data were summarized in an article by Bell, Cleveland, Hanson, and O'Connell (1969). The program was cautiously considered successful as noted in a 70% reduction in citizen complaints about police behavior and no further rioting, including during the contentious summer of 1968 when other cities were experiencing rioting after the assassinations of Martin Luther King Jr., and Robert F. Kennedy. Each member of the VA psychology staff at the Houston VA received a commendation from the VA Central Office in 1968 for their work in this community project.

The success of the Houston VA psychology service in using human relations training in treatment and in community intervention also received attention by the VA Central Office when it needed help with some system problems. In the late 1960s the VA was receiving large numbers of complaints from patients who described clerks and first-contact employees as rude. Cecil Peck, then chief psychologist for the VA, began discussions with Hanson and Cleveland about the possibility of developing a human relations training program to improve the behavior of VA employees toward patients. Peck asked Hanson to attend a meeting in Washington that was also attended by Ralph Fingar (Boston) and Roy Brener (Hines), two prominent VA chiefs of psychology at the time, and a pilot training program was developed for 13 VA hospitals. The success of the pilot convinced the VA to implement this program in all of its hospitals.

With the support and encouragement of Cleveland, Hanson put together a team to design and implement this national human relations training program for employees. With three other Houston VA staff psychologists and two non-VA training experts, a training schedule was developed and a manual for training trainers was published (Veterans Administration, 1973b).[7] The training-of-trainers program eventually prepared over 200 psychologists and other staff to conduct the training program in VA hospitals.

---

[7] In addition to Hanson, the group included Houston VA staff psychologists Rodney Baker, Quentin Dinardo, and Richard Ermalinski. Joyce Paris and Richard Brown-Burke joined the group as training experts from the Houston community.

The program was initially called Training in Individual and Group Effectiveness. A footnote to this story was Sid Cleveland's half-serious suggestion that an *R* word be added to the program title so that the program could be called TIGER. *Resourcefulness* was added to the title, and the program was henceforth affectionately known as the TIGER program.

The TIGER program was arguably the largest organizational development project to date to change the culture in a system. Over 40,000 VA employees were eventually trained by the TIGER program. Built into the program was VA Central Office funding and staffing to evaluate the program and demonstrate its successes. In later years, Cecil Peck noted that many influential hospital directors in the VA reported to him that the TIGER program was the most successful and influential training program ever undertaken for improving the care climate for VA patients (C. Peck, personal communication, July 3, 1992).

MENTAL HEALTH TREATMENT PROGRAMMING GROWTH IN THE 1970s AND 1980s

From 1970 to 1981, the specialized VA mental health treatment programs developed in the 1960s continued to grow in number (see Table 5.1). Several factors led to a significant growth in other specialized mental health treatment programs in the 1970s. These factors included a reorganization of mental health services in the VA Central Office, the influx of Vietnam veterans seeking treatment in the VA, and special congressional funding for treatment of substance abuse and posttraumatic stress disorder (PTSD).

The 1972 reorganization of the Psychiatry, Neurology, and Psychology Service in the VA Central Office resulted in neurology being established

TABLE 5.1
Growth of VA Specialized Mental Health Treatment Programs

Program	Number of units	
	1970	1981
Mental hygiene clinics	70	131
Day treatment centers	36	73
Day hospitals	9	39

Note. 1970 data were obtained from the VA administrator's 1970 annual report to Congress, and 1981 data were obtained from a special survey by the Mental Health and Behavioral Sciences Service in June 1981.

as a separate, independent service. The psychology and psychiatry services were combined into a redesignated Mental Health and Behavioral Sciences Service to better reflect the expanding role of mental health treatment in the VA. The administrator's 1972 annual report to Congress (Veterans Administration, 1973a), for example, reported that the VA's 73 MHCs were providing treatment to over 60,000 veterans with over 1.25 million treatment visits per year. That report acknowledged that the demands for psychologists were steadily expanding as a result of the influx of Vietnam veterans and a greater diversity of responsibilities in the new Mental Health and Behavioral Sciences Service.

During the 1970s, Congress passed special legislation to fund increases in treatment of substance abuse, one of the most frequently encountered diagnoses in the VA, either as a primary or secondary treating condition. Inpatient alcohol treatment units grew from 30 in 1970 to 113 in 1981. In 1981 the VA operated 110 outpatient alcohol treatment programs with a staff psychologist assigned to most of these programs.

The drug dependency treatment programs in the VA could and did draw on the treatment experience of non-VA psychologists and mental health professionals in the development of these programs. The increasing number of Vietnam-era veterans coming to the VA seeking treatment for PTSD, however, presented a unique problem for the VA. Other than in the Department of Defense, the PTSD treatment experience in the non-VA sector was primarily limited to noncombat trauma experiences in such areas as sexual assault and trauma produced by natural disasters. Both the Department of Defense and the VA also initially struggled with whether the PTSD diagnosis involved dynamics other than the "combat fatigue" experience of veterans in World War I and World War II. VA psychologists had little to draw on from the non-VA sector in building programs to meet the needs of veterans with combat-related PTSD (Shepard, 2000).

The pressures for change in the VA resulting from the special treatment needs of Vietnam veterans resulted in a series of five 1-day conferences held around the country in April and May of 1971. The conferences were organized and moderated by Charles Stenger in his role as chair of the VA's Vietnam Veterans Committee and in his leadership role in psychology in the VA Central Office (Stenger, 2003). The conferences were specifically designed to acquaint VA leadership with the issues of Vietnam veterans and were attended by the directors of VA hospitals and heads of veterans' benefits offices in the area as well as other VA field leaders responsible for care of veterans. Donald E. Johnson, then administrator of the VA, attended and presented at all sessions in each conference. A unique feature of these conferences was that Vietnam veterans were invited to participate in the conferences in addition to VA staff. Panels of Vietnam veterans talking about their experiences in the VA supplemented other presentations.[8]

Johnson's presence and presentations during these conferences were an acknowledgment of the problems that the VA was having in providing treatment to Vietnam veterans; it also gave a strong message to top leadership in the field that Johnson wanted to improve treatment services to this population of veterans. The conference noted that a number of factors set Vietnam veterans apart from other veterans: (a) they were younger than other veterans; (b) improved military medical care in Vietnam resulted in a greater proportion who had sustained and survived serious physical disabilities and emotional trauma from their combat experience than in previous wars; (c) abused substances for Vietnam veterans tended to be drugs as opposed to alcohol for other veteran groups; and (d) unlike previous generations of veterans, many Vietnam veterans were angry and felt alienated from mainstream society as a result of their experiences in Vietnam. Contributing to the problems that the VA had in responding to the needs of the Vietnam veteran was the prolonged and inconclusive nature of the Vietnam conflict itself and the public's contentious response to that war.

The conferences were used to propose initiatives and programs to address these problems. By 1988, the VA was operating 31 inpatient PTSD programs, 65 general outpatient PTSD programs, and an additional 30 special funded PTSD clinical team programs. These programs almost universally included a staff psychologist position on the team, and, together with the increase in psychology staffing for the drug dependence treatment programs, this resulted in a significant increase in psychology positions in the VA during the 1970s and 1980s.

Legislation in 1979 also created the Vietnam Veteran Readjustment Counseling Program, which established new community-based VA treatment teams operating outside of the VA hospital grounds in what were called Vet Centers (Veterans Health Care Amendments of 1979; Public Law 96-22). The Readjustment Counseling Program was initially assigned to the Mental Health and Behavioral Sciences Service and headed by psychologist Donald Crawford. By 1985 there were 189 Vet Centers treating 371,000 Vietnam-era veterans and 80,000 family members (Cranston, 1986).

By the time of the VA's survey of mental health treatment programs in June 1988, the VA was employing over 1,400 psychologists in these and

---

[8] Although reproduced for dissemination within the VA, the proceedings of the five conferences were never published. A copy of the comprehensive summary of the conference proceedings, titled "The Vietnam Era Veteran: Challenge for Change" (Veterans Administration, 1971), is on file in the VA psychology archive collection at the Archives of the History of American Psychology at The University of Akron.

TABLE 5.2
Mental Health Treatment Programs, June 1988

Program	Number of programs
Inpatient alcohol units	129
Outpatient alcohol programs	130
Inpatient drug units	60
Outpatient drug programs	66
Inpatient PTSD units	31
Outpatient PTSD programs	65
Special PTSD treatment teams	30
Mental hygiene clinics	153
Traveling mental hygiene clinics	27
Day treatment centers	90
Day hospitals	37
Vocational assessment counseling and placements	120
Compensated work therapy programs	44
Programs for homeless veterans	62
Biofeedback programs	101
Neuropsychology evaluation clinics	107
Pain clinics	67
Sexual dysfunction clinics	58
Sleep disorder clinics	26

Note. Data were obtained from the 1988 Mental Health Program Survey conducted by the Mental Health and Behavioral Sciences Service. They cover 172 VA medical centers, outpatient clinics, domiciliaries, and regional offices with outpatient clinics. PTSD = posttraumatic stress disorder.

other treatment programs. Table 5.2 indicates the diversity and number of these VA mental health treatment programs in a partial listing.

AUTOMATED PSYCHOLOGICAL ASSESSMENT

Completing this review of the contributions of psychology to the treatment of veterans is an account of the development of the VA's automated behavioral and psychological assessment program referred to as the Mental Health Package (MHP). The origins of the MHP can be traced to psychology field efforts during the late 1970s when psychologist Bob Luschene at the VA in Bay Pines, Florida, wrote software drivers that are still used in the VA to administer psychological tests. Jim Johnson helped start the preassessment unit at the VA in Salt Lake City (later headed by Doug Gottfredson), which used computerized assessment in evaluating all new psychiatry admissions. In the 1980s a group of psychologists and psychiatrists at the Dallas VA took the work being done at Salt Lake City and provided critical support work in developing the MHP.[9] The MHP was

---

[9] This group included Bob Fowler and Rob Kolodner, the chief and assistant chief of psychiatry, Dale Cannon, the chief of psychology, and Allan Finkelstein, a staff psychologist.

distributed throughout the VA in late 1985 as part of the VA electronic medical record (Cannon, 1985).

The development of the MHP was undertaken at a time when computer applications were not universally supported in the VA. When Doug Gottfredson was hired to head up the new Program Automation and Evaluation Section created in 1985 in the Mental Health and Behavioral Sciences Service in the VA Central Office, personal computers were rare in the field because of regulations constraining their use. In what was a significant step at the time, Gottfredson supplied personal computers and software to substance abuse and PTSD treatment programs in the field to support program evaluation efforts in addition to his work helping to develop the MHP.

In 1994, Dale Cannon succeeded Gottfredson to head what became known as the Informatics Section of the Mental Health Strategic Health Group. Under Cannon's leadership until his retirement in 2004, the number of psychological tests and behavioral rating scales such as the Minnesota Multiphasic Personality Inventory and the Beck Depression Inventory grew to 55 instruments and 24 clinical interviews in fiscal year 2004. That year also saw the MHP register over 2.1 million automated assessments and interviews by psychologists and other mental health professionals in the VA.[10]

SUMMARY AND CONCLUSIONS

The earliest reports of the activities of VA psychologists indicated that they were spending most of their time in diagnostic activities with very little time in treatment. Training and research activities took up the remainder of their time. By 1956 their role had substantially changed. Diagnostic and assessment activities accounted for 22% of their time with the same percentage in treatment activities. Training represented 20% of their time with 12% devoted to research. The remaining 24% of their time went into a variety of activities ranging from consultation and work placement program assignments to work on various management problems, administrative work, and vacation leave (Wolford, 1956). Thirty years later, VA psychologists were spending 75% of their time in direct patient care or patient care support activities (see chap. 6, this volume).

The significant numbers of psychologists employed by the VA and the contributions of VA psychologists to treatment programming summarized in this chapter provide support for Wolman's observation that the VA

---

[10] The author thanks Dale Cannon and Allan Finkelstein in the Informatics Section of the Mental Health and Behavioral Sciences Service in the VA Central Office for information on the MHP used in this section.

provided a significant impetus to the emergence of psychologists as health care practitioners in the country (Wolman, 1965). This chapter, however, illustrates only part of the story of the role of psychology and the VA in the mental health treatment of veterans. The topics chosen are meant to characterize rather than fully describe these contributions. Space limitations have required difficult decisions about what to include and in what depth. Omissions include the role of VA psychologists in the 1940s in the treatment of tuberculosis, the role of psychologists in the treatment of spinal cord injury and other medical conditions, the work of psychologists in developing neuropsychological assessment techniques and other diagnostic instruments, the treatment of former prisoners of war, and the contributions of psychologists in the treatment of elderly veterans. It is hoped that these contributions can be more fully developed in future publications.

In many ways, the values of psychology and the skills of VA psychologists promoted a greater sensitivity of VA health care programs to the human needs of veterans served. Together with their colleagues in psychiatry and social work, psychologists helped transform the VA into a major mental health care program in this country, a role continued to this day.

6

DEFINING AND DEFENDING THE PRACTICE OF PSYCHOLOGY IN THE VA

The years immediately following World War II marked an important time period for defining the practice of psychology for the entire profession, as well as for VA psychology. In addition to developing standards for internship training and determining qualifications for practice, the profession was struggling with the emergence and functioning of psychologists as independent practitioners. Just as mainstream psychology in the American Psychological Association (APA) had difficulty in understanding the interest of psychologists in institutional practice in the VA (see the introduction to this volume), an uneasy relationship existed in APA between the academic community and the early proponents of independent practice. The reorganization merger finalized in 1945 between APA and the American Association of Applied Psychology was a step taken that had much to do with the emerging advocacy of psychologists as practitioners within the profession (Fowler, 1996; Wolfle, 1946).

Several events occurred in 1946 that were important to the practice of psychology. Discussions on advanced credentials for practice led APA to establish the American Board of Examiners in Professional Psychology, later named the American Board of Professional Psychology (ABPP). The National Mental Health Act (1946; Public Law 79-487) created the National

Institute of Mental Health (NIMH) and, together with the VA's training program established the same year, provided substantial support for the clinical training of psychologists and other mental health professionals. The reorganization of APA also created the first divisions in APA, many of which were centered on practice issues such as the divisions of Clinical Psychology, Counseling Psychology, and Psychologists in Public Service. The activities of these divisions within APA served an important role in helping the practice community develop and define itself. The APA journals started in 1946 also contributed to this effort.

With the growth and influence of the practice community, the first 2 decades of advocacy after World War II can be characterized by efforts to define and legitimize the practice of psychology. In their review of the history of the growth of the practice areas of psychology, for example, Benjamin and Baker (2004) noted the 30-year effort by APA and state psychological associations to define the practice of psychology in state licensing laws. Those efforts resulted in Virginia passing the first licensing law for psychologists in 1946 and ended in 1977 when Missouri became the 50th state to pass a psychology licensing law.

If the first 2 decades can be characterized as advocacy to define the practice of psychology, the next 2 decades extended the definition of *practice* and also added advocacy efforts to defend the profession. In this time period, for example, reports by the APA Practice Directorate detailed numerous legislative and legal efforts by the profession to obtain Medicare and other insurance reimbursement for services by psychologists and continued with its efforts and early successes in obtaining prescriptive authority for psychologists.

Similar defining and defending advocacy activities surfaced for VA psychology to those that occurred for the rest of the profession, albeit with some differences noted later in this chapter. For example, the early role of VA psychology in helping the profession define practice in training, accreditation, and qualification standards has been noted in chapters 1 and 2. In the 1970s and 1980s, VA psychology obtained clinical privileges and medical staff membership for staff psychologists and established licensure as an employment criterion. That time period also had VA psychology defending the practice and functioning of psychology and its training program during periods of budget challenges and other forces that threatened the role and status of psychology in the VA.

Although VA psychology was involved early in advocacy within the profession in addressing a number of practice issues, especially in the area of training and accreditation, its leaders tended to develop parallel rather than interactive advocacy efforts with the rest of the profession. It was not until the late 1970s and 1980s that this trend was reversed when VA psychology and APA began forging advocacy alliances to affect federal legislation for funding of psychology training (see chap. 2, this volume) and other issues described in this chapter.

One of the reasons for VA psychology developing its own advocacy initiatives in the early years was that many practice and employment issues were uniquely defined by practice in a large federal organization. Employment qualifications, pay, and other working conditions for VA psychologists were, in fact, often determined by federal agencies other than the VA, such as the Civil Service Commission and the Office of Personnel Management (OPM). The VA was also governed by federal legislation that added an even more diverse arena for advocacy and change efforts in that different congressional committees had oversight for different aspects of the VA's operation affecting psychology.

Early efforts to define the role and practice of psychology in the VA led VA psychology leaders to a natural involvement with psychology leadership in other federal agencies. An informal informational network among psychology leaders in the VA, Public Health Service, Department of Defense, Indian Health Service, and the Federal Bureau of Prisons worked on such issues as professional, classification, and qualification standards for psychologists in all federal agencies. Cecil Peck (personal communication, July 3, 1992) noted that these meetings had to deal with a number of areas of disagreement among the psychology agency leaders over strategy and political realities. Not all federal agency psychology leaders, for example, believed that the organizational independence of psychology and psychiatry was desirable or could be realized in their agencies, but this was an important agenda for the VA.[1]

At the local level, in VA hospitals and clinics, psychologists had to deal with an organizational structure frequently governed by administrators who did not fully appreciate how the professional role and services of a psychologist fit into the technical aspects of law and regulation that defined the functioning of the VA's medical care programs. VA and other federal psychologists had to work in settings with a considerable amount of administrative control (L. S. Rogers, 1956). In his listing of professional frustrations of psychologists working under this administrative control, Chase (1947) observed that nonpsychologically sensitive administrators employing psychologists as professional experts were not concerned with the advancement of psychology as a profession. Their interest in the functioning of psychologists ended when that functioning produced the minimal results provided by law. Doing only what was considered administratively necessary led to

---

[1]According to Cecil Peck, these meetings of federal agency psychology leaders were irregularly scheduled, usually once a year, often at American Psychological Association meetings or in Washington, DC, and by agreement, no records or minutes were kept.

conflict for psychologists, who were interested in rendering the maximum possible service under a code of ethics.

These early administrative control issues had more impact on the role and practice of psychologists in the VA than any professional discipline issues between psychology and psychiatry. Although psychology in the VA Central Office has been included under the administrative leadership of psychiatry during its history, VA Central Office psychologists and psychiatrists worked together in a collaborative and mutually respectful relationship in meeting the needs of veterans (Stenger, 2003, 2005). The advantages and disadvantages of separating psychiatry and psychology into separate services in the Central Office to reflect the organizational independence of the two disciplines in the field were discussed in the late 1970s. The same issue of separating psychiatry and psychology in the VA Central Office surfaced a decade later, but in neither case did these discussions result in an official proposal to the VA Central Office leadership. The prevailing opinion was reflected in Oakley Ray's comments (Ray, 1979) that psychology and psychiatry in the VA had more in common than they had differences and that the disciplines needed to continue to work together to promote mental health issues. In his previously referenced oral history interview in 2003, Stenger also noted that mental health was battling the medical side of the house, which had all the money.

The early vision by the VA Central Office psychology leadership and its advocacy for the practice of psychology was clearly focused in its interactions with the rest of the profession in training standards, accreditation, and establishing the doctoral degree as the journeyman credential for practice. This advocacy role has already been described in chapters 2 and 3 and this description is not repeated here. That role, however, will likely be considered one of the primary legacies of VA psychology in contributing to the development of psychological practice in this country.

A significant part of the VA practice advocacy story was the joint advocacy between the VA Central Office and field psychology leaders with other psychology groups. This advocacy was first focused within APA's Division 18 (Psychologists in Public Service) and, later, within the Association of VA Chief Psychologists (AVACP). These two groups served important roles in helping define and defend the role and practice of psychology in the VA.

EARLY ADVOCACY IN DIVISION 18: PSYCHOLOGISTS IN PUBLIC SERVICE

As one of the 19 original divisions created by the APA reorganization in 1946, Division 18 quickly became a home in APA for VA psychologists and other psychologists employed in state and federal programs. In his review of the history of Division 18, however, R. R. Baker (1996b) noted that discussions regarding the formation of this division were met with some opposition, as reported by Margaret Ives, an early historian for Division 18. She noted that it was observed by some APA leaders that most practicing psychologists at that time were employed in public service settings and that if everyone eligible to join this division did so it would become the largest division in APA. To offset this advantage, the first president of the division had to agree that the division would not have a newsletter or a program at the APA convention. The uneasy relationship between the academic and practice communities was still in evidence as was the early competition between practice groups.

In addition to increasing psychological services in public agencies and improving the quality of those services, one of the goals of the division was to help management of these agencies define the role and practice of psychology in the agency health care programs. The early officers of the division came from personnel management positions in government and used that expertise to promote personnel management goals. With James Quinter Holsopple's election as president of the division in 1954, there tended to be a shift toward clinical practice psychologists, many from the VA or NIMH, serving as officers, with a focus on the role of clinical practice in public agencies.

R. R. Baker (1996b) cited Lee Gurel's observation that the division started as what Gurel called a union organization with bread-and-butter issues such as establishing psychology in the civil service. Early division presidential addresses spoke to these concerns as reflected in Roger Bellows's address in 1949 on selling psychological services to administrators and Holsopple's address in 1954 arguing for a fair and realistic research salary in government.

As civil service employees, VA psychologists shared many of the concerns of their public service federal colleagues in Division 18. Recruitment and pay led the list of VA psychology issues. The recruitment problem for VA psychology was twofold. Already noted in previous chapters was the fact that the VA generally found it difficult to recruit the large numbers of psychologists to fill the positions authorized by the VA. The other recruitment problem was the requirement to follow cumbersome procedures and resulting delays encountered in the civil service recruitment and employment application process. This problem was addressed in 1946 for physicians, dentists, and nurses in the VA when legislation established the Department of Medicine and Surgery (DM&S) in the VA and also created a new employment system for those professions in the Title 38 United States Code (USC; To Establish a Department of Medicine and Surgery, 1946; Public Law 79-293). Psychologists, social workers, pharmacists, and other professional groups in the VA remained in the civil service and were governed by Title 5 USC laws and civil service rules and regulations.[2]

In addition to recruitment issues, the Title 5 and Title 38 employment systems also had different pay systems. Title 5 employees were appointed to what were called *grade levels*, in which pay was based on job descriptions and minimum qualifications for those defined jobs. Title 38 allowed the VA to set pay on the basis of the professional credentials and qualifications of the individual rather than the job. In 1975, Title 38 legislation also authorized special pay bonuses for board certification and other credentials for physicians and dentists—pay bonuses not available to psychologists and other Title 5 employees. As noted later in this chapter, the Title 5 and Title 38 recruitment and pay issues surfaced in the early 1980s as an important advocacy issue for VA psychologists.

Many of the early discussions regarding the employment status and role of federal psychologists tended to be focused in the Civil Service Commission. In 1949, for example, the commission followed the example set by the VA and agreed to include both service and research duties in the position descriptions of federally employed psychologists. It was not until the 1960s, however, that Division 18 became more involved in policy decisions in state and federal government. This interest and involvement was noted by APA in 1966 when APA asked Division 18 to help respond to a request from the Civil Service Commission for assistance in studying pay comparability for psychologists in the civil service (R. R. Baker, 1996b). Although the VA had early established the doctoral degree and internship as qualifications for employment, there was still great variability in other federal programs regarding education and training requirements, which were closely tied to salary rates. The VA had also been successful in developing an independent service status within the VA with the chief of psychology reporting directly to the chief of staff (the title of the top medical care officer in VA hospitals) rather than reporting to the chief of psychiatry, which was more common in non-VA health care settings. The VA experience was useful in helping Division 18 and APA suggest qualification modifications to the civil service that moved other federal agencies closer to the qualifications for employment that existed in the VA.

Although the division's members still held a common bond in serving the public by working in public settings, specialized interests among its members resulted in a bylaw change in 1974 to establish sections within the division (R. R. Baker, 1996b). VA psychologists saw this as an opportunity to

---

[2] In 1946, James G. Miller pointed out to General Bradley that psychologists also needed to be placed in Title 38 along with physicians, dentists, and nurses and obtained a verbal commitment from Bradley to include this in the VA's next legislative agenda, a step never taken.

develop a formal advocacy group within APA to help its leaders in the VA Central Office better deal with a number of professional issues. The VA section of Division 18 was proposed and approved in 1977 with Ralph Fingar (chief of psychology at the Boston VA) as its first chair.

Shortly after its formation, the VA section quickly became the largest section in Division 18.[3] The section became active in promoting bonus pay for board-certified VA psychologists and in discussions regarding Title 38 employment. Other issues that the section worked on with psychologists in the Central Office included the study of recruitment and retention problems of psychologists in the VA and support and funding of internship training and research.

The advocacy for VA psychology issues by the VA section, Division 18, and APA had its primary impact in directly presenting VA psychology concerns to top leaders in the VA, a route not available to psychology leaders in the VA Central Office, who had to follow an organizational chain of command in surfacing the same issues. APA used its contacts with Congress to have congressional members write letters to the administrator of the VA and other VA officials asking for explanations of or expressing concerns about policy decisions. As a result, the issues were not easily ignored even though the sometimes contorted responses to these inquiries did not always produce the desired effect.[4]

Although the advocacy efforts for VA psychology by the VA section and Division 18 were partially met within APA, VA chiefs of psychology began discussing the need for another advocacy voice. At a meeting of psychology chiefs at the APA meeting in August 1977 in San Francisco, the formation of an independent VA psychology organization was discussed. Support for such an organization at that meeting resulted in a decision to form the AVACP.[5]

---

[3] Sidney Cleveland, president of Division 18 in 1980, and Harold Dickman, president-elect of the division, both influential chiefs of psychology in the VA, had to reassure the division membership that VA psychologists were public service psychologists first and that there was no plan to turn Division 18 into a VA division (Cleveland, 1980b).

[4] For example, in a November 4, 1980, letter by Donald L. Custis, chief medical director for the VA, to Senator Daniel K. Inouye, Custis acknowledged the senator's letter (which was requested by APA) expressing an interest in including chief psychologists as voting members of the Clinical Executive Board and including psychologists on the medical center staff. In his reply, Custis noted that his department supported these steps and observed that over half of the psychology services in the VA had such membership but that he did not feel that a strong policy statement to this effect would be helpful at the time.

[5] In 2003, the Association of VA Chief Psychologists, then named the Association of VA Psychologist Leaders, voted to turn its archive collection over to the Archives of the History of American Psychology at The University of Akron to be included with the VA psychology archives. Copies of all association newsletters from 1978 to the present referenced in this chapter as well as correspondence between association presidents and APA staff and congressional members and staff are included in that collection.

ADVOCACY BY THE ASSOCIATION OF VA
CHIEF PSYCHOLOGISTS

In forming the AVACP, VA psychology was following the lead of VA chiefs of medicine and chiefs of surgery, who had developed similar organizations to assist their VA Central Office leaders with professional and guild issues. As organizations independent of the VA, these groups could directly bring up their issues with top VA officials without having to follow the VA's chain of command, a benefit already noted with VA psychology and its advocacy efforts within Division 18 in APA. As an additional advocacy voice, however, AVACP had the advantage of moving more quickly on issues without having to use the governance structure within APA. AVACP could also address issues of importance to VA psychology that were not directly relevant to APA, such as the need for administrative training for new chiefs of psychology.

With support received during the August 1977 meeting of VA chiefs of psychology, a planning group was formed and chaired by Oakley Ray, chief of psychology at the VA in Nashville, to develop bylaws for the proposed organization. The bylaws were ratified by chiefs of psychology in the field in late 1977 and elections were held in early 1978 with Oakley Ray selected as the first president of the association (Cummings, 1998). An association newsletter was also started in January of 1978 with Phil Laughlin, chief of psychology at the VA in Knoxville, Iowa, as newsletter editor. The newsletter became an important source of information to the field in tracking the advocacy efforts of the association and contributed to important networking support among VA psychologists.

The formation of AVACP occurred at a time when psychologists had clearly established themselves as important health care providers in the VA, but they lacked the status of psychiatrists, an important goal of James G. Miller in establishing VA psychology (see chap. 1, this volume). The lack of status was frequently tied to such issues as psychologists not having clinical privileges to independently practice their profession without implied medical supervision. The fact that psychologists did not require licensure for employment in the VA contributed to the indifference and lack of recognition of psychologists by the physician-controlled leadership of the hospitals. Both of these issues were at the time similar to those of psychologists functioning in independent practice and other practice settings. Early surveys conducted by AVACP identified numerous professional and administrative challenges for VA psychologists.

As important as these guild issues were to the entire profession, the interest of VA psychologists in improving their status within the hospital was not simply related to lack of status per se but was also driven by a conviction that psychologists had an important voice that needed to be heard in meeting the mental health needs of veterans and in helping to define and establish quality care in VA programs. By not being included as members of the medical staff in a hospital's bylaws psychologists were frequently overlooked as members of important boards and committees. In spite of their important role and expertise in research, for example, psychologists were rarely included as members of the important and prestigious hospital research committee. The Title 5 status of psychologists also contributed to the perception that psychologists were not "professionals" but were grouped with other technicians employed by the hospital who did not need representation on the hospital Professional Standards Board. Chiefs of psychology were also not regularly included with physician service chiefs as members of the Clinical Executive Board (CEB), which was given oversight for clinical care in the hospital.

With these issues as a background, AVACP began developing a list of topics to address in advocacy. High on the list were a number of professional practice issues: establishing psychologists as members of the medical staff, obtaining clinical privileges for psychologists, and developing licensure requirements for psychologists. Other topics emerged on the list, such as obtaining bonus pay for psychologists with the ABPP, moving psychologists to Title 38 employment, and an almost unanimous agreement in the field regarding the need to develop an administrative training program for new chiefs of psychology.

The most immediate problem that faced the new association, however, was the concern over whether the VA psychology training program would be continued and supported at the same funding levels as in past years. Information had been received about pending cuts in that training budget. Funding for the continuation of the training program was clearly a topic of interest not only within the VA but within APA and the universities participating in the training program, and plans were made to enlist congressional support for maintaining funding for the program through APA's advocacy network.

The Growth of Advocacy With APA

In the fall of 1978, AVACP president Oakley Ray began a vigorous letter-writing campaign on threats to funding for the VA's psychology training program. Included were letters to Ludy Benjamin (administrative officer for the APA Education Affairs Office), Patrick DeLeon (chair of the APA Board of Professional Affairs), and Carolyn Jackson (APA Office of

Accreditation). Early contacts for support of the VA psychology training budget were also made by AVACP and APA to U.S. senators Alan Cranston and Daniel Inouye.[6]

As noted in chapter 2, the anticipated cuts in the VA's training program surfaced in 1979. APA and AVACP were successful in reversing most of these cuts, but similar cuts surfaced the following year. With support by APA and the Association for the Advancement of Psychology, AVACP president Harold Dickman testified before Congress on the proposed cuts and, again, the cuts were mostly reversed. In succeeding years, AVACP and APA remained vigilant in monitoring and working together on advocacy for a number of VA psychology training issues. The success of that joint effort on training issues led to further joint advocacy on other issues.

In 1980, at the suggestion of Ludy Benjamin in the APA Education Affairs Office, AVACP president Harold Dickman wrote to Michael Pallak, then executive director of APA, to propose a jointly funded annual spring meeting of AVACP officers with key APA officers and staff. That proposal was accepted, and the first meeting was held in the spring of 1981. The success of that meeting led to the meeting becoming an annual event that continues to the present and helped to develop advocacy agendas and action steps for the AVACP and APA.

The spring meeting with APA staff was later expanded, with AVACP officers meeting with other groups. Meetings with top VA leaders were first added to the agenda of those spring AVACP meetings. Later, the meetings also included contacts with representatives of the veterans' organizations and visits to congressional offices.

In 1990, Raymond Fowler, chief executive officer of APA, invited chief psychologists from all federal agencies to a meeting to discuss the new directorate structure in APA and to share information about psychology programs and issues among each of the agencies (Sieracki, 1991). In addition to the VA, attendance included representatives from the Army, Navy, Air Force, Bureau of Corrections, and the Bureau of Indian Affairs. That meeting led to the idea of forming the Council of Federal Agency Practicing Psychologists. Ed Sieracki, deputy director of the Mental Health and Behavioral Sciences Service in the VA Central Office, was asked to chair the formation phases of the proposed council. Three organizational meetings of the group were held in 1991 (E. Sieracki, personal communication, October 28, 2004), but with Sieracki's retirement from the VA later that year, the council never became fully functional.

---

[6] As noted previously, copies of these letters and other materials referenced in this section are on file in the VA psychology collection at the Archives of the History of American Psychology at The University of Akron.

Administrative Training for VA Chiefs of Psychology

As noted earlier, there was almost universal agreement among AVACP members of the need for a training program to help new chiefs of psychology better respond to their professional and administrative leadership responsibilities. Discussions with the VA Office of Academic Affairs (OAA), however, were not successful in obtaining support for such a program. In 1983, AVACP president Rodney R. Baker organized an administrative training program for new chiefs that was funded by AVACP. The program was held in Washington, DC, and a strategic decision was made to invite VA Central Office education and personnel staff to help evaluate the program. Both the education and personnel evaluations were highly positive and led to the funding of the program by the OAA in 1984.[7]

The program was logistically assigned to the VA's Regional Medical Education Center (RMEC) in Minneapolis, which hosted the program from 1984 to 1997. In 1998 the program was moved to the RMEC in St. Louis and expanded to include new chiefs of psychiatry in a move by AVACP to broaden VA Central Office funding support. Social work and nursing leaders were added as participants in 1999 when the program was moved to the education training center in Little Rock, which hosted the program through 2003. In a decision by the VA to concentrate training dollars on other established leadership programs, the 2003 program was the last year the program was funded. Psychology was included, however, in a new administrative training program for all VA professional service chiefs in the fall of 2005.

In addition to supporting an information network among chief of psychology participants, the training program served an important advocacy role in helping new chiefs develop strategies for implementing the emerging practice agendas in VA psychology in such areas as developing clinical privileges for psychologists. Participants were given VA policy information and sample clinical privilege policies developed in other medical centers, and strategy discussions for establishing clinical privileges in the field supplemented the formal documents. Training resources and strategy discussions were provided in the program in other areas such as personnel recruitment, job descriptions, performance evaluation, and use of the VA's workload and databases in planning and advocacy at the local medical center level. The training materials for the 1983 class were reproduced by AVACP and

---

[7]In addition to Rodney R. Baker, the planning staff and faculty for the 1st years of the training program from 1983 to 1987 drew on experienced chiefs of psychology from the field including Jonathan Cummings (Washington, DC), Kenneth Klauck (Milwaukee), Philip Laughlin (Knoxville, Iowa), Orville Lips (North Chicago), and Edmund Nightingale (Minneapolis).

distributed throughout the VA as a handbook for VA chiefs of psychology. A similar handbook with updated materials was also reproduced by AVACP and distributed to the field in 1993.[8]

During its 21-year history, over 300 chiefs of psychology and other psychology leaders in the field had attended the training program. The networking and practice advocacy goals of the administrative training program clearly added to the successes in practice advocacy efforts described in the following sections.

Licensure and Internship Employment Standards

One of the early issues addressed by AVACP and psychology in the VA Central Office in the late 1970s concerned standards for employment of psychologists in the DM&S. Since its inception in 1946, VA psychology had established the goal of hiring the best-qualified psychologists to work with veterans. For VA psychology leadership in the 1970s this included a preference for hiring psychologists who were licensed and had an APA-approved internship. Because most state licensing laws exempted psychologists from licensure if they worked in a state or other public agency setting and the status of APA-approved internships had not yet reached importance as a practice credential, these credentials had not been included as a requirement for employment in the VA. As a result, the civil service register from which VA psychologists had to be recruited had many psychologist applicants seeking employment without these credentials, but they had to be given consideration in the recruitment process and often complicated the process of hiring the best-qualified applicants.

Although the VA had been successful in recruiting psychologists who were licensed (two thirds were licensed at the time) and the majority had received an APA-approved internship in the VA or in other internship settings, the goal of hiring only psychologists with these credentials led VA psychology to seek legislative action to make this change. In 1979, legislation added licensure in a state or obtaining such licensure within 2 years to the requirement for employment as a psychologist in the DM&S (Veterans Health Programs Extension and Improvement Act of 1979; Public Law 96-151). Also in the law was language that required psychologist applicants to

---

[8]The 1983 and 1993 training handbooks distributed to the field offer important insights into professional and administrative issues for psychology leadership in local medical centers as well as changes in those issues from the 1980s to the 1990s (Association of VA Chief Psychologists, 1983, 1993). Both are on file in the VA psychology collection at the Archives of the History of American Psychology at The University of Akron. Starting in 2001, the training files were put on compact discs. A detailed history of the training program was also added. The training discs for 2001 and 2003 are also on file in the VA psychology archive collection (Department of Veterans Affairs, 2001, 2003b).

have an internship acceptable to the administrator of the VA. VA policy issued in 1982 indicated that all APA-approved internships and internships received in the VA would automatically be acceptable to the administrator (Veterans Administration, 1982). A psychologist without an APA-approved or VA internship could be employed by making an application to the administrator, an option rarely sought and even more rarely approved since the law's passage. Together with the previous employment requirement of a doctoral degree from an APA-approved graduate program in clinical or counseling psychology, Public Law 96-151 established the highest standards for employment and psychological practice in the country for the largest employer of clinical and counseling psychologists.[9]

Medical Staff Membership and Clinical Privileges for Psychologists

In setting a goal for medical staff membership, VA psychologists were continuing their efforts to obtain an equal status with physicians as health care providers. As members of the medical staff, psychologists could be expected to participate in the various clinical boards and committees that set policy and monitored clinical practice in the hospital. Especially sought was membership of the chief of psychology on the CEB, which included physician chiefs of services and was the hospital oversight body for clinical activities. Noted earlier, the congressional advocacy network of APA had an impact in bringing this issue to the attention of VA Central Office officials, but this was one case where the persistent efforts of chiefs of psychology at the local level assisted by the training materials and focus of the administrative training program had a major impact. By 1981, over two thirds of chiefs of psychology were functioning as voting members of the CEB.

Closely tied to the issue of including psychologists as members of the medical staff in VA medical centers was the equally important task of establishing clinical privileges, that is, the delineation of those professional services that could be performed by psychologists without medical super-vision. Two concerns were raised in the field—were clinical privileges for psychologists permitted by the Joint Commission on Accreditation of Hospitals (JCAH), and what privileges for psychologists could be agreed on and supported by their psychiatry colleagues?

---

[9] It is important to note the distinction between the VA's Department of Medicine and Surgery (DM&S) and the Department of Veterans Benefits (DVB). DM&S was the primary health care treatment arm of the VA whereas DVB administered the many benefits to veterans in such areas as education, employment, and compensation for injury and illness resulting from their military service. Both employed psychologists but under different professional practice credentials. For example, nondoctoral psychologists could be employed in DVB but not in DM&S. The practice initiatives of VA psychologists described in this chapter refer only to psychology practice in DM&S.

As an illustration of the collaboration between psychology and psychiatry in the VA Central Office, a clinical privilege template for psychologists was agreed to by the Mental Health and Behavioral Sciences Service and published by the VA that recommended a number of areas for the independent practice of psychology in the VA (Veterans Administration, 1978). That publication further referenced a prior information letter from the chief medical director that provided basic departmental policies on this matter and contained areas of agreement between the VA and JCAH on giving privileges to psychologists. The template included as suggested privileges the traditional areas of practice of VA psychologists prepared through doctoral-level education in clinical or counseling psychology in the areas of assessment, general individual and group psychotherapy services, and consultation. The template also suggested specialized proficiencies for psychologists, achieved through additional training or certification, in such areas as neuropsychology, hypnotherapy, family therapy, and group behavioral management techniques involving token economy programs. The template finally included suggestions for inclusion of privileges for psychologists in new or emerging treatment approaches in such areas as biofeedback, pain management, and aversive conditioning.

The publication of the clinical privileges template in 1978 gave medical centers both guidance and support for granting privileges to psychologists. Medical centers according privileges to psychologists eventually became an almost universally accepted practice in the VA.

Threats to Funding and Staffing

The late 1970s and early 1980s marked a time period in the country when federal budgets were closely scrutinized. Special concerns over the expenditure of health care dollars began to receive attention during this period, including funding for the VA. Already noted were the pressures to reduce funding for training, and in 1978 a proposal surfaced to reduce funding for research that would eliminate central office research funding in up to 65 VA hospitals. The need to defend funding for the VA's health care programs, especially its professional and administrative staffing, which accounted for 69% of its health care budget, led the VA to contract a study with the National Academy of Sciences (NAS) to develop staffing guidelines for its patient care workload. The NAS study, completed in 1977, was unable to develop the requested guidelines, in part over disagreement on how to project needed workload, and NAS recommended that the VA redirect its focus to productivity.

The VA essentially ignored the NAS recommendation to focus on productivity. As a result, a Government Accounting Office report issued in March 1981 criticized the VA for not having developed a uniform, centrally directed system to measure productivity. The VA's chief medical director subsequently established what was called the *staffing guideline project* for this purpose. The involvement of VA psychology in this project resulted in one of the largest databases describing psychology workload ever developed.

Acknowledging the psychology staff resource limitations in the Central Office as the project proceeded, John E. Davis Jr., then deputy director of the Mental Health and Behavioral Sciences Service, asked AVACP for assistance with this project. AVACP president Rodney R. Baker appointed a task group of chiefs of psychology to respond to this request. Baker headed the task group, which also included Sidney Cleveland (Houston), Kenneth Klauck (Milwaukee), Joseph Rickard (Temple, Texas), and Jon Barrett (Livermore, California).

A 1981 survey and pilot study helped make the decision to divide the psychology workload for the study into 11 direct patient care workload categories (a list of different types of assessments and therapy services), five patient care support activities (including informal consultation, team planning meetings, and supervision of interns), and 6 professional and administrative categories (such as psychology service administration, research, and continuing education provided or received by staff). A stratified sample of 28 VA psychology services was selected for the study, representing large and small services, and included 16 services with a psychology internship training program and 12 without such training programs.

Workload data were collected in 1984 on a daily basis for 3 months from 285 doctoral psychology staff, 80 psychology technicians, and 90 psychology interns and represented almost 200,000 hours of work activities. For the direct patient care workload categories both the number of assessments and therapy episodes were recorded as well as the time spent for each episode to determine average time required for the activity as a baseline from which needed staff levels would be calculated. For the nondirect patient care categories, only time spent in the category was recorded. The direct patient care database included 29,000 assessments (including over 1,000 brief and full neuropsychological assessments), 38,000 individual therapy sessions, and 88,000 group therapy contacts.

The results of the study (R. R. Baker, Barrett, & Klauk, 1986) indicated that psychology staff in psychology services with internship training programs were spending 47% of their time in direct patient care workload categories, 26% of their time in patient care support activities, and 27% of their time in professional and administrative activities. For those psychology services without an internship training program the percentages were 53%, 25%, and 22%, respectively.

The VA psychology staffing guideline project was successful in determining baseline levels for the productivity and activities of psychologists.

However, derivations of "needed" staff levels based on the average time needed to perform the workload produced were never mandated for field use but rather left to local management action. The study demonstrated what most psychology chiefs already knew, that is, that psychology services were understaffed for the workload being produced. A second study conducted in 1986 to refine the workload coefficients showed similar results, with the model suggesting that the needed psychology staffing for the VA was 20% higher than actual staffing (R. R. Baker, 1987). Anecdotal data indicated that the staffing guideline data helped some psychology services get additional staffing, but there were also examples of staffing loss in psychology services where actual levels of staffing were higher than that suggested by the projected staff need level. The data collection process used in the psychology staffing guideline study was subsequently incorporated into the annual VA psychology workload report and became an important data source used by the VA Central Office psychology, AVACP, and APA in legislative testimony and other advocacy efforts on behalf of VA psychology.

One of the most effective uses of this data occurred in 1994 to counteract the arguments of a national VA planning group headed by an influential hospital director who proposed that the VA reduce psychology staffing by half and contract out needed psychological services. In preparing a response to this proposal, AVACP helped develop a study of the annual staffing guideline-based workload and fiscal accounting cost data for VA psychology operations in fiscal year 1993 and compared these costs with the costs for contracting out these services (R. R. Baker, 1996a). To obtain an estimate of the costs to contract out direct patient care workload, Civilian Health and Medical Program of the United States (CHAMPUS) reimbursement rates were used as an estimate of fair market value in that CHAMPUS reimbursement rates were generally based on some discount of community fee-for-service rates. The estimated fair market value of psychology's assessment and therapy treatment services totaled $264 million. Annual costs of the VA's psychology program were calculated to include salary of doctoral staff, technicians, psychology interns, and secretarial staff. Fringe benefit costs and costs for office space, utilities, supplies, and administrative support were also included. The costs came to $177 million or $87 million less than the fair market value of contracting out the same assessment and therapy services.

The study also pointed out the fact that the comparison did not place a dollar value estimate on the other, nondirect patient care services provided by psychologists in the VA such as research, intern training and supervision, supervisory training, and time spent in treatment planning and program development. Also not given a dollar value was time spent by psychologists in other hospital-wide programs such as counseling employees in employee assistance programs and providing consultation to hospital management on work-related personnel and organizational issues.

The study's finding that contracting out psychological services in the community for direct patient care services would increase costs by 55% and that the employment of VA psychologists was fiscally sound helped lead to a dropping of the proposal to reduce psychology staffing and contract out psychological services in the VA. The study also helped defend the value and costs of the psychology training program in other advocacy situations.

Resource Allocation Methodologies

The hoped-for increase in psychology staffing as a result of the staffing guideline project ran counter to the funding pressures on the VA in the 1980s. By 1982, the VA was beginning to study methods for allocating budgets to medical centers on the basis of workload performed. One of the first models used by the VA for this purpose was the diagnostic-related groups (DRG) method, which was first used in 1984 to develop medical center budgets. By this time, the DRG model had also started receiving attention in Medicare as a retrospective reimbursement system. For the VA, however, the DRG method served as a prospective reimbursement budget model for medical centers, that is, an estimate of dollars needed to treat a patient in a diagnostic group in future years based on a case-mix workload performed in the past.

The DRG resource allocation model in the VA worked best for surgery, less well for acute medicine, and was not kind to mental health (Nightingale, 1986).[10] One reason for the model not serving mental health well was the fact that fewer than 30 DRGs were mental health related in a listing of over 400 DRGs. Because the mental health workload in terms of numbers of patients treated was the largest in the VA and consumed the most dollars for lengths of stay, the small number of DRGs in mental health tended to collapse diverse groups of patients into a small number of groups. Even with adjustments for extreme lengths of stay, for example, the size of the standard deviation of lengths of stay for some DRGs would almost equal the mean (Nightingale, 1982).

With the DRG and use of other resource allocation models that followed, the VA started seeing shifts of funding among medical centers and drops in lengths of stay and staffing. A survey by AVACP of psychology service staffing levels between October 1984 and March 1987 showed a

---

[10] The reader may be interested in reviewing the January 1986 issue of *American Psychologist*, which contained several other articles on the problems and issues with using diagnostic-related groups as a basis for medical cost reimbursement.

drop of 8% (Bloom, 1987). Noted was the fact that medical centers that generally fared well in the resource allocation budget process were showing fewer losses and even some gains in psychology staffing.

Although reductions were also being made in levels of staffing for psychiatry and other disciplines, VA psychology saw for the first time a reduction in its own staffing after the growth in prior decades. Staff reductions and delays in recruitment also affected psychology leadership positions in the VA Central Office. During a planned reduction in staffing throughout the Central Office and with retirements, resignations, and delays in recruitment in 1985, there was a period from August 1985 to October 1987 with no psychologists employed in the Mental Health and Behavioral Sciences Service (Lips, 1985).[11] It was left to AVACP and psychology leadership in the field to help fill the VA Central Office leadership gap and provide leadership for the profession in attempting to understand and argue for changes in the resource allocation models as well as address other critical issues. For the resource allocation models, for example, Edmund J. Nightingale (chief of psychology at the VA in Danville, Illinois, and later at the VA in Minneapolis) chaired the AVACP Committee on Resource Allocation Methodologies and frequently led VA psychology's efforts to understand the implications of and need to alter these budget allocation models for mental health program funding and staffing. It was not until the late 1980s, however, with congressional expansion of substance abuse and PTSD treatment funding (see chap. 5, this volume), that VA psychology staffing levels approached the pre-DRG staffing levels.

VA PSYCHOLOGY PRACTICE INITIATIVES AND APA

As previously noted, the 1970s and 1980s not only saw APA take an active interest in VA psychology training advocacy, but the APA practice community began to see that VA psychology was pursuing, with some successes, issues that were generally important to the independent practice of psychology in the health care field. In a 1980 survey by AVACP president-elect Sidney Cleveland, for example, the top two practice issues given priority by 97% of respondents were placing the chief of psychology as a voting member on the hospital CEB and naming doctoral-level, licensed

---

[11]During this 2-year period, Paul Errera, the psychiatrist director of the Mental Health and Behavioral Sciences Service, appointed a field psychology advisory committee to advise him on psychology issues. During other subsequent leadership absences in the VA Central Office, Washington-area chiefs of psychology were appointed as acting deputies for psychology and mental health. These included Robert C. Gresen (chief of psychology at the VA in Washington, DC) from 1991 to 1992 and 1999 to 2000 and Christine LaGana (chief of psychology at the VA in Baltimore) from 1994 to 1998.

psychologists as members of the medical staff in the medical center's bylaws (R. R. Baker, 1980). Other issues in the priority list were allowing staff psychologists to write "doctor's orders" of a nonmedical nature and giving doctoral-level, licensed staff psychologists the authority to admit and discharge patients. With VA psychology advocacy in the field and in the Central Office, the percentage of psychology chiefs serving as voting members of the CEB between 1979 and 1981 grew from 54% to 69% (Cleveland, 1981). The same time period saw a tenfold increase in the percentage of VA hospitals in which psychologists were named to the medical staff (3% in 1979 and 30% in 1981).

The APA practice community was interested in these issues for psychologists in other settings and believed its support for these VA psychology issues would set a precedent in federal organizations that could be used to build on advocacy for these issues in other health care arenas (Peck, 1978). VA psychology was clearly interested in this support, especially in APA's congressional advocacy network.

As the practice community began to mature and assume prominence in APA, a contentious issue arose between the APA practice community and VA psychology. The practice leaders in APA in the 1980s tended to define and promote practice issues in terms of the independent, private practice of psychologists. Institutional practice in the public sector was not included in this definition of practice. While president of Division 18 and later as that division's representative on the APA Council of Representatives, Rodney R. Baker was involved in many discussions with APA practice leaders about whether VA and other public sector psychologists were really practitioners and whether issues concerning VA psychologists should be included in the practice agenda of APA. There was an assumption among APA practice leaders that as APA promoted clinical privileges and medical staff membership in the independent practice sector this would benefit public sector psychologists, an assumption not held by those practicing in the public sector.

The disagreement regarding whether institutional practice should be specifically included in the APA practice agenda became even more pronounced with the reorganization of APA into directorates in the late 1980s. With the substantial support of independent practice practitioners, the Practice Directorate was able to institute a special assessment fee to be levied against all licensed psychologists in APA. The fee was to be used to support practice advocacy projects. Because VA psychologists were required to be licensed by then, all VA psychologists and many other public sector psychologists in Division 18 were assessed the fee and were hopeful the fee would be partially used to advance public sector psychology issues.

Even though Division 18 agreed to be patient as the special assessment fees were initially used to support agreed-on critical practice projects for independent practice practitioners in state psychological associations, patience grew thin. The use of the special assessment fee also started creating unhappiness among other divisions in APA, including those licensed psychologists in nonpractice divisions and in academia. Rodney R. Baker introduced a resolution in the APA Council of Representatives, with 30 other council members signing on as cosponsors, that would levy the special assessment fee against all APA members, who could then choose which of the four directorates would receive the fee to support their advocacy efforts. The resolution clearly represented a threat to the income for practice advocacy projects with the concern that VA psychologists and other dissatisfied licensed psychologists would designate their special assessment fee to be given to one of the other directorates. Although this resolution was withdrawn by Baker 3 years later, it served to focus more attention on the use of the special assessment fee for a more broadly defined practice agenda. Division 18 was subsequently included on the Executive Roundtable of Practice Divisions and Baker was appointed to the platform committee of the Association of Practicing Psychologists.

In spite of this disagreement over whether VA psychologists were practitioners or not, APA and VA psychology continued to develop significant joint practice advocacy efforts, albeit with some difficulties. Best illustrating the rocky history in this joint advocacy was the inclusion of VA psychologists in Title 38, an advocacy effort spanning 25 years.

As noted earlier, recruitment delays and pay status concerns of VA psychologists in Title 5 had been an issue since the beginning of the VA psychology program. In 1978, a Senate bill was introduced that would have placed VA psychology under Title 38. Only indirectly and by accident, however, did the existence of this bill come to light for VA psychology. As reported by Oakley Ray (1978), the Senate bill placing VA psychologists into Title 38 was initiated by professional psychology interest groups in APA, not by VA psychology. The move was seen by APA, presumably as noted previously, as a step to improve the professional status of psychologists in federal government, especially the provisions of Title 38 to set pay on the basis of professional credentials, on which other advocacy steps for psychologists in the health care delivery field could be based.

Following notice of the bill's existence, a telephone survey by VA Central Office psychologists found that psychologists in the field were overwhelmingly opposed to conversion. Although the move was popular with some chiefs of psychology, staff psychologists were opposed to the move because of their concerns that they would not be able to continue their part-time independent practice activities, which were generally prohibited for full-time Title 38 employees. Because about two thirds of VA staff psychologists at the time had a part-time independent practice outside of their VA employment, the opposition was substantial. Concerns over job security under Title 38 also surfaced. The Senate bill was shelved when it appeared that many VA psychologists would want to testify against it.

In 1980, interest in Title 38 resurfaced. This time a number of forces threatening the pay and promotion of psychology in the VA led to more support for the move. The proposed 1978 Civil Service Reform Act was gaining momentum. This legislation not only proposed the establishment of the Office of Personnel Management, under which VA psychologists and other federal employees would be placed, but also included provisions for what was called *merit pay promotion*, which required that promotion be based on merit, a provision that many staff psychologists believed would be used to limit the promotion of psychologists. Notably, this provision would not be applied to health care providers in Title 38.

VA psychology leadership in the field and in the VA Central Office was also becoming concerned about the retention of senior and experienced staff psychologists. Pay for the newly trained or entry-level staff psychologist in the VA was highly competitive. Pay for senior or experienced staff was not as competitive, however, and there was a concern that the VA might be losing its experienced senior psychologists to jobs outside of the VA, especially those psychologists with the ABPP. In addition, a move by the VA to reduce managerial positions, which again excluded Title 38 positions, also raised concerns over the impact of this proposal on psychology. Finally, other health care disciplines in the VA were starting to express interest in Title 38 in dealing with the recruitment delays and competition for health care providers experienced by psychology.

In a review of the Title 38 issue, AVACP president Sidney Cleveland (1980c) noted that a real concern existed that all health care providers (social workers, pharmacists, licensed vocational nurses, etc.) might be placed under Title 38 and that psychology's opposition to a move to Title 38 might place psychology in the position of not being classified as a health care provider profession. AVACP and APA again began exploring congressional support for legislation that would place psychologists in Title 38 and together helped develop a Senate bill in 1980 that called for, among other things, a study by the VA to determine which categories of DM&S health care personnel should be converted from Title 5 to Title 38 to improve patient care, alleviate recruitment and retention problems, and improve employee morale.

Cleveland's review of the Senate bill cited a report from the Committee on Veterans Affairs in the U.S. Senate, chaired by Senator Alan Cranston, regarding the Title 38 study as it pertained to VA psychology. That report acknowledged that there was significant disagreement among VA psychologists on the move to Title 38 and asked the VA to address in the study whether it was necessary or desirable to bar outside professional activities for remuneration if psychologists were placed under Title 38 and whether current VA psychologists might appropriately be given the option of remaining under Title 5 rather than converting to Title 38. The language of this report clearly dealt with the overriding emotional issues of conversion to Title 38 for staff psychologists—permission to earn outside professional income and an option to remain in Title 5 for perceived job security concerns. The official VA Central Office study, however, did not support VA psychology's claim of a retention problem with senior staff psychologists, and the VA continued to oppose the move of psychologists (and other health care disciplines) to Title 38.

Strong opposition to the Title 38 move during this time continued to exist among many VA staff psychologists, again focused on concerns over independent practice restrictions and job security. The resistance to the Title 38 move was one of the issues that led to the formation of Nova Psi in 1982, an organization composed primarily of VA staff psychologists. Nova Psi and the AVACP had divergent positions and interests with respect to the Title 38 issue, and, as both claimed to represent the interests of VA psychologists (as did the VA Section of Division 18), APA was unwilling to push forward on Title 38 legislative efforts until the groups reached agreement on the issue.

Meanwhile, other professional groups in the VA increased their efforts to become involved in the Title 38 employment issue. In 1983, the Veterans Health Care Amendments (Public Law 98-160) gave the VA authority to establish qualifications and special pay for appointment of licensed physical therapists, respiratory therapists, and board-certified clinical and counseling psychologists under what was called hybrid Title 38. This hybrid authority used the Title 38 system to recruit and appoint professional employees and establish salary rates but retained Title 5 coverage for other personnel matters including job security. In 1985, the VA made the decision to exercise the option given in Public Law 98-160 to include physical therapists and respiratory therapists in the new hybrid Title 38 employment system but, again, failed to include psychologists under the VA's official position that there were no recruitment or retention problems involving psychologists.

Between 1985 and 1989, a number of other professional groups in the VA were placed under the new hybrid Title 38 employment system, including pharmacists. Support for hybrid Title 38 was increasing among VA psychologists, in part because of changes in Title 38 that now allowed outside independent practice and other professional employment activities, and AVACP continued to seek congressional support for the move of psychologists to this hybrid employment system.

As late as 1993, however, the APA Practice Directorate was urging VA psychologists to reject the hybrid Title 38 system because of their belief that the hybrid system would not adequately address bonus pay and professional treatment issues. In his article updating the field on hybrid

Title 38 issues, which included the memorandum outlining the Practice Directorate's recommendation that hybrid Title 38 status not be sought, Gresen (1993) reported that AVACP would not be accepting this recommendation and would continue to seek support for inclusion of psychologists in hybrid Title 38.

The VA itself had started seeing the hybrid Title 38 system as effective in helping keep the VA competitive in recruitment of its needed professional staff and began supporting legislative agendas to place more professional groups into hybrid Title 38, including psychologists. In 2003, with support by both AVACP and APA, legislation was finally passed that converted psychology and a number of other health care occupational groups to the hybrid Title 38 personnel system (Veterans Health Care, Capital Asset, and Business Improvement Act of 2003; Public Law 108-170). This legislation opened the way for VA psychologists to be recruited and paid for their individual credentials, accomplishments, and responsibilities.[12]

CONCLUSION AND SUMMARY COMMENTS

The emergence of psychology as a health care profession in the VA and non-VA settings was due as much to advocacy in defining and defending the practice of psychology as to the profession's many advancements and contributions through research and treatment services. Credentialing and employment standards as well as hospital privileges added to the status of psychology as a health care profession.

In the VA, the scope of activities in support of the profession can be appreciated in an article by Charles Stenger on the role of the associate director of psychology in the VA Central Office (Stenger, 1979). The article, published in the AVACP newsletter, was published at the request of AVACP pending the retirement of Stenger to let potential applicants for the position know what the position entailed. Stenger listed 52 activities in which he was involved in seven broad areas ranging from personnel matters and field visits to psychology services, attendance at professional meetings, training and research, general duties and functions, and specific projects. The latter category included projects addressing the needs of Vietnam veterans and former prisoners of war, serving on the President's Commission on Mental Health, representing psychology in Congress and APA groups, and proposing new legislation and interagency agreements. The previously noted categories included contacts with OPM and VA personnel on employment standards, rating and ranking psychology applicants for employment, and interactions

---

[12] It can be noted that with less opposition among VA staff psychologists to hybrid Title 38 and other organizational issues, Nova Psi had been disbanded in 1998.

with other medical disciplines in the VA Central Office to promote the use of mental health concepts in treatment. Although Stenger noted that others in the Mental Health and Behavioral Sciences Service, both psychologists and psychiatrists, played very active and supportive roles in the list of activities that led to the satisfaction he had with his job, it was noted by some that his list was overwhelming for a number of potential applicants.

The practice advocacy activities described in this chapter clearly resulted in a sound professional role for psychology in the VA. These initiatives and the joint advocacy by VA psychology and APA helped determine a model for practice in the profession based on a recognition of the value of psychology as a health care profession.

7

PAST TO PRESENT: CONTRIBUTIONS OF VA PSYCHOLOGY TO HEALTH CARE AND THE PROFESSION

Although this book primarily focuses on the mid-1940s through the 1980s, this history reflects issues and activities in defining psychology as a health care profession that still exist for both VA psychology and the profession at large. Before offering a summary and perspective of this history, we present a brief summary of the VA and the VA psychology program as it existed in 2005, including events over the past 15 years that have shaped the current status of psychology.

RECENT HISTORY OF THE VA AND VA PSYCHOLOGY

The VA was designated a Cabinet-level department in 1989, reflecting its important role in assisting veterans. The agency was renamed the Department of Veterans Affairs that year but is still referred to as the VA.

The VA has continued its leadership role in many aspects of health care. For example, the VA developed a computerized medical record system that is the envy of many health care organizations. The computerization of medical records provided an accessible patient database for practitioners, but the advantages of the database go beyond simple access. Basic patient data, along with progress notes, laboratory findings, medication history, and health care screenings are quickly available to health care providers. This has allowed the VA to develop a sophisticated monitoring system called the Decision Support System (DSS). DSS provides a summary of the database in such areas as clinical indicators, clinical performance, and clinical pathways. DSS has allowed the VA to document an impressive improvement in the care of veterans over the years, with the VA leading other health care organizations in many aspects of care, especially in using health care screenings and practice guidelines to improve primary care.

In the throes of health care reform during the Clinton administration, the VA developed its own health care reform office in 1993. Although federal reforms never materialized, the goals of the VA's health care reform program continued—to modernize the VA and ensure participation in state health care reform activities. Reform goals also included a blueprint for decentralizing program operations in what later became known as Veterans Integrated Service Networks (Taylor, 1994). The reforms put in place over the next decade had a far-reaching impact on VA program operations. In the service of reform, for example, the VA developed its own managed care program with an emphasis on outpatient primary care and a reduced focus on inpatient care.

The VA had always functioned under a *managed care* framework, with a specific health care benefit for a veteran population defined in legislation and a budget for health care based on projected usage for the next year. The VA's newest managed care programs under reform, however, were driven by best practices and accountability for performance built into the contracts and performance plans of key VA medical center administrators, executives, and service chiefs. These reforms resulted in changes to VA operations with many parallels to concerns that managed care presented to the American Psychological Association (APA) and other professional groups around the country.

With the emphasis on outpatient primary care in the 1990s, for example, the VA eliminated many of its inpatient general medicine, surgery, and psychiatric and substance abuse disorder beds. These bed closures contributed to a reduction in professional staffing in all areas of medical care, including psychology and the other mental health disciplines.[1] The number of full-time, nonresearch doctoral psychologists employed in the VA had peaked at 1,582 on September 30, 1994; 3 years later that number had dropped to 1,437, a 9% loss (R. R. Baker, Cannon, Jansen, & LaGana, 1998). For the same period, a similar loss of 8% occurred in full-time psychiatry positions

---

[1] The unsuccessful proposal to cut psychology staffing and contract out psychological services also emerged in this time period (see chap. 6, this volume).

(1,517 to 1,402), with a 16% loss in part-time psychiatry positions (680 to 574). The part-time clinical positions in psychology remained fairly stable over that period (170 to 166). According to R. R. Baker et al. (1998), these cuts in psychology and psychiatry staffing levels were similar to an overall 8% reduction of employment in the VA's health care programs for the same period.

With legislation that gave more veterans access to primary care and other services, the number of veterans receiving care in the VA substantially increased. Between 1990 and 2004, the number of veterans receiving mental health services increased by 71% (Department of Veterans Affairs, 2005). Together with tight budgets and the aforementioned loss in staffing, psychologists in the VA were faced with a demand for services and insufficient resources not experienced since the early years after World War II. The focus on health care screenings and clinical performance indicators that helped the VA strengthen its health care reputation among other health care organizations added still additional demands on the professional time of psychologists and other clinicians.

Practice patterns were substantially altered. With fewer beds and reduced lengths of stay, inpatient psychiatry treatment was frequently focused on medical stabilization of the patient and early discharge to outpatient care. The prevalent individual and group psychotherapy services of psychologists in the past simply did not fit into an average length of stay of 10 days on an acute psychiatry unit.

The earlier discharge of veterans to outpatient care combined with the general increase of veterans seeking outpatient care forced psychologists to decrease the frequency of outpatient treatment visits. Instead of weekly or every other week, the scheduling of outpatient therapy visits dropped to monthly or even every other month visits. In many cases, the traditional 50-minute therapy hour was reduced to 30 minutes.

The new performance standards stressed by the VA added to the pressures. For example, medical centers were evaluated on whether or not mental health patients discharged from inpatient care received their first outpatient mental health visit within 30 days. Although a high quality-of-care standard was intended, scheduling new patients within 30 days after discharge contributed to the less frequent scheduling or shortening of treatment visits for other patients already enrolled in treatment.

It should not go unnoticed that the pressures on psychiatrists were similar to those on psychologists. The 15-minute medication management visit for psychiatrists started becoming the norm for many of their patients, with less time being spent on more traditional psychotherapy services. Even within the highly charged political debate between psychology and psychiatry over prescriptive authority for psychologists, Rodney R. Baker had a number of conversations with VA psychiatrists who half jokingly and half seriously expressed the wish that psychologists had prescriptive authority to help them with their medication management workload. The reluctance of some VA psychologists to seek prescriptive authority was similarly based on the concern that they, too, would be faced with altering their practice for this medication management workload with less time for therapy.

Product and Service Line Management

At the same time that VA psychology was struggling with increased workload and inadequate staffing, the VA began experimenting with what were called alternative management structures as part of the VA's reform plan to reduce management redundancy and increase efficiency. This experimentation with organizational models led to significant changes that affected the autonomy of psychology in the field. A popular management model used in this experiment, for example, was the product or service line organization in which fiscal and program management activities were consolidated across several professional services. Typical service lines included ambulatory care, extended care and geriatrics, and mental health care.

The mental health service line, which had emerged in many hospitals by the mid-1990s, involved a grouping of psychiatry and psychology into a single management unit, and, in some cases, included social work, psychiatric nursing, and other staff, such as recreation therapists. The original professional discipline services and their service chief positions were often abolished with the establishment of the service line. A mental health service line director position was established to manage the new organizational unit. In the majority of these new mental health organizational units, the service line director position was filled by the former chief of psychiatry with the former chief of psychology appointed as deputy director, given some other leadership role, or simply assigned to a nonsupervisory clinical position. With the emergence of these new organizational units, the number of independent psychology services and chief of psychology positions showed a dramatic drop. From the early 1990s to 2001, the number of VA chief of psychology positions was reduced from 150 to 30. Although psychology was eventually successful in promoting a directive stipulating that medical centers should recruit from all mental health disciplines for the top leadership role in mental health service lines, this directive was difficult to monitor and enforce. In 2001, approximately 60% of the mental health service line director positions were filled by psychiatrists. Psychologists occupied this leadership position in about 30% of cases with the remainder filled by social workers, nurses, or other discipline leaders.

Not unexpectedly, these new organizations were extremely unpopular with VA psychology. Although APA again used its congressional advocacy network to help argue against merging psychiatry and psychology, these efforts were not successful. The loss of many psychology chief positions and the difficulty in maintaining psychology oversight for internship training, research, and professional staff development had a definite negative effect on morale among psychologists in the field.

With the reduction in chief of psychology positions in the VA, AVACP changed its name to the Association of VA Psychologist Leaders (AVAPL) in 1997 and expanded its membership to all VA psychologists in management, supervisory, or other leadership positions. The reorganized association also began looking at new ways to promote the role and value of psychology in the VA's evolving health care system.

AVAPL/APA Psychology Leadership Conference

The loss of many psychology chief positions in the VA also resulted in the loss of the chief of psychology information and support network that had served VA psychology so well in the past. To compensate for this loss, the idea of a national VA psychology leadership conference emerged in discussions among psychology leaders, with Russell Lemle, chief of psychology at the VA in San Francisco, serving as the prime mover. Under Lemle's planning leadership, the idea took shape and AVAPL approached Russ Newman and Randy Phelps in the APA Practice Directorate for their guidance and support. These discussions resulted in the scheduling of a leadership conference in Dallas in 1998 that was jointly funded by AVAPL and APA's Practice Directorate.

The first leadership conference brought together close to 100 psychology leaders from more than 50 VA medical centers and was a somber event as workload, budget, and reorganization problems in the field were discussed in formal and informal sessions. APA leaders speaking to conference participants included immediate past president Norman Abeles, Russ Newman (Executive Director for Professional Practice), and Paul Nelson (Deputy Executive Director for Education). Their presentations emphasized the important partnership of APA and VA psychology, offered strategies and support for coping with the changes in VA health care, and underscored the strong investment that APA had made in the conference.

An important conference planning decision was to ask participants to develop planning interest groups around some of the critical problems facing psychology in the VA. Work begun during and after the conference on such issues as promotion and advancement concerns, developing leadership credentials, and promoting psychologists' role as value-added providers began to reverse some of the feelings of loss and impotence among participants. The success of that conference led to the program becoming an annual event that continues to the present, serving an important function in energizing psychology in the field.

Subsequent conferences grew in importance as conference planners became successful in inviting both APA and VA leaders to speak to participants. In every conference to date, current or past presidents of APA have participated and offered their support for advocacy agendas. The focus broadened, as well, with each succeeding conference following a patient care theme ranging from innovative clinical programming to incorporation of outcome research and program evaluation into ongoing care.

With the focus on care for veterans, the conference was able to attract top VA leaders as speakers, including either the secretary of the VA or the undersecretary for health. The conferences have provided an important interchange of ideas among APA and VA leaders. They have improved morale issues in the field, helped build a new advocacy and support network, and helped psychology become proactive rather than reactive in a changing environment. The conferences clearly helped psychology remain a viable health care profession in the VA. Over the past several years, with medical center disillusionment with the product and service line management organization, a small number of new independent psychology services and new chief of psychology positions began emerging in the VA. In addition, an ambitious strategic mental health plan was funded in fiscal year 2005 that was expected to increase the number of psychologists in mental health programs as well as improve funding for mental health programs.

Growth of Mental Health Programs and Psychology

In spite of the organizational turmoil and budget concerns of the 1990s, the VA continued to expand attention to mental health concerns and treatment programs for veterans that included important roles for psychologists. The 1990s saw the VA creating its first Mental Illness Research, Education, and Clinical Centers (MIRECCs). MIRECCs were established to provide centers of excellence for mental health research, training, and clinical care and were modeled after similar centers of excellence in geriatrics and extended care that the VA had established earlier. The first three MIRECCs were funded in October 1997. Three additional MIRECCs were funded in October 1998, two more were funded in October 1999, and two more were added in October 2004, bringing the total to 10.

Each of the MIRECCs focused on a specific mental health topic, including dual diagnosis of drug and alcohol dependence, effective treatment of those with severe mental illness, comorbidity of psychiatric diagnoses, quality and cost-effectiveness of services for veterans with schizophrenia, long-term functional outcome treatment of chronic mental disorders, and suicide prevention. All centers were expected to disseminate information produced by their research, education, and clinical activities throughout the VA. Annual reports of the MIRECC activities describe research and clinical topics covering virtually all aspects of mental health care of importance in the VA in the 1990s.[2]

In addition to the recruitment of psychologists for administrative, clinical, and research roles, the MIRECCs' education mission also included new funding for postdoctoral training positions. Sixteen postdoctoral positions were funded in the first eight MIRECCs. The two new MIRECCs created in 2004 added four additional postdoctoral training positions to the 2005 training year (L. Johnson, personal communication, July 11, 2005).

The expansion of mental health programs in the 1990s was frequently supported by specific congressional funding mandates. For example, with emerging data showing that one fifth to one half of the nation's homeless were veterans in different parts of the country, many needing mental health care, the VA had started addressing the health care needs of the homeless veteran toward the end of the 1980s. The 1990s saw significant funding increases from Congress for homeless treatment programs and services.

A new focus on psychosocial rehabilitation also emerged during this time. Work therapy programs, which had lost favor by the late 1970s, again started receiving attention. The VA's Compensated Work Therapy programs, now renamed Veterans Industry, received a special boost from legislation that permitted Veterans Industry to contract with and provide patient-based work services to federal agencies, including the VA itself (Sheldon, 1993). Many VA medical centers chose to use this program to obtain services for their facility operations that, in some cases, could not otherwise be provided because of staff funding shortfalls. The benefits to the medical center were matched by the vocational rehabilitation work opportunities for patients in the program, most of whom were mental health patients.

Also reaching prominence by the mid-1990s were the VA's psychosocial rehabilitation residential care programs. By providing stable housing as part of the overall rehabilitation treatment goals, these residential care programs partially offset losses in mental health care beds. Under this program, the target treatment population could be chosen to meet the needs of the medical center's mental health patients. Special rehabilitation residential care programs emerged for the homeless and for substance abuse and PTSD patients in addition to programs for the general psychiatry patient population. By the end of fiscal year 2002, there were 97 of these programs around the country with 1,858 residential care beds. In fiscal year 2002, these programs treated over 11,000 patients (Department of Veterans Affairs, 2003a).

---

[2] The VA report to Congress on Mental Illness, Research, Education, and Clinical Centers activities for 2001 is on file in the VA psychology archive collection at the Archives of the History of American Psychology at The University of Akron.

TABLE 7.1
Number of Veterans Provided Care by the VA in Special Treatment
Groups in Fiscal Year 2004

Group	Number treated
Homeless	40,491
PTSD	56,228
Psychotic disorders	284,493
Seriously mentally ill	314,208
Substance abuse	86,785

Note. For purposes of classification, psychotic disorders include the affective disorders (bipolar and other psychotic disorders), and patients with severe mental illness include those with diagnoses of schizophrenia and dementia.

The number of women veterans seeking care in the VA had been steadily increasing along with the increased role of women in the military. In fiscal year 2004, 60,000 female veterans received mental health services in the VA (Department of Veterans Affairs, 2005). The 1990s saw funding increases helping to establish general health care clinics for women veterans. Special clinics with psychologists and other mental health professionals were also established in VA medical centers and Vet Centers for female veterans who had experienced sexual trauma while in the military.

The VA was also taking advantage of the advances in telecommunication technology. By the end of the 1990s, many medical centers had established telehealth communication systems and psychologists began using this technology to provide assessment and other mental health care services to veterans in rural areas distant from a mental health care clinic.

Finally noted is the important assessment and treatment role of psychologists in traumatic brain injury centers, a role that gained prominence in the 1990s. As highlighted in the introduction to this book, these established roles led to a natural and important inclusion of psychologists in the new regional polytrauma centers established in 2005 to care for the severely wounded veteran with multiple and complex injuries.

During the fiscal year ending September 30, 2004, the VA had provided mental health services to over 847,000 veterans representing over 17% of the total 4.9 million veterans treated in the VA that year (Department of Veterans Affairs, 2005). Expenditures for mental health care were almost $2.2 billion. Table 7.1 displays the number of veterans treated in fiscal year 2004, categorized into several special treatment groups.

As of June 2005, the VA employed over 2,000 individuals in full-time ($n = 1,960$) and part-time ($n = 174$) psychology positions in patient care, research, and clinical training. According to Robert Gresen, again serving as acting deputy of mental health in the VA Central Office, this included over 1,500 full- and part-time clinical and counseling psychologists in nonresearch positions and over 400 in the VA psychology training program (Robert Gresen, personal communication, July 11, 2005).

The 2005 Mental Health Strategic Plan

In 2005, the VA began an ambitious effort to look at ways it could better respond to the challenges of meeting the VA's health care mission. As part of that effort, a planning group was established to look at the organization of mental health services in the VA Central Office. That group was also given the task of developing a long-range strategic plan for mental health services in the VA.

The work of the mental health planning group was, in part, based on an appreciation that the funding of mental health services in the VA had lagged far behind the need for those services by veterans. In addition to proposed changes that gave psychology a greater role in program management in the Central Office, the planning group proposed substantial increases in the VA's funding for mental health programs.

In early 2005, the action elements of the strategic mental health plan were approved by the secretary of the Department of Veterans Affairs. As noted by Antonette Zeiss, a psychologist member of the mental health strategic planning committee, special funding was subsequently approved to implement the plan (A. Zeiss, personal communication, September 4, 2005). The funding provided an increase of $100 million for mental health programs in fiscal year 2005 with that funding to be carried over for the next 2 years. An additional $100 million was approved for fiscal year 2006, also to be carried over for the subsequent fiscal year. The approved plan with its special funding was expected to result in increases in staff psychologist and other mental health profession positions to support programs in such areas as substance abuse and PTSD treatment and care of the patient with severe mental illness. These programs would continue the emphasis on psychosocial rehabilitation with a recovery orientation. Zeiss also noted that Veterans of the Gulf wars and the war in Afghanistan would also benefit from this new program funding.[3]

The 2005 mental health strategic plan took an important step forward in closing the gap between resources and the mental health treatment needs of veterans. It will be left to future historians to evaluate the impact of the plan and the wisdom of mental health leaders in the VA in its implementation.

---

[3] It can parenthetically be noted that in August 2005, Antonette Zeiss was appointed deputy chief consultant in the VA Office of Mental Health Services, still another title change in this position, in filling the vacancy left by the reassignment of Mary Jansen.

SUMMARY AND PERSPECTIVE ON THE FUTURE

The VA after World War II, like the institutes of the National Institutes of Health, benefited from the concern for the health of the nation that was emphasized by the administration of Franklin Delano Roosevelt. Roosevelt's New Deal emphasized that the government should and would act to positively impact the health of its citizenry. The reform and expansion of the VA after the war incorporated this ethos. Clinical psychology, then primarily concerned with assessment, rapidly expanded its roles to treatment and research and, today, joins psychiatry, social work, and psychiatric nursing as a fundamental health care profession in the VA. During the period described in this volume, psychologists from other subdisciplines also played important parts, including, but not limited to, social, counseling, rehabilitation, and experimental psychology.

The year 2006 marked the 60th anniversary of VA psychology and its clinical psychology training program. As this volume indicates, psychologists in the VA have functioned in a wide variety of capacities, many more than space here allows. An enduring legacy of the VA for psychology is its role in training, accreditation, and establishment of credentials for psychology as a mental health profession. However, as this volume documents, the contributions of VA psychology to innovative mental health treatment programming and to diverse and important research is also a part of the legacy.

The story of the commitment of the VA and the federal government to assisting the nation's veterans offers a number of observations. In addition to the continued support of the psychology training program by the federal government and the VA, the VA and its treatment programs, especially over the last 2 decades, have provided an important health care safety net in American society to millions of uninsured and underinsured citizens. Since World War II, psychologists in the VA have provided mental health care services to patients in medical care programs for tuberculosis and those with spinal cord injuries, programs caring for the aging veteran, and programs for patients with numerous other medical conditions in addition to the psychologist's role in more traditional mental health programs. The impact on society of educational benefits to millions of veterans by the VA after World War II has only been briefly mentioned but adds still another facet to the influence of the VA and the federal government on our society.

A final note must include the reciprocal and interactional roles of VA psychology with the rest of the profession, especially with APA and the VA's training universities, in developing psychological practice, training, and research. Without the involvement and support of the many graduate departments of psychology in training and research affiliations, especially in the early years, it is doubtful whether VA psychology could have had the growth and impact referenced in this volume. The interest and support of APA and its leaders have also been of significant importance in helping VA psychology build and maintain a health care, training, and research presence in the profession. Psychologists in the VA have modeled innovative treatment programming and have helped non-VA psychologists understand how different models of patient care can work to benefit patients.

Accurately predicting the future is difficult, if not impossible. However, if past is indeed prologue, then it is likely that psychologists in the VA will continue to be of importance both within the VA and in psychology generally. To do so, psychologists in the VA must evolve to meet the changing political, professional, and health care landscape. The evolving landscape includes the lack of adequate funding for health care and insurance for both veterans and nonveterans. It includes the future of guild issues such as prescriptive authority. And it includes the question of whether our nation will continue a well-deserved commitment to care for those who have borne the battle. It is our hope that this historical account will be of service to this evolution.

APPENDIX:

Timeline of VA and Psychology Historical Events and Key VA Psychology Leadership Appointments: 1930 Through 1999

1930   Congress authorized President Herbert Hoover to establish the VA to "consolidate and coordinate government activities affecting war veterans."

1940   The VA's annual report to Congress described construction under way for 6,500 additional beds under a grant from the Public Works Administration with plans for an additional 14,000 beds. Of patients hospitalized on June 30, 1940, 58% were being treated for psychiatric disorders with an average length of stay of 519 days.

1944   Passage of the Servicemen's Readjustment Act (Public Law 78-346), commonly known as the GI Bill of Rights, authorized occupational, educational, and health assistance for veterans.

1945   The VA opened its first mental hygiene clinic for outpatient mental health services at the regional office in Los Angeles.

1945   General Omar Bradley, administrator of the VA, appointed George A. Kelly as the first VA psychology consultant to help design the new VA psychology program.

1946   To Establish a Department of Medicine and Surgery in the Veterans Administration (Public Law 79-293) gave the department responsibility for providing medical care to veterans and officially created an organization of professional departments or services within the VA. Clinical psychology became a section in the new Neuropsychiatry Service in the VA Central Office along with the psychiatry and neurology sections.

1946   VA Policy Memorandum Number 2 established affiliations with medical schools to help train physicians and other medical personnel needed to work in VA hospitals. Affiliations with 63 of the nation's 77 medical schools were developed.

1946   James Grier Miller was appointed the first chief clinical psychologist for the Psychology Section in the Neuropsychiatry Division of the VA Central Office.

1946 Urie Bronfenbrenner was appointed associate chief clinical psychologist for research and administration in the VA Psychology Section, and Iris Stevenson was appointed assistant chief psychologist for training and personnel.

1946 Maurice Lorr succeeded Urie Bronfenbrenner as the assistant chief clinical psychologist for research in the Psychology Section in the VA Central Office and Jane D. Morgan succeeded Iris Stevenson as assistant chief psychologist for training and personnel.

1946 The VA adopted the doctoral degree as the minimum qualification standard for employment of clinical psychologists.

1946 The first appointments were made of students with part-time employment status for VA training in clinical psychology (over 200 positions from 22 universities).

1946 The American Psychological Association's (APA's) Division 18 (Psychologists in Public Service) was established as one of the 19 charter divisions in APA and became a division of interest for VA psychologists.

1947 The first register of civil service positions was published for the recruitment of clinical psychologists in the VA.

1948 Harold M. Hildreth was appointed chief clinical psychologist in the Psychology Section of the VA Central Office to succeed James Miller.

1949 James Quinter Holsopple and Harold M. Houtchens were appointed assistant chief clinical psychologists in the Psychology Section in the VA Central Office.

1952 Vocational counseling became an independent service and program in the VA. Robert S. Waldrop was appointed director of vocational counseling in the VA Central Office.

1952 The VA adopted the doctoral degree as the minimum qualification standard for employment of counseling psychologists.

1953 The first appointment of students for VA training in counseling psychology was established (55 positions).

1953 Maurice Lorr was asked to head the new outpatient psychiatry research laboratory in the VA Central Office.

1953 The Department of Veterans Benefits was established within the VA to coordinate education, training, and disability benefits for veterans.

1954 The Neuropsychiatry Division in the VA Central Office was renamed the Psychiatry and Neurology Service, with clinical psychology a section in that service.

1955 The Psychiatric Evaluation Program was established to study effective treatment of patients with psychiatric disorders. Psychiatrist Richard Jenkins served as its first project director; it was later headed by psychologist Lee Gurel. In one of the first large-scale research projects in the VA, 13 VA hospitals collaborated in the study, using the VA's cooperative research model.

1956 Max Houtchens was appointed chief clinical psychologist in the VA Central Office to succeed Harold Hildreth.

1956 Cecil Peck was brought into the VA Central Office as chief consulting psychologist.

1956 The VA's deputy chief medical director presented a report at the APA convention noting that one third of all research in the VA was being carried out by psychologists and that the VA employed 20% (628) of all psychologists in the country who met VA qualification standards (doctoral degree and internship).

1956 The Cooperative Studies of Chemotherapy in Psychiatry program was established in 1956 and activated in 1958 to study the new phenothiazines being used in psychiatric treatment. The administration of this research program was assigned to the Central Neuropsychiatric Research Laboratory at the VA hospital in Perry Point, Maryland, which was briefly headed by James Quinter Holsopple and then Ned N. Springer, followed by Julian "Jack" Lasky and James Klett.

1956 The cooperative study of psychological factors in tuberculosis was established. The central planning committee included George Calden, Claire Vernier, Robert Barrell, Jonathan Cummings, and Joseph Dickerson.

1956 The *Newsletter for Psychologists in Tuberculosis* was started, and in 1959 it became the *Newsletter for Cooperative Research in Psychology*. This quarterly publication continued in 1961 as the *Newsletter for Research in Psychology* and in 1973 became the *Newsletter for Research in Mental Health and Behavioral Sciences*, which was discontinued in 1976.

1957 The Central Neuropsychiatric Research Laboratory started publication of the *Newsletter for Cooperative Studies in Psychiatry*.

1957 The staff and training programs for clinical and counseling psychology were combined into one service in the VA Central Office.

1958 Legislation amended Title 38 of the U.S. Code to add medical research to the mission of the Department of Medicine and Surgery in the VA (To Consolidate Into One Act; Public Law 85-857).

1960 The VA published the *Manual of Group Therapy*, authored by Abrahams Luchins, Lewis Aumack, and Harold Dickman at the VA in Roseburg, Oregon; it was one of the first publications with practical suggestions for conducting group therapy.

1962 Cecil Peck succeeded Max Houtchens as chief clinical psychologist in the Clinical Psychology Division in the VA Central Office.

1962 Frederick Elton Ash was appointed chief consulting psychologist in the VA Central Office and later became the first chief for psychology education and training in 1966.

1963 Richard N. Filer was appointed chief of psychology research in the VA Central Office.

1963 The VA psychology training stipend program was established; psychology trainees were no longer part-time employees but were paid from funds specifically appropriated for training.

1964 Charles A. Stenger was brought into the Clinical Psychology Division in the VA Central Office as chief of psychology for medical and surgical hospitals.

1965 The VA sponsored a psychology conference in Chicago to highlight nontraditional treatment approaches being used by psychologists. Presentations included those of Joseph McDonough at the Palo Alto VA on token economy programs; Earl Taulbee at the Tuscaloosa VA on attitude therapy; Harold Dickman at the VA in Roseburg, Oregon, on therapeutic milieu programs; and Roy Brener at the Hines VA in Chicago on the work of psychologists in domiciliary restoration centers.

1966 The Veterans Hospitalization and Medical Service Modernization Amendments (Public Law 89-785) made education a part of the VA's mission along with patient care and research, including a mandate to train health professionals for the nation in addition to training them for its own staffing needs.

1966 John E. "Jack" Davis Jr. was appointed chief of outpatient psychology in the Clinical Psychology Division in the VA Central Office, and Harold Dickman was appointed chief of psychology for psychiatric hospitals.

1971 In a VA Central Office reorganization, the Psychiatry and Neurology Service became the Mental Health and Behavioral Sciences Service with Cecil Peck given the title of associate director for psychology. Neurology became an independent professional service.

1973 The Office of Academic Affairs was established in the VA Central Office. Elton Ash and the administration of the VA training program were transferred out of mental health into this new office.

1973 The TIGER program (Training in Individual and Group Effectiveness and Resourcefulness) was established to provide leadership and interpersonal training throughout the VA. The program was headed by Philip Hanson and a group of psychologists at the Houston VA Hospital and from the Houston community.

1973 The cemeteries operated by the Army were transferred to the VA, excepting only the Arlington National Cemetery, and the National Cemetery System was created within the VA.

1974 The psychology training program at the VA Hospital in Topeka, Kansas, received APA accreditation for predoctoral internship training, the first in the VA.

1975 Cecil Peck was promoted to deputy director of the Mental Health and Behavioral Sciences Service in the VA Central Office.

1975 Jule D. Moravec succeeded Elton Ash and took over the administration of the VA Psychology Training Program as educational specialist for psychology training in the Office of Academic Affairs.

1976 Charles A. Stenger became the associate director for psychology in the VA Central Office.

1977 The Association of VA Chief Psychologists was formed with Oakley Ray elected its first president.

1977 The VA section was established within APA's Division 18 (Psychologists in Public Service) with Ralph Fingar elected its first chair.

1977 Dana L. Moore succeeded Jule D. Moravec as educational specialist for the VA Psychology Training Program in the Office of Academic Affairs.

1979 Congress authorized the establishment of the Readjustment Counseling Service and its Vietnam Veterans Readjustment Counseling Program in the Veterans Health Care Amendments of 1979 (Public Law 96-22). The program was headed by psychologist Donald Crawford and was initially assigned to the Mental Health and Behavioral Science Service in the VA Central Office.

1979 Legislation required psychologists in the Department of Medicine and Surgery to be licensed in a state, have a doctoral degree in clinical or counseling psychology, and have an internship acceptable to the administrator of the VA (Veterans Health Programs Extension and Improvement Act of 1979; Public Law 96-151).

1980 Joseph Mancusi succeeded Charles Stenger as associate director for psychology in the VA Central Office.

1981 The Former Prisoner of War Benefits Act (Public Law 97-37) established special treatment examinations and benefits for former prisoners of war.

1981 The VA psychology training program reduced funding for practicum training and became primarily focused on internship training, which required 1,900 hours of training and provided interns with a $10,000 stipend.

1982 The National Organization of VA Psychologists was formed with Leila Foster elected its first president.

1982 On the basis of 1979 legislation, the VA published a policy that established the doctoral degree in clinical or counseling psychology from a graduate school approved by APA as the credential for employment as a psychologist providing health care in the Department of Medicine and Surgery. An APA-approved internship was also required as was state licensure or certification within 2 years of appointment.

1983 John "Jack" Davis Jr., succeeded Cecil Peck as deputy director of the Mental Health and Behavioral Sciences Service in the VA Central Office.

1983 The Association of VA Chief Psychologists piloted a leadership training program for new chiefs of psychology that became an annual event through 2003.

1985 Eighty-five VA medical centers had APA-approved internship programs.

1985 Dorothy Stringfellow was appointed educational specialist for the Psychology Training Program to replace Dana Moore.

1987 Edward Sieracki succeeded John Davis as deputy director of the Mental Health and Behavioral Sciences Service in the VA Central Office.

1988 Gloria Holland was appointed educational specialist for the Psychology Training Program, replacing Dorothy Stringfellow.

1988 Legislation to elevate the Veterans Administration to cabinet status was signed into law by President Reagan.

1989 The VA was redesignated the Department of Veterans Affairs and became the 14th department in the President's Cabinet. The Department of Medicine and Surgery, which was responsible for all medical care in the VA, was renamed the Veterans Health Services and Research Administration (shortened to Veterans Health Administration in 1991), and the Department of Veterans Benefits was renamed the Veterans Benefits Administration.

1991 The VA funded the first postdoctoral psychology fellowship training positions in substance abuse at the VAs in Dallas and Seattle for the 1991–1992 training year.

1992 Martha Rae Barnes succeeded Edward Sieracki as deputy director of the Mental Health and Behavioral Sciences Service in the VA Central Office.

1992 The VA funded the first postdoctoral psychology fellowship training positions in geropsychology at six VA medical centers for the 1992–1993 training year.

1993 Linda D. Johnson was appointed educational specialist for the Psychology Training Program to replace Gloria Holland.

1997 The Association of VA Chief Psychologists was renamed the Association of VA Psychologist Leaders with membership expanded to all VA psychologists in management, supervisory, or other leadership positions.

1997   The first three Mental Illness Research, Education, and Clinical Centers were funded by the VA.

1998   The National Organization of VA Psychologists was disbanded.

1998   Mary Jansen assumed the top leadership position in psychology in the VA Central Office, replacing Martha Rae Barnes. This position was now called deputy chief consultant of the Mental Health Strategic Health Group under a reorganization in the VA Central Office.

1998   The first annual VA Psychology Leadership Conference was held in Dallas, jointly sponsored and funded by the Association of VA Psychologist Leaders and the Practice Directorate of APA.

1999   The postdoctoral psychology training program at the VA medical center in San Antonio, Texas, became the first VA training program to receive APA postdoctoral accreditation and the third such approved program in the nation.

1999   For the 2000–2001 training year the VA requested proposals to expand the number and types of postdoctoral psychology training programs requiring APA accreditation or substantial progress toward that accreditation for continued funding.

REFERENCES

Acker, M., & McReynolds, P. (1965). The Obscure Figures Test: An instrument for measuring "cognitive innovation." *Perceptual and Motor Skills, 21*(3), 815–821.

Adler, M. H., Futterman, S., & Webb, R. (1948). Activities of the mental hygiene clinics of the Veterans Administration. *Clinical Psychopathology, 9,* 517–527.

Adler, M. H., Valenstein, A. F., & Michaels, J. J. (1949). A mental hygiene clinic. *Journal of Nervous and Mental Disease, 110,* 518–533.

Alexander, F. (1934). The influence of psychologic factors upon gastro-intestinal disturbances: A symposium: I. General principles, objectives, and preliminary results. *Psychoanalytical Quarterly, 3,* 501–539.

American Psychiatric Association. (1952). *Diagnostic and statistical manual of mental disorders.* Washington, DC: Author.

American Psychiatric Association. (1980). *Diagnostic and statistical manual of mental disorders* (3rd ed.). Washington, DC: Author.

American Psychological Association. (1949). Doctoral training programs in clinical psychology. *American Psychologist, 4,* 331–341.

American Psychological Association. (1956). Internships for doctoral training in clinical psychology approved by the American Psychological Association. *American Psychologist, 11,* 710–711.

American Psychological Association and American Association for Applied Psychology, Subcommittee on Graduate Internship Training. (1945). Graduate internship training in psychology. *Journal of Consulting Psychology, 9,* 243–266.

Ash, E. (1968a). The Veterans Administration psychology training program. *Clinical Psychologist, 21,* 67–69.

Ash, E. (1968b). Issues faced by the VA psychology training program in its early development. *Clinical Psychologist, 21,* 121–123.

Association of VA Chief Psychologists. (1983). *Handbook for new VA chief psychologists.* (Available from the Archives of the History of American Psychology, The University of Akron, Polsky Building, LL10A, 225 South Main Street, Akron, Ohio 44325-4302)

Association of VA Chief Psychologists. (1993). *Manual for VA chiefs and assistant chiefs of psychology.* (Available from the Archives of the History of American Psychology, The University of Akron, Polsky Building, LL10A, 225 South Main Street, Akron, Ohio 44325-4302)

Baker, D. B., & Benjamin, L. T., Jr. (2005). Creating a profession: The National Institute of Mental Health and the training of psychologists, 1946–1954. In W. E. Pickren & S. F. Schneider (Eds.), *Psychology and the National Institute of Mental Health: A historical analysis of science, practice, and policy* (pp. 181–207). Washington, DC: American Psychological Association.

Baker, R. R. (1980, October). Research summaries and administrative issues. *Newsletter for the Association of VA Chief Psychologists, 3,* 14–15.

Baker, R. R. (1987, January). Second generation staffing guideline data. *Newsletter for the Association of VA Chief Psychologists, 10,* 11.

Baker, R. R. (1996a). Comparing VA and community practitioner costs. *Federal Practitioner, 13,* 76–78.

Baker, R. R. (1996b). A history of Division 18 (Psychologists in Public Service). In D. A. Dewsbury (Ed.), *Unification through division* (Vol. 1, pp. 137–155). Washington, DC: American Psychological Association.

Baker, R. R., Barrett, J., & Klauck, K. (1986, August). *Productivity standards for psychology staffing in treatment institutions.* Paper presented at the annual meeting of the American Psychological Association, Washington, DC.

Baker, R. R., Cannon, D., Jansen, M., & LaGana, C. M. (1998, April). Employment of VA psychologists and other mental health staff: A status report. *Newsletter for the Association of VA Chief Psychologists, 21,* 22.

Baker, R. R., & Gurel, L. (2003, August). The VA affiliation contribution to the development of clinical psychology. In W. E. Pickren (Chair), *Growth stimulus: Federal funding of American psychology after World War II.* Symposium conducted at the annual meeting of the American Psychological Association, Toronto, Canada.

Ball, J., Klett, C. J., & Gresock, C. (1959). The Veterans Administration study of prefrontal lobotomy. *Journal of Clinical and Experimental Psychopathology, 20,* 205–217.

Barker, R. G., Wright, B. A., & Gonick, M. R. (1943). *Adjustment to physical handicap and illness.* New York: McGraw-Hill.

Barrell, R. P. (2003, September 5). *Oral history with Wade Pickren* [Transcript]. (Available from American Psychological Association, 750 First Street, NE, Washington, DC 20002)

Bell, R. L., Cleveland, S. E., Hanson, P. G., & O'Connell, W. E. (1969). Small group dialogue and discussion: An approach to police–community relationships. *Journal of Criminal Law, Criminology and Police Science, 60,* 242–246.

Benjamin, L. T., Jr., & Baker, D. B. (2004). *From séance to science: A history of the profession of psychology in America.* Belmont, CA: Wadsworth/Thomson Learning.

Blain, D. (1947). The psychiatrist and the psychologist. *Journal of Clinical Psychology, 3,* 4–10.

Blain, D. (1948). Priorities in psychiatric treatment of veterans. *Military Surgeon, 102,* 85–95.

Bloom, K. (1987, November). Survey of psychology service staffing losses October 1984–March 1987. *Newsletter for the Association of VA Chief Psychologists, 10,* 27–33.

Bradley, O. N., & Blair, C. (1983). *A general's life: An autobiography by General of the Army, Omar N. Bradley.* New York: Simon & Schuster.

Brady, J. V. (1953). Does tetraethylammonium reduce fear? *Journal of Comparative and Physiological Psychology, 46*, 307–310.

Brady, J. V. (1956, June 8). Assessment of drug effects on emotional behavior. *Science, 123*, 1033–1034.

Bronfenbrenner, U. (1947). Research planning in neuropsychiatry and clinical psychology in the Veterans Administration. *Journal of Clinical Psychology, 3*, 33–38.

Buchanan, R. (2003). Legislative warriors: American psychiatrists, psychologists, and competing claims over psychotherapy in the 1950s. *Journal of the History of the Behavioral Sciences, 39*, 225–249.

Caffey, E. M. (2003, December 10). *Oral history with Wade Pickren* [Transcript]. (Available from American Psychological Association, 750 First Street, NE, Washington, DC 20002)

Calden, G., Thurston, J. R., Stewart, B. M., & Vineberg, S. E. (1955). The use of the MMPI in predicting irregular discharge among tuberculosis patients. *Journal of Clinical Psychology, 11*, 374–377.

Campbell, H. M. (1947). The role of the clinical psychologist in a Veterans Administration mental hygiene clinic. *Journal of Clinical Psychology, 3*, 15–21.

Cannon, D. (1985, November). Computer update. *Newsletter of the Association of VA Chief Psychologists, 9*, 22.

Capshew, J. H. (1999). *Psychologists on the march: Science, practice, and professional identity in America, 1929–1969.* New York: Cambridge University Press.

Casey, J. F., Bennett, I. F., Lindley, C. J., Hollister, L. E., Gordon, M. H., & Springer, N. N. (1960). Drug therapy in schizophrenia: A controlled study of the relative effectiveness of chlorpromazine, promazine, phenobarbital, and placebo. *Archives of General Psychiatry, 2*, 210–220.

Casey, J. F., Lasky, J. J., Klett, C. J., & Hollister, L. E. (1960). Treatment of schizophrenic reactions with phenothiazine derivatives. *American Journal of Psychiatry, 117*, 97–105.

Casner, D. (1953). Staff-centered clinical psychology in a tuberculosis hospital. *Journal of Clinical Psychology, 9*, 151–155.

Chase, W. P. (1947). Professional frustration in government psychologists. *American Psychologist, 2*, 73–75.

Clark, K. E. (1957). *America's psychologists: A survey of a growing profession.* Washington, DC: American Psychological Association.

Cleveland, S. E. (1980a). Counseling psychology: An endangered species. *Professional Psychology, 11*, 314–323.

Cleveland, S. E. (1980b, Fall). President's message: Division 18 will not become VA division. *Public Service Psychology, 1*, 6.

Cleveland, S. E. (1980c, July). Title 38 revisited. *Newsletter of the Association of VA Chief Psychologists, 3*, 14–15.

Cleveland, S. E. (1981, August). VA psychology services survey 1981. *Newsletter of the Association of VA Chief Psychologists, 43*, 5–8.

Cleveland, S. E., & Patterson, T. W. (1979, April). On applying for APA internship accreditation. *Newsletter for the Association of VA Chief Psychologists, 2,* 14–16.

Cohen, A. J., Klett, C. J., & Ling, W. (1983). Patient perspectives of opiate withdrawal. *Drug and Alcohol Dependence, 12,* 167–172.

Cole, J. O., & Gerard, R. W. (Eds.). (1959). *Psychopharmacology: Problems in evaluation.* Washington, DC: National Academy of Sciences.

Cook, S. W. (1958). The psychologist of the future: Scientist, professional, or both. *American Psychologist, 13,* 635–644.

Cranston, A. (1986). Psychology in the Veterans Administration: A storied history, a vital future. *American Psychologist, 41,* 990–995.

Cummings, J. W. (1998). In the beginning . . . the startup. *Newsletter of the Association of VA Psychologist Leaders, 21,* 5–6.

Cushman, P. (1992). Psychotherapy to 1922: A historically situated interpretation. In D. K. Freedheim (Ed.), *History of psychotherapy: A century of change* (pp. 21–64). Washington, DC: American Psychological Association.

Darley, J. G., & Marquis, D. (1946). Veterans' guidance centers: A survey of their problems and activities. *Journal of Clinical Psychology, 2,* 109–116.

Darley, J. G., & Wolfle, D. (1946). Can we meet the formidable demand for psychological services? *American Psychologist, 1,* 179–180.

Davis, J., & Dickman, H. (1983, April). The end of an era: Cecil Peck retires. *Newsletter of the Association of VA Chief Psychologists, 6,* 29.

Delay, J., Deniker, P., & Harl, J. M. (1952). The treatment of excitation and agitation states by a method of medication derived from hibernotherapy. *Annals of Medical Psychology, 110,* 267.

DeLeon, P. H. (1982, February). An outsider speaks. *Newsletter for the Association of VA Chief Psychologists, 5,* 15–20.

Department of Veterans Affairs. (2001). *Training manual files for the behavioral health leadership training program, June 11–15* [Text files on CD-ROM]. (Available from the Archives of the History of American Psychology, The University of Akron, Polsky Building, LL10A, 225 South Main Street, Akron, Ohio 44325-4302)

Department of Veterans Affairs. (2003a, May 21). *Psychosocial residential rehabilitation treatment program: Fiscal year 2002 report.* Washington, DC: Author.

Department of Veterans Affairs. (2003b). *Training manual files for the behavioral health leadership training program, June 9–13* [Text files on CD-ROM]. (Available from the Archives of the History of American Psychology, The University of Akron, Polsky Building, LL10A, 225 South Main Street, Akron, Ohio 44325-4302)

Department of Veterans Affairs. (2005, April 15). *National mental health program monitoring system: Fiscal year 2004 report.* Washington, DC: Author.

Dickman, H. R. (1981, May). The cutting edge. *Newsletter for the Association of VA Chief Psychologists, 4,* 8–9.

Dosier, C. (2000). Report of roundtable on internship and training of clinical psychologists. *Journal of Clinical Psychology, 56,* 319–325. (Original work published 1947)

Fairweather, G. W. (Ed.). (1964). *Social psychology in treating mental illness: An experimental approach.* New York: Wiley

Fairweather, G. W. (1967). *Methods for experimental social innovation.* New York: Wiley.

Fairweather, G. W. (1994). *Keeping the balance: A psychologist's story.* Austin, TX: Author.

Fairweather, G. W., Sanders, D. H., Cressler, D. L., & Maynard, H. (1969). *Community life for the mentally ill: An alternative to institutional care.* Chicago: Aldine.

Farberow, N. L., & Shneidman, E. S. (1955). A study of attempted, threatened, and completed suicide. *Journal of Abnormal and Social Psychology, 50,* 230.

Farberow, N. L., & Shneidman, E. S. (1961). *The cry for help.* New York: McGraw-Hill.

Farreras, I. G. (2005). The historical context for National Institute of Mental Health support of American Psychological Association training and accreditation efforts. In W. E. Pickren & S. F. Schneider (Eds.), *Psychology and the National Institute of Mental Health: A historical analysis of science, practice, and policy* (pp. 153–179). Washington, DC: American Psychological Association.

Ferguson, J. T., McReynolds, P., & Ballachey, E. L. (1953). *The Hospital Adjustment Scale.* Palo Alto, CA: Consulting Psychologists Press.

Filer, R. N. (1973, February). A current overview of the Veterans Administration Mental Health and Behavioral Sciences research program. *Newsletter for Research in Mental Health and Behavioral Sciences, 15,* 2–28.

Former Prisoner of War Benefits Act of 1981, Pub. L. No. 97-37, 95 Stat. 935 (1981).

Fowler, R. D. (1996). Preface. In D. A. Dewsbury (Ed.), *Unification through division* (Vol. 1, pp. xv–xxiv). Washington, DC: American Psychological Association.

Fox, R. E. (1990). The history of the APIC selection process: A personal prequel. *APIC Newsletter, XV,* 27–28.

Freeman, W., & Watts, J. (1942). *Psychosurgery: Intelligence, emotion, and social behavior following prefrontal lobotomy for mental disorders.* Springfield, IL: Charles C Thomas.

Galbrecht, C. R., & Klett, C. J. (1968). Predicting response to phenothiazines: The right drug for the right patient. *Journal of Nervous and Mental Disease, 147,* 173–183.

Gresen, R. C. (1993, June). Update on hybrid title 38. *Newsletter of the Association of VA Psychologist Leaders, 16,* 22–25.

Grob, G. N. (1991). *From asylum to community: Mental health policy in modern America.* Princeton, NJ: Princeton University Press.

Gurel, L. (1964, September). *Correlates of psychiatric hospital effectiveness.* Paper presented at the annual meeting of the American Psychological Association, Los Angeles, CA.

Gurel, L. (1975). The human side of evaluating human services programs: Problems and prospects. In M. Guttentag & E. L. Struening (Eds.), *Handbook of evaluation research* (Vol. 2, pp. 11–28). Beverly Hills, CA: Sage.

Gurel, L. (1999, August 11). *Oral history with Wade Pickren* [Transcript]. (Available from American Psychological Association, 750 First Street, NE, Washington, DC 20002)

Gurel, L. (2003, August). *Contributions of VA research to developments in American psychology.* Paper presented at the annual meeting of the American Psychological Association, Toronto, Ontario, Canada.

Hale, N. G. (1995). *The rise and crisis of psychoanalysis in the United States: Freud and the Americans, 1917–1985.* New York: Oxford University Press.

Hanson, P. G. (2004, March 25). *Oral history with Rodney Baker* [Transcript]. (Available from American Psychological Association, 750 First Street, NE, Washington, DC 20002)

Hanson, P. G., Rothaus, P., Johnson, D. L., & Lyle, F. A. (1966). Autonomous groups in human relations training for psychiatric patients. *Journal of Applied Behavioral Science, 2,* 305–324.

Harrower, M. R. (1955). *Medical and psychological teamwork in the care of the chronically ill.* Springfield, IL: Charles C Thomas.

Healy, D. (1998). *The psychopharmacologists I.* London: Hodder Arnold.

Healy, D. (1999). *The psychopharmacologists II.* London: Edward Arnold.

Healy, D. (2000). *The psychopharmacologists III.* London: Oxford University Press.

Healy, D. (2002). *The creation of psychopharmacology.* Cambridge, MA: Harvard University Press.

Herman, E. (1995). *The romance of American psychology: Political culture in the age of experts.* Berkeley: University of California Press.

Hildreth, H. M. (1954). Clinical psychology in the Veterans Administration. In E. A. Rubinstein & M. Lorr (Eds.), *Survey of clinical practice in psychology* (pp. 83–108). New York: International Universities Press.

Hirsch, J. (1987). *The history of the National Training Laboratories, 1947–1986: Social equality through education and training.* New York: Peter Lang.

Hollister, L. E., Overall, J. E., Meyer, F., & Shelton, J. (1963). Perphenazine combined with amitriptyline in newly admitted schizophrenics. *American Journal of Psychiatry, 120,* 591–592.

Houtchens, H. M. (1959). Forward. *Newsletter for Cooperative Research in Psychology, 1,* 1.

Jackson, D. D. (Ed.). (1960). *The etiology of schizophrenia.* New York: Basic Books.

Jacobsen, C., Wolfe, J. B., & Jackson, T. A. (1935). An experimental analysis of the functions of the frontal association areas in primates. *Journal of Nervous and Mental Diseases, 82,* 1–14.

Jenkins, R. L., & Holsopple, J. Q. (1953). Criteria and experimental design for evaluating results of lobotomy. *Annals of Nervous and Mental Disease, 31,* 319–327.

Kelly, E. L., & Fiske, D. W. (1950). The prediction of success in the VA training program in clinical psychology. *American Psychologist, 5*, 395–406.

Kelly, G. A. (1955). *Psychology of personal constructs: Vol. 2. Clinical diagnosis and psychotherapy.* New York: Norton.

Kelly, G. A. (1965). Moments I remember. In E. L. Hoch, A. O. Ross, & C. L. Winder (Eds.), *Professional preparation of clinical psychologists.* Washington, DC: American Psychological Association.

Kelly, J. G. (2005). The National Institute of Mental Health and the founding of the field of community psychology. In W. E. Pickren & S. F. Schneider (Eds.), *Psychology and the National Institute of Mental Health: A historical analysis of science, practice, and policy* (pp. 233–259). Washington, DC: American Psychological Association.

Klett, C. J. (2003, August 13). *Oral history with Wade Pickren* [Transcript]. (Available from American Psychological Association, 750 First Street, NE, Washington, DC 20002)

Klett, C. J., & Lasky, J. J. (1960). A clinical trial of five phenothiazines using sequential analysis. *Journal of Clinical and Experimental Psychopathology and Quarterly Review of Psychiatry and Neurology, 21*, 89–100.

Klett, C. J., & Moseley, E. C. (1965). The right drug for the right patient. *Journal of Consulting Psychology, 29*, 546–551.

Lasky, J. J. (1958, June). *A progress report of the Central NP Research Unit.* Paper presented at the annual research conference of Chemotherapy Studies in Psychiatry, Washington, DC.

Lasky, J. J. (1959a, July). Development of the Inpatient Multidimensional Psychiatric Scale. *Newsletter: Cooperative Studies in Psychiatry, Central NP Research Laboratory, 3*, 2.

Lasky, J. J. (1959b, July). Small Scale Mutual Aid Research Group. *Newsletter: Cooperative Studies in Psychiatry, Central NP Research Laboratory, 3*, 2.

Lasky, J. J. (1960). Veterans Administration cooperative chemotherapy projects and related studies. In L. Uhr & J. G. Miller (Eds.), *Drugs and behavior* (pp. 540–554). New York: Wiley.

Lasky, J. J. (2003, June 20). *Oral history with Wade Pickren* [Transcript]. (Available from American Psychological Association, 750 First Street, NE, Washington, DC 20002)

Laties, V. G. (2003). Behavior analysis and the growth of behavioral pharmacology. *Behavior Analyst, 26*, 235–252.

Laughlin, P. R. (1979, November). Editorial. *Newsletter for the Association of VA Chief Psychologists, 2*, 1–2.

Laughlin, P. R. (1985, August). Some components of education and training within American psychology. *Newsletter for the Association of VA Chief Psychologists, 8*, 9–10.

Laughlin, P. R., & Worley, J. L. (1991). Roles of the American Psychological Association and the Veterans Administration in the development of internships in psychology. *American Psychologist, 46,* 430–436.

Lips, O. J. (1985, August). President's column. *Newsletter of the Association of VA Chief Psychologists, 1,* 1–2.

Lorr, M. (1953). Multidimensional Scale for Rating Psychiatric Patients. *Veterans Administration Bulletin, 10-507,* 1–44.

Lorr, M. (1954). Rating scales and check lists for the evaluation of psychopathology. *Psychological Bulletin, 51,* 119–127.

Lorr, M., Jenkins, R. L., & O'Connor, J. P. (1955). Factors descriptive of psychopathology and behavior of hospitalized psychotics. *Journal of Abnormal and Social Psychology, 50,* 78–86.

Lorr, M., Klett, C. J., McNair, D. M., & Lasky, J. J. (1962). Evidence of ten psychotic syndromes. *Journal of Consulting Psychology, 26,* 185–189.

Lorr, M., Klett, C. J., McNair, D. M., & Lasky, J. J. (1963). *The Inpatient Multidimensional Psychiatric Scale* [Manual]. Palo Alto, CA: Consulting Psychologists Press.

Lorr, M., O'Connor, J. P., & Stafford, J. W. (1960). A psychotic reaction profile. *Journal of Clinical Psychology, 16,* 241–245.

Luchins, A. S. (1959). *A functional approach to training in clinical psychology.* Springfield, IL: Charles C Thomas.

Luchins, A. S., Aumack, L., & Dickman, H. R. (1960). *Manual of group therapy.* Roseburg, OR: Veterans Administration Hospital.

Lyerly, S. B., & Abbott, P. S. (1966). *Handbook of psychiatric rating scales.* Washington, DC: U.S. Government Printing Office.

Magnuson, P. (1960). *Ring the night bell: An American surgeon's story.* Boston: Little, Brown.

McReynolds, P. (1951). Perception of Rorschach concepts as related to personality deviations. *Journal of Abnormal and Social Psychology, 46,* 131–141.

McReynolds, P. (1953). Thinking conceptualized in terms of interacting moments. *Psychological Review, 60,* 319–330.

McReynolds, P. (1954a). *The research program at the VA, Palo Alto.* Unpublished manuscript.

McReynolds, P. (1954b). The Rorschach concept evaluation technique. *Journal of Projective Techniques, 18,* 60–74.

McReynolds, P. (1956). A restricted conceptualization of human anxiety and motivation. *Psychological Reports, 2*(Suppl. 6), 293–312.

McReynolds, P. (1958). Anxiety as related to incongruencies between values and feeling. *Psychological Reports, 8,* 57–66.

McReynolds, P. (1960). Anxiety, perception, and schizophrenia. In D. D. Jackson (Ed.), *The etiology of schizophrenia* (pp. 248–292). New York: Basic Books.

McReynolds, P. (1963). Reactions to novel and familiar stimuli as a function of schizophrenic withdrawal. *Perceptual and Motor Skills, 16(3),* 847–850.

McReynolds, P. (1965). *Manual: Rorschach concept evaluation technique.* Los Angeles: Western Psychological Services.

McReynolds, P. (1966). A comparison of normals and schizophrenics on a new scale of the Rorschach CET. *Journal of Projective Techniques and Personality Assessment, 30,* 262–264.

McReynolds, P. (Ed.). (1968a). *Advances in psychological assessment* (Vol. 1). Palo Alto, CA: Science and Behavior Books.

McReynolds, P. (1968b). The Hospital Adjustment Scale: Research and clinical applications [Monograph]. *Psychological Reports, 23,* 823–835.

McReynolds, P. (1969, July). *Exploratory behaviors in C57 BL/10J mice.* Film presented at the International Congress of Psychology, London.

McReynolds, P. (1971). The three faces of cognitive motivation. In H. I. Day & D. E. Berlyne (Eds.), *Intrinsic motivation: A new direction in education* (pp. 33–45). Minneapolis, MN: Winston Press.

McReynolds, P., Collins, B., & Acker, M. (1964). Delusional thinking and cognitive organization in schizophrenia. *Journal of Abnormal and Social Psychology, 69,* 210–212.

McReynolds, P., & Weide, M. (1959). The prediction and assessment of psychological changes following frontal lobotomy. *Journal of Mental Science, 105,* 971–978.

McReynolds, P., & Weide, M. (1960). Psychological measures as used to predict psychiatric improvement and to assess behavioral changes following prefrontal lobotomy. *Journal of Mental Science, 106,* 256–273.

Miller, G. A. (1969). Psychology as a means of promoting human welfare. *American Psychologist, 24,* 1063–1075.

Miller, J. G. (1946). Clinical psychology in the Veterans Administration. *American Psychologist, 1,* 181–189.

Moore, D. L. (1979a, April). Psychology training program. *Newsletter for the Association of VA Chief Psychologists, 2,* 18–19.

Moore, D. L. (1979b, November). VA internships with APA approval. *Newsletter for the Association of VA Chief Psychologists, 2,* 16.

Moore, D. L. (1983, July). Psychology training program. *Newsletter for the Association of VA Chief Psychologists, 6,* 23.

Moore, D. L. (1992). The Veterans Administration and the training program in psychology. In D. K. Freedheim (Ed.), *History of psychotherapy* (pp. 776–800). Washington, DC: American Psychological Association.

Moreno, J. L. (1953). *Who shall survive? Foundations of sociometry, group psychotherapy, and sociodrama* (2nd ed.). New York: Beacon House.

Morgan, J. D. (1947). Training clinical psychologists in the Veterans Administration. *Journal of Clinical Psychology, 3,* 28–33.

National Mental Health Act of 1946, Pub. L. No. 79-487, 60 Stat. 421 (1946).

Nightingale, E. J. (1982, July). Here come the DRGs: Some thoughts about adjustment to a model of prospective reimbursement intradistrict methodology (PRIME). *Newsletter for the Association of VA Chief Psychologists, 5,* 18–23.

Nightingale, E. J. (1986). Experience with prospective payment in the Veterans Administration and its impact on the delivery of mental health services. *American Psychologist, 41*, 70–72.

O'Neill, W. (1986). *American high: The years of confidence, 1945–1960.* New York: Free Press.

Overall, J. E., & Gorham, D. R. (1962). The Brief Psychiatric Rating Scale. *Psychological Reports, 10*, 799–812.

Overall, J. E., Hollister, L. E., Bennett, J. L., Shelton, J., & Caffey, E. M., Jr. (1963). Benzquinamide in newly admitted schizophrenics: A search for patients best treated with a specific drug. *Current Therapeutic Research, 5*, 335–342.

Overall, J. E., Hollister, L. E., Prusmack, J. J., Shelton, J., & Pokorny, A. (1969). Controlled comparison of SK & F 14336 and chlorpromazine in newly admitted schizophrenics. *Journal of Clinical Pharmacology, 9*, 328–338.

Overall, J. E., & Klett, C. J. (1972). *Applied multivariate analysis.* New York: McGraw-Hill.

Paré, W. P. (1962). The effect of conflict and shock stress on stomach ulceration in the rat. *Journal of Psychosomatic Research, 6*, 223–225.

Paré, W. P. (2003, October 29). *Oral history with Wade Pickren* [Transcript]. (Available from American Psychological Association, 750 First Street, NE, Washington, DC 20002)

Peck, C. (1978, May). Provisions for employment of psychologists in the Department of Medicine and Surgery. *Newsletter for the Association of VA Chief Psychologists, 1*, 13–16.

Peffer, P. A. (1955, March). The member-employee program. *Department of Medicine and Surgery program guide for psychiatric and neurology service* (G-1, M-2, Pt. X). Washington, DC: Veterans Administration.

Penk, W. E. (2005, August). *Roots and contributions of VA psychology in mental health research.* In W. E. Pickren (Chair), *VA psychology treatment and research contributions after World War II.* Symposium conducted at the annual meeting of the American Psychological Association, Washington, DC.

Pickren, W. E. (1995). Psychologists and physicians in the borderlands of science, 1900–1942. *Dissertation Abstracts International, 56*, 11B. (UMI No. 6373)

Pickren, W. E. (2003). Obituary of James Grier Miller (1916–2002). *American Psychologist, 58*, 760.

Pickren, W. E. (2005). Science, practice, and policy: An introduction to the history of psychology and the National Institute of Mental Health. In W. E. Pickren & S. F. Schneider (Eds.), *Psychology and the National Institute of Mental Health: A historical analysis of science, practice, and policy* (pp. 3–15). Washington, DC: American Psychological Association.

Pickren, W. E., & Schneider, S. F. (Eds.). (2005). *Psychology and the National Institute of Mental Health: A historical analysis of science, practice, and policy.* Washington, DC: American Psychological Association.

Platz, A. R., Klett, C. J., & Caffey, E. M., Jr. (1967). Selective drug action related to chronic schizophrenic subtype. *Diseases of the Nervous System, 28,* 601–605.

Pokorny, A. D. (2004, August 18). *Oral history with Rodney Baker* [Transcript]. (Available from American Psychological Association, 750 First Street, NE, Washington, DC 20002)

Pottharst, K., & Kovacs, A. (1964). The crisis in training viewed by clinical alumni. In L. Blank & H. P. David (Eds.), *Sourcebook for training in clinical psychology* (pp. 278–300). New York: Springer Publishing Company.

Pressman, J. D. (1988). Sufficient promise: John F. Fulton and the origins of psychosurgery. *Bulletin of the History of Medicine, 62,* 1–22.

Prien, R. F., Caffey, E. M., & Klett, C. J. (1971). Lithium carbonate: A survey of the history and current status of lithium in treating mood disorders. *Diseases of the Nervous System, 32,* 521–531.

Problems of the Veterans Wounded in Vietnam: Hearings before the Subcommittee on Veterans Affairs of the Committee on Labor and Public Welfare, 91st Cong., 307–309 (1970) (testimony of Dr. Donald C. Klein).

Psychological notes and news. (1946a). *American Psychologist, 1,* 168–170.

Psychological notes and news. (1946b). *American Psychologist, 1,* 410–412.

Psychological notes and news. (1946c). *American Psychologist, 1,* 474–476.

Psychological notes and news. (1947a). *American Psychologist, 2,* 113–116.

Psychological notes and news. (1947b). *American Psychologist, 2,* 184–185.

Psychological notes and news. (1947c). *American Psychologist, 2,* 531–533.

Raimy, V. C. (Ed.). (1950). *Training in clinical psychology.* New York: Prentice-Hall.

Ray, O. S. (1978, May). President's column. *Newsletter for the Association of VA Chief Psychologists, 1,* 2–3.

Ray, O. S. (1979, November). Biting the big apple. *Newsletter for the Association of VA Chief Psychologists, 2,* 10–12.

Redei, E., Solberg, L., Kluczynski, J., & Paré, W. (2001). Paradoxical hormonal and behavioral responses to hypothyroid and hyperthyroid states in the Wistar Kyoto rat. *Neuropsychopharmacology, 24,* 632–639.

Rogers, C. R. (1951). *Client-centered therapy: Its major practice implications and theory.* Boston: Houghton Mifflin.

Rogers, L. S. (1956). Psychologists in public service and the public. *American Psychologist, 7,* 307–313.

Rosenbaum, M., Lakin, M., & Roback, H. B. (1992). Psychotherapy in groups. In D. K. Freedheim (Ed.), *History of psychotherapy: A century of change* (pp. 695–724). Washington, DC: American Psychological Association.

Rosner, R. I. (2005). Psychotherapy research and the National Institute of Mental Health, 1948–1980. In W. E. Pickren & S. F. Schneider (Eds.), *Psychology and the National Institute of Mental Health: A historical analysis of science, practice, and policy* (pp. 113–150). Washington, DC: American Psychological Association.

S. Rep. No. 96-926 at 97 (1980).

Sawrey, W. L., & Weisz, J. D. (1956). An experimental method of producing gastric ulcers. *Journal of Comparative and Physiological Psychology, 49*, 269–270.

Scherer, I. W., Klett, C. J., & Winne, J. F. (1957). Psychological changes over a five-year period following bilateral prefrontal lobotomy. *Journal of Consulting Psychology, 21*, 291–295.

Scherer, I. W., Winne, J. F., Clancy, D. D., & Baker, R. W. (1953). Psychological changes during the first year following prefrontal lobotomy. *Psychological Monographs, 67*(Whole No. 357).

Schneider, S. F. (2000). The National Institute of Mental Health. In A. E. Kazdin (Ed.), *Encyclopedia of psychology* (Vol. 5, pp. 391–394). Washington, DC: American Psychological Association; and New York: Oxford University Press.

Schneider, S. F. (2005). Reflections on psychology and the National Institute of Mental Health. In W. E. Pickren & S. F. Schneider (Eds.), *Psychology and the National Institute of Mental Health: A historical analysis of science, practice, and policy* (pp. 17–28). Washington, DC: American Psychological Association.

Schneidler, G. (1947). The role of the psychologist in the counseling program of the Veterans Administration. *Educational and Psychological Measurement, 7*, 117–125.

Sears, R. R. (1946). Graduate training facilities: I. General information; II. Clinical psychology. *American Psychologist, 1*, 135–150.

Sears, R. R. (1947). Clinical training facilities: 1947. *American Psychologist, 2*, 199–205.

Seidenfeld, M. A. (1966). Clinical psychology. In R. S. Anderson (Ed.), *Neuropsychiatry in World War II* (Vol. 1). Washington, DC: Office of the Surgeon General, Department of the Army.

Selye, H. (1952). *The story of the general adaptation syndrome.* Montreal, Quebec, Canada: Acta.

Servicemen's Readjustment Act of 1944, Pub. L. No. 78-346, 58 Stat. 284 (1944).

Shaffer, L. (1947). Clinical psychology and psychiatry. *Journal of Consulting Psychology, 11*, 5–11.

Shakow, D. (1972). The Worcester State Hospital research on schizophrenia (1927–1946). *Journal of Abnormal Psychology, 80*, 67–110.

Sheldon, J. (1993, December). The world of work. *Newsletter for the Association of VA Chief Psychologists, 16*, 12–14.

Shepard, B. (2000). *A war of nerves: Soldiers and psychiatrists in the twentieth century.* Cambridge, MA: Harvard University Press.

Shneidman, E. S., & Farberow, N. L. (1961). Suicide: The problem and its magnitude. *Veterans Administration Medical Bulletin 7.* Washington, DC: Veterans Administration.

Sidle, A. (1962). *The Life Problems Test: Manual for administration and scoring* (Research Rep. No. 35). Palo Alto, CA: Veterans Administration Hospital, Behavior Research Laboratory.

Sieracki, E. (1986, February). Meeting of the APA Committee on Graduate Education and Training. *Newsletter for the Association of VA Chief Psychologists, 9,* 6–7.

Sieracki, E. (1991, January). Items from VACO. *Newsletter of the Association of VA Chief Psychologists, 14,* 2–3.

Skocpol, T. (1992). *Protecting soldiers and mothers: The political origins of social policy in the United States.* Cambridge, MA: Harvard University Press.

Sokal, M. M. (Ed.). (1987). *Psychological testing and American society, 1890–1930.* New Brunswick, NJ: Rutgers University Press.

Stenger, C. A. (1979, November). What it is like to be associate director for psychology. *Newsletter for the Association of VA Chief Psychologists, 2,* 23–26, 28.

Stenger, C. A. (2003, December 3). *Oral history with Wade Pickren* [Transcript]. (Available from American Psychological Association, 750 First Street, NE, Washington, DC 20002)

Stenger, C. A. (2005, August 20). *VA psychology in Central Office: A view from the top.* Paper presented at the annual meeting of the American Psychological Association, Washington, DC.

Stevens, R. (1999). *In sickness and in wealth: American hospitals in the twentieth century.* Baltimore: Johns Hopkins University Press.

Stockdill, J. W. (2005). National mental health policy and the community mental health centers, 1963–1981. In W. E. Pickren & S. F. Schneider (Eds.), *Psychology and the National Institute of Mental Health: A historical analysis of science, practice, and policy* (pp. 261–293). Washington, DC: American Psychological Association.

Taylor, R. R. (1994, September). Report: VA healthcare reform office (Issue no. 2, March 1994). *Newsletter for the Association of VA Chief Psychologists, 17,* 9–11.

Tejani-Butt, S., Paré, W. P., & Yang, J. (1994). Effects of repeated novel stressors on depressive behavior and brain noradrenergic function in Sprague-Dawley and Wistar Kyoto rats. *Brain Research, 649,* 27–35.

To Consolidate Into One Act All of the Laws Administered by the Veterans Administration, and for Other Purposes, Pub. L. No. 85-857, 72 Stat. 1105 (1958).

To Establish a Department of Medicine and Surgery in the Veterans Administration, Pub. L. No. 79-293, 59 Stat. 675 (1946).

Uhr, L., & Miller, J. G. (1960). *Drugs and behavior.* New York: Wiley.

Ullmann, L. P. (1967). *Institution and outcome: A comparative study of psychiatric hospitals.* Oxford, England: Pergamon Press.

Ullmann, L. P., & Krasner, L. (1965). *Case studies in behavior modification.* New York: Holt, Rinehart & Winston.

Uribe, B., Jr., & Tryk, H. E. (1967). *The Creative Production Session: A preliminary report* (Research Rep. No. 37). Palo Alto, CA: Veterans Administration Hospital, Behavior Research Laboratory.

Valenstein, E. S. (1986). *Great and desperate cures: The rise and decline of psychosurgery and other radical treatments for mental illness.* New York: Basic Books.

VA psychologists conduct nationwide study of TB patients. (1959, March). *The Challenge, 14,* 4–5.

Vernier, C. M., Barrell, R. P., Cummings, J. W., Dickerson, J. H., & Hooper, H. E. (1961). Psychosocial study of the patient with pulmonary tuberculosis. *Psychological Monographs, 75*(Whole No. 510).

Veterans Administration. (1941). *Administrator of Veterans Affairs annual report for fiscal year ending June 30, 1940.* Washington, DC: U.S. Government Printing Office.

Veterans Administration. (1947a). *Administrator of Veterans Affairs annual report for fiscal year ending June 30, 1946.* Washington, DC: U.S. Government Printing Office.

Veterans Administration. (1947b, June). *Department of Medicine and Surgery Information Bulletin IB 10-5-4.* Washington, DC: Author.

Veterans Administration. (1947c, September 5). *Department of Medicine and Surgery Technical Bulletin 10-35.* Washington, DC: Author.

Veterans Administration. (1948, August). *Department of Medicine and Surgery Information Bulletin 10-5-15.* Washington, DC: Author.

Veterans Administration. (1949). *Administrator of Veterans Affairs annual report for fiscal year ending June 30, 1948.* Washington, DC: U.S. Government Printing Office.

Veterans Administration. (1950). *Administrator of Veterans Affairs annual report for fiscal year ending June 30, 1949.* Washington, DC: U.S. Government Printing Office.

Veterans Administration. (1951). *Administrator of Veterans Affairs annual report for fiscal year ending June 30, 1950.* Washington, DC: U.S. Government Printing Office.

Veterans Administration. (1952). *Administrator of Veterans Affairs annual report for fiscal year ending June 30, 1951.* Washington, DC: U.S. Government Printing Office.

Veterans Administration. (1954). *Administrator of Veterans Affairs annual report for fiscal year ending June 30, 1953.* Washington, DC: U.S. Government Printing Office.

Veterans Administration. (1955a). *Administrator of Veterans Affairs annual report for fiscal year ending June 30, 1954.* Washington, DC: U.S. Government Printing Office.

Veterans Administration. (1955b, May). *Department of Medicine and Surgery Program Guide for Psychiatric and Neurology Service* [G-2, M-2, Part X]. Washington, DC: Author.

Veterans Administration. (1956). *Administrator of Veterans Affairs annual report for fiscal year ending June 30, 1955.* Washington, DC: U.S. Government Printing Office.

Veterans Administration. (1957). *Administrator of Veterans Affairs annual report for fiscal year ending June 30, 1956.* Washington, DC: U.S. Government Printing Office.

Veterans Administration. (1958). *Administrator of Veterans Affairs annual report for fiscal year ending June 30, 1957.* Washington, DC: U.S. Government Printing Office.

Veterans Administration. (1965). *VA psychology in the mid-sixties: Trends and developments.* (Available from the Archives of the History of American Psychology, The University of Akron, Polsky Building, LL10A, 225 South Main Street, Akron, Ohio 44325-4302)

Veterans Administration. (1967). *Medical care of veterans.* Washington, DC: U.S. Government Printing Office.

Veterans Administration. (1969). *Administrator of Veterans Affairs annual report for fiscal year ending June 30, 1968.* Washington, DC: U.S. Government Printing Office.

Veterans Administration. (1970). *Cooperative studies in psychiatry: 1956–1970.* Washington, DC: U.S. Government Printing Office.

Veterans Administration. (1971). *The Vietnam era veteran: Challenge for change.* Washington, DC: Author. (Available from the Archives of the History of American Psychology, The University of Akron, Polsky Building, LL10A, 225 South Main Street, Akron, Ohio 44325-4302)

Veterans Administration. (1973a). *Administrator of Veterans Affairs annual report for fiscal year ending June 30, 1972.* Washington, DC: U.S. Government Printing Office.

Veterans Administration. (1973b, June). *Department of Medicine and Surgery Individual and group effectiveness training: A handbook for trainers* [Information Bulletin 11-41]. Washington, DC: Author.

Veterans Administration. (1974). *Medical research in the Veterans Administration (fiscal year 1973).* Washington, DC: U.S. Government Printing Office.

Veterans Administration. (1975). *Department of Medicine and Surgery Information Bulletin 11-49.* Washington, DC: Author.

Veterans Administration. (1978, March 28). *Determination of clinical privileges for psychologists* [Professional Services Letter IL-78-17]. Washington, DC: Author.

Veterans Administration. (1982, August 10). *Department of Medicine and Surgery Supplement MP-5* [Pt. I, Appendix 338A, Change 35]. Washington, DC: Author.

Veterans Health Care Amendments of 1979, Pub. L. No. 96-22, 93 Stat. 47 (1979).

Veterans Health Care Amendments of 1983, Pub. L. No. 98-160, 97 Stat. 993 (1983).

Veterans Health Care, Capital Asset, and Business Improvement Act of 2003, Pub. L. No. 108-170, 117 Stat. 2042 (2003).

Veterans Health Programs Extension and Improvement Act of 1979, Pub. L. No. 96-151, 93 Stat. 1092 (1979).

Veterans Hospitalization and Medical Services Modernization Amendments of 1966, Pub. L. No. 89-785, 80 Stat. 1368 (1966).

Weiss, J. M. (1970). Somatic effects of predictable and unpredictable shock. *Psychosomatic Medicine, 32*, 397–408.

Wells, F. L. (1917). *Mental adjustments.* New York: Appleton & Co.

Wittkower, E. D. (1949). *A psychiatrist looks at tuberculosis.* London: National Association for the Prevention of Tuberculosis.

Wolfle, D. (1946). The reorganized American Psychological Association. *American Psychologist, 1,* 3–6.

Wolford, R. A. (1956). A review of psychology in VA hospitals. *Journal of Counseling Psychology, 3,* 243–248.

Wolman, B. B. (1965). *Handbook of clinical psychology.* New York: McGraw-Hill.

Yerkes, R. M. (1921). *Psychological examining in the United States Army.* Washington, DC: National Academy of Sciences.

INDEX

Clinical Psychology Section, VA, 7, 22, 32, 33
Cognitive psychology
    psychosis assessment, 78
    VA research program and, 77, 78
Cole, Jonathan, 57
Community psychology, 39
    VA research program and, 81–82
Compensated Work Therapy, 143
Compensation for psychologists, 117, 118
    Title 38 issues, 132–135
Computers
    automated assessment, 110–111
    data analysis in cooperative chemo-
        therapy studies, 61–62
    medical records management, 137–
        138
Continuity of care, 102
Contracting out psychological services, 128–129
Contributions of VA programs, 13–14, 116
    clinical psychology, 14, 92–93, 111–
        112
    community mental health
        movement, 81–82
    data sources, 14–15
    education and training of
        psychologists, 3–4, 13, 17, 49–51
    information management, 137–138
    professional development of
        psychology, 3–4, 6, 114–115,
        135–136, 146–147
    recent history, 137–145
    research, 14, 73, 74, 82, 89–90
    scope of, 14
Cooperative Psychology Research
    Laboratory, 69–70
Cooperative research
    chemotherapy studies, 56–64, 65
    definition, 53
    origins and early development, 53
    prefrontal lobotomy study, 54–56
    psychiatric evaluation project, 70–
        73
    rationale, 53
    shortcomings, 73–74
    significance of, for psychology
        profession, 73, 74
    substance abuse and addiction, 64
    tuberculosis studies, 66–70

Cooperative Studies in Psychiatry, 57–
    58, 63, 64, 74
Counseling psychology, 99–100
    current VA employment, 144–145
    development of training program for,
        28
    effectiveness of VA programs, 99
    evolution of VA system, 7, 8–9, 10,
        13, 99
    member–employee programs, 99–100
    postdoctoral training, 47
    rationale, 99
    services, 99
    VA training program, 39
Cranston, Alan, 122
Crawford, Donald, 108, 153
Credentialing and licensure, 135
    contributions of VA to psychology
        profession, 146
    development of professional
        psychology, 113, 114
    employment standards for VA
        psychologists, 124–125
    of psychologists for employment in
        VA, 120
Cummings, Jonathan, 16, 67, 68, 151

Daily, John M., 83
Davis, John E., Jr., 16, 38, 127, 152, 154
Day treatment centers, 101, 102
Decision Support System, 138
Deinstitutionalization movement, 40
DeLeon, Patrick, 121
Department of Defense, 3, 115
Department of Medicine and Surgery, 7,
    76, 117
Dews, Peter, 16
*Diagnostic and Statistical Manual of Mental
    Disorders*, 14, 64–65, 87–88
Diagnostic-related groups methodology,
    129–130
Dickerson, Joseph, 67, 68, 151
Dickman, Harold, 16, 38, 42, 101, 122,
    151, 152
Disabled American Veterans, 9
Dobson, William, 72
Doll, Edgar A., 24, 25, 26
Domiciliary restoration centers, 101
Double-bind concept, 79

ABOUT THE AUTHORS

Rodney R. Baker grew up in Breckenridge, Minnesota, and obtained his bachelor's degree from Moorhead State College in 1963. He spent 1 year at the University of Illinois planning for a doctorate in experimental psychology before turning his interest to the clinical field. He transferred to the University of Arizona, where he earned his PhD in clinical psychology. His almost 40-year career in the VA included 3 years of practicum training (Tucson VA), an internship (West Haven VA), a staff psychology position (Houston VA), and a 26-year position as chief of psychology and, later, director of the mental health service at the VA in San Antonio. As one of the first presidents of the Association of VA Chief Psychologists, Dr. Baker gained a leadership reputation for advocacy for VA psychology and served on multiple national VA psychology projects. He retired from the VA in 2004 and continues to provide leadership training in the VA.

Wade E. Pickren earned his PhD in the history of psychology with a minor in the history of science under the direction of Don Dewsbury at the University of Florida. He served as the American Psychological Association (APA) Historian and Director of Archives from 1998 to 2006. He is currently on the psychology faculty at Ryerson University in Toronto and continues to serve as APA Historian. He has two edited books, *Evolving Perspectives on the History of Psychology* (APA, 2002) and *Psychology and the National Institute of Mental Health: A Historical Analysis of Science, Practice, and Policy* (APA, 2005). He has served as a guest editor and contributor for several issues of the *American Psychologist*: "The Contributions of Kenneth and Mamie Clark," "Psychology and the Nobel Prize," and "50 Years After *Brown* *v. Board of Education.*" Dr. Pickren's scholarly interests include the history of efforts to make psychology truly inclusive in both theory and practice, the history of psychology and health care, and the history of indigenous psychologies. He enjoys classroom teaching and aims to help students develop a disciplined curiosity about psychology and life.